JUE

THE CORPORATION AND THE INDIAN

TRIBAL SOVEREIGNTY AND
INDUSTRIAL CIVILIZATION IN
INDIAN TERRITORY, 1865-1907

❋

H. CRAIG MINER

UNIVERSITY OF OKLAHOMA PRESS : NORMAN AND LONDON

Library of Congress Cataloging-in-Publication Data

Miner, H. Craig.
  The corporation and the Indian.

  Bibliography: p.
  Includes index.
  1. Indians of North America—Indian Territory—Economic conditions. 2. Cor-
porations—Indian Territory. 3. Indians of North America—Indian Territory—
Tribal government. 4. Indian Territory—Economic conditions. 5. Indians of North
America—Indian Territory—Land tenure. I. Title.
E78.I5M63 1989   305.8'970766   88-40550
ISBN 0-8061-2205-6

CONTENTS

Preface, vii

Acknowledgments, xi

Abbreviations in Footnotes, xiii

   I. The Invisible Hand, 1

  II. "They Take Stock in Our Destruction," 20

  III. Capitalists and Strangers, 38

  IV. Coal and Ties: The Confrontation, 58

   V. The Territorial Ring, 77

  VI. "The Philistines Are Upon Us," 97

  VII. The Cattle Syndicates, 118

VIII. The Politics of Petroleum, 143

  IX. Cable Osage, New York, 164

   X. "A Corps of Clerks," 186

  XI. The Syndicated Indian, 207

Bibliography, 217

Index, 227

PREFACE TO THE PAPERBACK EDITION

When the Civil War resolved the moral and economic arguments between North and South, Americans turned to the West and the "Indian Question." There were moral and economic issues there also, and they were not neatly separated. But nineteenth-century industrial civilization —represented by its most stunning flower, the corporation—had confidence that the "underdeveloped" West was a fine target for a magic mixture of Adam Smith and Jesus of Nazareth and that the desert and its people would shortly be transformed.

In practice, the accommodation between American Indians and American business was more complicated and more painful. It did not proceed according to the expectations that Americans had looking forward to it, nor, interestingly, did it conform to the models that they have created looking back on it through history. The role played by business in Indian policy has been neglected and misunderstood. The layperson was likely to believe that there was doubtless little contact, much less serious negotiation, between what they took to be blanketed tribesmen riding ponies, and cigar-smoking magnates in capes and private railroad cars.

However, it is only common sense to note that corporate representatives, government agents, and Indians did not play stereotyped roles, but rather acted as complete human beings with a full range of motives and a variety of interests and degrees of understanding. Indians could be devious speculators ready to sell the graves of their ancestors, and whites could be romantics about Indian survival, ready to protect the tribes even against themselves. "Robber Barons" could make effective deals to preserve tribal control, while "do-gooders" could destroy tribal sovereignty in exchange for supposed philosophical benefits that the Indians would appreciate in time.

Intercultural business negotiations represented a far more prevalent and satisfactory way of working toward coexistence than military force. Contracts were as effective as cannon, and much more palatable. In business development of the Indian and Indian lands, it was possible to argue that both white and Indian could benefit and share in the wealth that was created in the West through the application of the most clever of modern arts.

This book is a study of the badly flawed attempt to implement that vision in Indian Territory, where it showed most promise. The story of the tribes' relationship with American business, especially corporations, is contained in the voluminous record groups in the National Archives at Washington and Fort Worth, and in the several million pieces of tribal archives at the Oklahoma State Historical Society. Organization of the archives is less than perfect, especially for the years between 1880 and about 1900. There is much dross to sift through, but with time and patience surprising truths emerge.

That these have remained hidden in most written histories is no shock, considering the reluctance of imaginative writers seeking an overview to check out things like the ninety-six boxes at the National Archives entitled "Osage leases." These same authors have been loath also to have delivered to the reading room the hundreds of spring-loaded walnut boxes containing the records of the Interior Department's Indian Territory Division. It has seemed hopeless to try reading and analyzing the two thousand microfilm frames of records of investment of Indian Trust funds. The Osage boxes are a mishmash of legal documents, minutes, and correspondence. The Indian Territory Division files are papers folded and pressed for nearly one hundred years, which have to be opened and weighted one by one. The trust records are endless rows of figures about transactions in stocks and bonds. Yet in the Osage records rest the real dynamics of the great Foster oil play. From the Indian Territory Division files came the bases for chapter 10, "A Corps of Clerks," illustrating the collusion of government officials in the notorious Indian Territory real-estate trust companies of the allotment period. The trust records showed the extent to which the Indians financed their own destruction by providing, indirectly, finance capital for the very corporations often pressing for their extinction.

None of the truths that can be drawn out of the paper labyrinth have been especially grist for the journalists' mill, then or since. Nor did the corporate principals or the Indian beneficiaries wish to make it easy. Modern historians, however, have the tools and access to make the "dullest" material speak. Since the initial publication of this book in 1976, I have been gratified to see how many are indeed doing so by concentrating in a sophisticated way on the previously neglected periods of the late nineteenth and early twentieth centuries in Indian history. The economic dimension of cross-cultural contact is getting more attention now than ever before.

The failure of Indians, corporations, and government to work out a satisfactory economic coexistence over the period documented in this book was a major factor in creating the state of Indian "dependency" and rootlessness that had such tragic consequences in the twentieth century. The possibility existed in 1865 of a culture and economic life in Indian Territory that was recognizably Indian as well as satisfactorily integrated with U.S. industrial needs. That possibility did not exist in 1907. Indians still reap the whirlwind of that time, finding that their history, including prominently the "unromantic" part recorded here, makes either neglect or paternalism by the United States an unsatisfactory solution to the by now incomparably muddled question of the status of the American Indian.

Did it have to be that way?

I think not.

A market meeting of the two cultures would have been filled

with mistakes and inefficiencies, injustices, even tragedies. Indeed, this book illustrates several of the more sinister possibilities.

Yet, through Indian Territory—wide meetings and conferences as early as the 1870s, Indians *did* move to solve the intratribal differences that hindered them in their dealings with corporations. They did form their own corporations. They did petition to be allowed to carry out their own negotiations. They did suggest alternative treaty terms. They did learn that a competitive enterprise system has capability to accommodate diversity and recognize interests, including cultural ones, through contracts.

But they found that in the end politics, not the market, dominated. The U.S. government felt it was its duty to intervene in the Indians' growth as business thinkers and to impose an "improved" plan on the seeming chaos of intercultural capitalism. In its role as "protector," it dispatched "disinterested" agents who were neither businessmen nor Indians and who stood to gain or lose nothing but power from the economic and political transactions in Indian country. In market-based, wealth-creating economics, sometimes both sides win. In political situations, someone always loses.

Possibly, savvy and realistic Indian leaders like Peter Pitchlynn and Dennis Bushyhead, whose market activities and corporate strategies are detailed here, could have done no better than the bureaucrats and agents. Maybe the interplay of interest and the evolution of negotiating skill would have done no better with the "Indian Question" than the methods that are now our history.

But they could hardly have done any worse.

H. CRAIG MINER

Wichita, Kansas

ACKNOWLEDGMENTS

Since, as a consequence of my perception of the relationship between the corporation and the Indian, I decided upon an intertribal and intercorporate approach, a great number of people, especially archivists who looked at their collections from a new angle, helped me. Richard Crawford and Robert Kvasnika were of special help at the National Archives, where it was necessary for me to learn a great deal about the organization of the files of the Office of Indian Affairs between 1880 and 1900 to proceed at all. At the Federal Records Center at Fort Worth, I must thank George Yonkin, who, from the time I walked in out of a sleet storm, provided great academic and personal service. Likewise, Rella Looney of the Oklahoma Historical Society should be singled out. She has worked with the Indian archives there for thirty years and knows them as no one else does. She was of immense help at the very beginning of my research, when she was able to translate my vague ideas into advice to look at specific groups of documents. Jack Haley of the Western History Manuscript Collection at the University of Oklahoma was very helpful in insuring that I found germane materials in that important collection. The staff at the Gilcrease Institute in Tulsa did yeoman's duty also in providing me with the hundreds of rare individual pamphlets, so important to this study, in which that library's collection is rich. Special thanks too to Thorburn Taggart of the Wichita State University Library for dealing expertly with my sometimes unusual requests for interlibrary loans, to Phyllis Nickel for typing, and to the Wichita State University Research Committee for generous and flexible financial support. Finally, my appreciation to William Unrau for sharing with me his expertise and encouragement in many discussions of the problem of the Indian and the white economy.

ABBREVIATIONS IN FOOTNOTES

AR CIA—Annual Report of the Commissioner of Indian Affairs. National Cash Register Microfiche Edition. Year of publication follows.

The following abbreviations are used to identify National Archives microfilm publications:

M—Microcopy number

R—Roll number

F—Frame number

LR—Letters received

LS—Letters sent

FRC—Federal Records Center, Fort Worth, Texas

Gilcrease—Archives, Gilcrease Institute, Tulsa, Oklahoma

HR—House Report

H.R.—Records of the U.S. House of Representatives

IAD—Indian Archives Division, Oklahoma Historical Society, Oklahoma City

ID—Records of the Indian Division, Department of the Interior, Record Group 48, National Archives, Washington, D.C.

ISP—Irregularly shaped papers, Record Group 75, National Archives, Washington, D.C.

ITD—Letters Received by the Indian Territory Division, Record Group 48, National Archives, Washington, D.C.

KSHS—Kansas State Historical Society, Topeka

L&RR—Records of the Lands and Railroads Division, Department of the Interior, Record Group 48, National Archives, Washington, D.C.

NA—National Archives building, Washington, D.C.

OIA—Records of the Office of Indian Affairs, Record Group 75, National Archives, Washington, D.C.

OU—Archives Division, University of Oklahoma Library, Norman, unless another collection is specified

RG—Record Group, in the National Archives, Washington, D.C.

S—Serial number, in the government documents set

SC—Special Case number, Record Group 75, National Archives, Washington, D.C.

SED—Senate Executive Document

SF—Special File number. Record Group 48, National Archives, Washington, D.C.

SMD—Senate Miscellaneous Document

SR—Senate Report

T—Microcopy number for privately filmed documents at the National Archives, Washington, D.C.

THE CORPORATION AND THE INDIAN

Indian Territory and Oklahoma Territory, 1890

CHAPTER I

THE INVISIBLE HAND

The year 1865 marked the beginning of corporate dominance in America and the decline of Indian sovereignty. The rise of the one seemed directly related to the decline of the other, all set after the Civil War, when the nation was not only tired of rhetoric and ideals but also frantic to encourage any movement that seemed practical, constructive, and even, for a change, selfish. The generals became in that time presidents of corporations, and the corporations in that time turned the talents of these strategists to other fields and other weapons than those with which they had been of late acquainted. The philosophers in New England, who had said the slave should be free, now said that the Five Civilized Tribes residing in the Indian Territory must be allowed to continue, free of interference, to operate their tribal agricultural economies and to hold their lands in common. This was written in the treaties negotiated at bayonet point when the Indians were moved from their homelands in the Southeast, it was included in the Trade and Intercourse Acts passed by the Congress, and should be engraved on the heart of every fair man. But crusades had, for the present, been at center too long.[1] The Indians in Indian Territory controlled potential railway routes to the Gulf of Mexico; they grazed a few cattle over land underlaid with coal and oil; they were destitute, politically divided, and vulnerable to temptations of material progress in exchange for traditional values. Therefore men in the surrounding states of Kansas, Arkansas, and Texas spoke dis-

---

1. Recent books on removal that are especially revealing concerning the business aspects are Arthur DeRosier, *The Removal of the Choctaw Indians*, and Mary Young, *Redskins, Ruffleshirts, and Rednecks: Indian Allotments in Alabama and Mississippi, 1830–1860.*

paragingly of the "Chinese Wall," the "Ring of Fire," which the Indian Territory presented to ambitious capitalists in the West. Congressman Sidney Clarke of Kansas drew cheers from constituents along the border of the Territory when he castigated the Office of Indian Affairs in Washington for delaying the removal of all the Kansas tribes to the Indian Territory and for hesitating to allow corporate representatives to follow the fleeing aborigines south in order there to "achieve the bloodless victories of a new civilization, inspired and accelerated by the spirit of a new and regenerated republic."[2]

There had been some warning of this attitude in the 1850s, when "Young America," flush with Mexican War victories, had directed its attention briefly to the question of industrial civilization and the Indian. The 1854 debate on the Kansas-Nebraska bill, which organized former Indian lands into U.S. territories, had ominous implications. Some Easterners argued then that the Indian would disappear naturally when the western railroads commingled the civilization of Europe and Asia around his present hunting grounds. Others thought his inevitable extermination should be helped along, since Joshua upon entering the promised land had been ordered by God to exterminate the Canaanites, an Indian-like people, and was punished for hesitating. John Pettit of Indiana had said that the Indian must give way to "a race of men heavier physically, and heavier mentally. The wild grass amid which he lay, the woods where he built his moon fire, . . . and all the accomplishments of the wild men, are to pass away, and the heavier race come on with their accomplishments." Could not the two cultures coexist, locomotive next to tepee? Not a chance, said Pettit: "You might as well attempt to tame a partridge and make a dunghill fowl of it." The very next year treaties were negotiated with the Choctaws, Chickasaws, and Creeks, granting a right of way to the United States or to any incorporated company to build a railroad through their Indian Territory lands. Only the Creeks added the proviso that the tribal legislature should dictate terms. A member of the governmental thirty-fifth parallel

2. *Kansas Tribune*, Sept. 20, 1865.

railway surveying party reported in 1853 that there were "progressive" classes among the Indians who seemed ready for a new age, and in 1856 Commissioner of Indian Affairs George Manypenny did not doubt that, barring U.S. involvement in a war, before 1866 the Indian lands would be settled. In 1858, formal application was made to Washington for a railway right of way through the Cherokee Nation and the privilege of buying lands there. The Office of Indian Affairs refused, but it was evident that the tribes had few years of isolation remaining.[3]

Cherokee chief John Ross spoke clearly upon this subject in his annual message of 1857. The self-government of the Indian Territory tribes, he said, was threatened by the spirit of industrial America's corporations. "We cannot be insensible to the spirit of the age in which we live, nor to the circumstances which surround our lot, with a population increasing rapidly and rife with the impulses of restless progress and acquisition." Robert Walker, territorial governor of Kansas, had earlier suggested that Indian Territory be made into a state and claimed that the treaties in force there constituted "no obstacle, any more than precisely similar treaties did in Kansas." Walker had outlined several "essential" railways through the region and had predicted that the Indians, anxious for the value of their lands to increase, would consent. Chief Ross was shocked by this assumption, and he warned his listeners that they must guard against this temptation by strengthening their governments, sending delegations to Washington, and reconsidering the worth of their traditional values. The Indian must be prepared to respond to the "necessities" of American corporations, or these pleas of economic expedience would bring him "strife, injury and political destruction."[4]

3. *Congressional Globe*, 33d Cong., 1st sess., XXIII, Appendix, pp. 972, 213. Defenses of Indian rights are on pp. 153, 159, 545, 636. Charles J. Kappler, *Indian Affairs: Laws and Treaties*, vol. 2, pp. 706–14, 756–63. H. Craig Miner, *The St. Louis-San Francisco Transcontinental Railroad: The Thirty-Fifth Parallel Project, 1853–1890*, p. 7; AR CIA (see "Abbreviations in Footnotes," p. vii), 1856, p. 23. J. Thompson to Commissioner of Indian Affairs, Feb. 9, 1858, LR ID, M 606, R 3, F 0057.

4. AR CIA, 1857, p. 220.

Although Indian nationalists responded positively to Ross's position, there were practical types among the tribes as there were practical whites along the border of Indian Territory. These two classes shared an overriding concern with the material well-being, as contrasted with the abstract principles, of their respective societies. This division of motives among the Indians insured that Ross's idea of unity would remain merely an idea and that for the next several decades both cultures would be dominated by loud voices that, upon reflection of generations, neither would be proud of.

The Civil War was vastly important to the hopes of the corporations. Not only did the Union victory insure that industrialization would be equated with civilization but it also destroyed the economic self-sufficiency of the Indian Territory tribes. In addition the federal government charged them with disloyalty during the war, which provided an excuse to renegotiate old treaties. Because Union efforts were late and ineffectual in the region, some tribal factions signed agreements with the Confederacy. When help did come, officers acting as temporary Indian agents defrauded their wards by speculating in hides and tallow from the beef sent for relief of starving refugee Indians. Persons in the surrounding states stole about 300,000 cattle from the herds of the tribes during this period of crisis. The head of the Southern Indian Superintendency could only say, "It is utterly impossible to effectually break up this system of plunder from the Indians as long as the state, civil, and military authorities are in sympathy with the parties engaged in this species of brokerage." The number involved was great, and their social standing so high "that it is almost fatal to interpose obstacles in the way of their success." He even justified robbing further as expedient. After all, he wrote, "the rapid development and settlement of this portion of the west . . . by the various enterprises and discoveries of the age, will soon demand these lands for mineral and agricultural purposes." While government thus looked on, the tribes sustained a loss by plunder of $4 million, Cherokees alone lost $2 million.[5] It left them so dis-

5. James Harlan to W. G. Coffin, Jan. 2, 1865, LR OIA Southern Superintendency, M 234, R 836, F 076–8; AR CIA, 1865, pp. 257–58, 38.

couraged and destitute that they were ready in 1865 to agree to negotiate new treaties on almost any terms in return for some economic
aid. A resident found a dreary fatalism in the Cherokee nation of that
time. People were burning their improvements, and what little stock
remained was being sold at low prices. It seemed, he wrote, that they
were trying to destroy "all traces of civilization and enterprise" that
had grown up within the tribal hegemony. "Public and private distress seem to keep pace with each other in gloomy concert. The hand-
some farms, the neat cottages—the abodes of happiness and compe-
tency and the cattle that pastured upon a thousand hills . . . have all
passed away."[6]

As Indians wandered east to Fort Smith for the treaty conclave of 1865 to join with corporate lobbyists from the north, the
commissioner of Indian affairs could comment that the "obliquity
of conscience" that had brought them to such a pass was almost at-
tractive in its zeal and "would be amusing if the thing were not
outrageously criminal." Congressman Clarke was more positive
still, saying that promoting railroads was like wooing a sweetheart,
and ardor should not cool in the pale cast of thought, just when "we
had a pretty thing, a good thing, a sure thing." If the Indians at
Fort Smith were "sweethearts," they were so anesthetized at their
first major contact with an aggressive suitor that a question of rape
was sure eventually to arise.[7]

The watchword everywhere was *circumstance*. It was as though
the modern age had eliminated men's freedom to do other than
adapt to the promptings of an "invisible hand," which had no arm
or brain it seemed, much less a soul. The loyalties of government
representatives at Fort Smith were questionable, and they gave am-
biguous rulings in adjudicating Indian and corporate rights. But
they were no more doubtful about how properly to weigh the demands of ethic and expedience than were the people they represented. In contrast, the corporate interests were positive of their

6. P. L. Thompson to W. P. Adair, May 23, 1866, SF 125 OIA, M 574,
R 24 (no file number).

7. AR CIA, 1865, p. 38. *Western Journal of Commerce*, July 30, 1864.

stance and about creating new necessities of circumstance if the old ones would not bring the economic development favorable to them. They did not get attention in the headlines at Fort Smith, which were reserved for such philosophical questions as the fate of the former Indian slaves and removal of plains tribes to the Indian Territory. Their influence was by all means evident, though. One of Congressman Clarke's correspondents told him that lobbyists from Wyandotte and Kansas City planned to attend the "grand gathering" where "treaties will be made—railroad grants fixed up and things done generally." A reporter from Kansas City attending the conference noticed that in the shadows, not participating in the grand ceremony of debates, were railwaymen unobtrusively speaking with a few Indians. He said that their presence was reassuring in making Fort Smith, filled now with the resounding and equally strange speeches of tribesman and government bureaucrats, "seem like America." Commissioner of Indian Affairs Denton N. Cooley telegraphed Washington: "All well. Shall we . . . make opening propositions, or say we are there to hear what they want?" The reply came back: "You will be controlled by circumstances."[8]

One prominent "circumstance" was the existence of factions within the tribes, some of which were willing to allow white business to enter Indian lands in order to gain political advantages within the tribes through the use of corporate and federal power. In the case of the Cherokees, the southern faction (the old Ridge faction) was agreeable to the government treaty plans, including rights of way for railroads through their lands. Thus, when Elias C. Boudinot, the leader of this group, spoke at Fort Smith in favor of a U.S. territorial government for the Indian Territory and submitted a number of treaty drafts generous to U.S. corporations, the faction was respected, even though it had been more involved with the Con-

8. William Meer (?) to Sidney Clarke, July 26, 1865, LR OIA Southern Superintendency, M 234, R 836, F 0200–1. *Western Journal of Commerce,* Sept. 30, 1865. D. N. Cooley to James Harlan (telegram), Aug. 24, 1865, Harlan to Cooley (telegram), Aug. 24, 1865, LR OIA Southern Superintendency, M 234, R 836, F 0384.

federacy than any other portion of the tribe. Similar divisions among the Choctaws prompted one of their leaders, Peter Pitchlynn, to urge against any overly broad interpretations of the implications of Indian consent to the Fort Smith treaties. White observers made much of these quarrels and suggested that the only way to protect Indians from destroying themselves in an orgy of tribal corruption occasioned by new economic opportunity was to divide their lands in severalty, eliminate trust funds and agencies, and form a territorial government—in short to destroy tribal sovereignty. With the necessity for common agreement thus eliminated, native ambition would "receive a new and powerful and hitherto unknown stimulus and all the great capabilities of the Indians will be developed." For this reason Indian nationalists regarded the "progressive" factions as traitors who were willing to trade a centuries-old tribal tradition for a "mess of pottage."[9]

Another "stress of circumstance" was the simple pressure of an expanding and ethnocentric white population. The commissioner of Indian affairs wrote in his 1864 annual report that, despite the "authoritative and imposing sanction" given to Indian treaties by all interpreting agencies, the rule of thumb through which the concrete drove out the abstract was bound to apply.[10] Commissioner D. N. Cooley wrote the next year that he could not understand why the Paiutes were complaining about the Union Pacific railroad passing near their agency, since, if the Indians were willing to work, the railroad could give them jobs and income. His attitude toward railroads through Indian Territory was similar. At the time of the Fort Smith conference, he spoke of the construction of internal

---

9. For background, see Morris Wardell, *A Political History of the Cherokee Nation, 1838–1907*, and M. Thomas Bailey, *Reconstruction in Indian Territory*. [P. P. Pitchlynn and Winchester Colbert], *Address . . . to the Choctaws and Chickasaws; Explanatory of the Circumstances Under Which the Treaty with the United States . . . Was Negotiated. . . .* (Washington, D.C., 1866) passim., 17664, Choctaw Federal Relations File, IAD. I. M. Tibbets to D. N. Cooley, March 30, 1866, SF 125 OIA, M 574, R 24, F 0396–0402.

10. AR CIA, 1864, p. 3.

improvements through the Indian Territory as an inevitable step in "the progress toward a final settlement of the questions remaining open in regard to the reorganization of the Indian country."

Treaties guaranteed the Five Tribes that Indian Territory would never be incorporated into a U.S. state or territory. Yet Cooley believed this development would occur soon, as railroads crisscrossed the region to connect the Gulf of Mexico with "the great central converging points of railroads in Kansas." "Whatever can properly be done by the government of the United States," wrote Cooley, "in paving the way for these improvements should . . . be done now, and thus avoid difficulties which may arise in the future."[11] Silas Armstrong, representing the Wyandottes at Fort Smith, was well aware of this trend and doused talk among tribesmen about being taken up onto a high mountain by Satan. He told fellow Indians that the only basis for unity in future was that "we are all in the suds" and that the only possible strategy was to try to adapt to industry. Wrote Armstrong on his first day at Fort Smith:

> I hear a proposition to run a railroad through the Indian Territory. An Indian told me you might as well knock an Indian in the head; but I told him it was useless to attempt to stop the railroad, for it would go through their country, and improve their lands, and make them valuable. If they do not like the railroads, let them move away from them as far as they can.[12]

While Armstrong's comment was the only analysis concerning railroads published in the proceedings of the twelve-day treaty conference at Fort Smith, the promotion of railroads was at issue. It was hidden, for example, in a seemingly positive statement about the protection of Indian rights. No white persons would be allowed to reside among the Indians, said the government representatives, except those adopted by the tribes, those given special licenses, and the officers and employees of internal improvement companies authorized by the federal government. In the face of the exceptions,

11. Ibid., 1865, pp. 15, 42.
12. Ibid., pp. 3, 7.

what was left of the rule? The provisions discussed for moving the tribes of Kansas to Indian Territory also directly affected railroad builders. Plans were being made in 1865 to transfer lands ceded by the Osages in Kansas directly to two railway corporations, one of which, the Union Pacific, Southern Branch (later Missouri, Kansas and Texas), would soon be pressing for Indian Territory lands as well.[13] The Five Tribes, recognizing better than others that corporate development was central here, did not sign treaties at Fort Smith but hired attorneys and proceeded to Washington for further negotiations, lasting through the summer of 1866.

Ironically, the Indians were placed in a position of giving ammunition to their enemies. The Cherokees were asked to provide a home for tribes to which the government had once guaranteed Kansas. Their removal to the south not only diminished the land base of the tribes already living in Indian Territory but upset intertribal relations and strengthened the hand of Kansas-based corporations, whose next step would be to connect their northern systems to the Gulf through the Indian Territory tribal reserves. Yet more strange, money that Indian tribes gained by the sale of lands they were forced to leave went to gird the loins of the industrial system that was responsible. Indian funds were usually not distributed per capita to the tribes, on the grounds that savages could not use them responsibly. Instead they were held in trust in Washington. These trust funds were sometimes invested by the Indian Office directly in the securities of railroad companies and often were invested in state and U.S. bonds, which were in turn pledged to guarantee corporate issues in manufacturing as well as transportation. In 1864 the Cherokee national fund and the Cherokee orphan fund were invested in a U.S. bond issue pledged to support the Union Pacific, Eastern Division railway, which was at the time illegally cutting timber on the Delaware reserve in Kansas, while the Delawares moved in with the Cherokees to the south. The U.S. bonds repre-

13. Ibid., pp. 34–35; Paul Gates, *Fifty Million Acres: Conflicts Over Kansas Land Policy, 1854–1890*, pp. 194–222. First published in 1954.

senting the Creek orphan fund were pledged to the Chesapeake and Ohio Canal Company.[14] In 1870, an attempt was made by the Treasury Department to tax the interest on bonds of the Nashville and Chattanooga railroad held in trust for the Chickasaw tribe and to debit the Chickasaw fund for defaults by the railroad company on payments of interest and principal. The Chickasaws successfully resisted this action with a stinging petition:

> The country [has] grown to be great and powerful in the same proportion that the Indians [have] diminished in numbers and . . . become poor and needy. . . . To aid in this mighty march of the white man, the United States . . . lent the poor and meager proceeds of the Indians' land to railroads, that brought wealth and population and built up cities in the old hunting grounds of the race. The Indians did not lend this money; the United States lent it, to increase the value of its multiplying states. It lent it for a session unwisely, but in good faith it provided for the default of the borrowers, and so it was hoped it would have continued to the end. But now the attempt is made to force the Indian to contribute his pittance to the growth of all this prosperity and power; and this, too, when the United States, triumphant over the perils that once surrounded it, is more than ever able to be liberal, although nothing more is asked of it than to be just.[15]

The significance of Indian trust funds as a source of capital for American industrialization cannot be overemphasized. It was one of the major mechanisms behind the casual observation, made by many at the time, that the strength of the corporation seemed inversely proportionate to that of the Indian. It diminishes the force of

14. HR 98, 42d Cong., 3d sess., March 3, 1873 (S 1578), pp. 392, 409, 410. Numerous letters exist complaining that the holding of trust funds allowed the government to exert pressure on the tribes by paying claimants directly without consulting Indians.

15. Holmes Colbert et al., *Letter from Hon. Holmes Colbert . . . And Other Indian Delegates to Hon. J. D. Cox . . . in Relation to the Attempt of the Commissioner of Internal Revenue to Collect Taxes on the Interest Due the Chickasaws and Other Indian Nations on Bonds Held in Trust by the U.S.* (Washington, D.C., 1870), LR OIA Choctaw Agency, M 234, R 180, F 0316–20.

the argument that this change was inevitable because God intended a new culture to rise, and it raises the question whether money held in trust for the "protection" of the Indians ought to have been used to support the instrument of the ultimate doom of their sovereignty without some more formal due process.

Unfortunately, however, for the legend of native intransigence, there is evidence that when the tribes moved to Washington for the negotiations of 1866 treaty clauses providing for the introduction of railways were promoted by white attorneys hired by the tribes and by progressives within the tribes. Douglas Cooper, the Choctaw agent, contacted his friend and relative John H. B. Latrobe, as the tribal representatives moved through Baltimore on the way to Washington. Latrobe later testified that the Indians were despondent, sure that they would lose everything as they had in the 1830s and willing to give up all claims they had upon the federal government. He agreed to represent them in exchange for a $25,000 fee and convinced them that they might control the industrial future and profit from it. Latrobe argued that individual ownership of land, combined with privileges for railroads, would give the tribes the economic strength to postpone disaster. He suggested to officials in Washington that not only should rights of way for railroads be included in the Choctaw-Chickasaw treaty but that Indians might trade their lands for stock in railroad companies if the railroads would agree to resell the land only to Indians. When later investigators charged him with taking advantage of the Choctaws, Latrobe insisted that his plan represented the only hope for them and that they had fully understood and agreed to it. These were sophisticated Indians, he noted, and not "the blanketed and feathered delegates whose savage ignorance requires the protection of the government as a merciful kindness." A House investigating committee looking into the Indian attorney business in 1872 was less kind, concluding that an Indian claim agent would "buy or sell, corrupt or be corrupted, whichever promises the most money."[16]

16. HR 98 (S 1578), pp. 92, 76; John Latrobe to D. N. Cooley, Aug. 1866, LR OIA Choctaw Agency, M 234, R 176, F 0634–38.

One might dismiss the activities of Latrobe and his ilk as insignificant pressure salesmanship were it not for corroboratory actions by the Indians. At Washington in 1866, the southern Cherokees said they were willing to agree to railroad rights of way, land division in severalty, and even a territorial government because "they harmonize with the progress of the age and the spirit of the Government, and because they indicate a desire on the part of the government to improve the condition of the Indian race and to elevate them in the scale of being."[17] Most of the preliminary drafts of the Cherokee treaty of 1866 made more liberal provisions for the railroads than those that were finally ratified, including large land grants, sales of land with the proceeds going to railroads, blanket permission for railroads to build without consulting Indian legislatures, and plans for the tribes to become railroad stockholders. In the final treaties with the Choctaws, Chickasaws, and Seminoles there were clauses giving three-mile wide strips of Indian land to the railroads if the companies would restrict their sales of land to Indians. While the southern Cherokees advertised themselves especially as the "party of civilization," even the northern faction submitted treaty drafts giving rights of way to specific railway companies, though it was more reticent about land grants.[18] As late as 1870, when the beginning of actual railroad construction had damaged the Indian dream of controlling the actions of the corporations, Choctaw chief Sampson Folsom lectured a native critic of railroads for forgetting that he lived "in the blessed age of Progressivism," when red, white, and

17. John Ridge, W. P. Adair, et al. to Secretary of Interior, n.d., SF 125 OIA, M 574, R 24, F 0212.

18. The treaty drafts may be traced in the following documents: Project of Treaty submitted to James Harlan by Cherokee delegation, March 15, 1866; Agreement with Southern Cherokees, June 13, 1866; and various unmarked drafts (F 0063–80, 0083–0116, 0134–0418), all in SF 125 OIA, M 574, R 24. Also, John Ross et al. to James Harlan, March 22, 1866, LR OIA Cherokee Agency, M 234, R 100, F 0714–15. For the final treaty forms, see Kappler, *Indian Affairs*, vol. 2, pp. 912, 920, 934, 945.

black people could unite in promoting a single economic and political system.[19]

One may go one step more and state that, remarkably enough, in 1866 whites acted at times as a restraining influence upon the enthusiasm for corporations exhibited by some Indian delegates. The secretary of the interior spoke to the delegations in May 1866 and advised them to allow limited rights of way, but no land grants. The Indians remembered that he "stated the evil effects of such grants with ... much ... emphasis." The delegates in general agreed but asked that the tribal councils be given power to make land grants to railroads later without additional treaty negotiations. At another point in the negotiations Daniel Vorhees, an attorney for the southern Cherokees, proposed selling all the land of the Cherokee Indian Territory west of ninety-six degrees longitude and the 800,000-acre Cherokee Neutral Tract in Kansas "on behalf of railroads." The Kansas lands were sold in 1866 to a Kansas railroad, and sale of the western land (the Cherokee Outlet) was included in the 1866 treaty. The Cherokee legislature passed an act that very year granting the proceeds from the Outlet to a railroad. Opposing this was a white man, Thomas Ewing, himself a principal promoter of the Union Pacific, Eastern Division. Ewing, representing for the moment the northern Cherokees, said that such action would not benefit Indian agriculture and would only "break down the barriers between the Indian people and the agressive [sic] whites on the border." William A. Phillips, a former Union officer who was at the conference with the Cherokees, remembered later that the Ross delegation was reluctant to admit the "disturbing element" of railroads, but that this was "positively demanded." Whether it was demanded most positively by the government or by other Indians, he did not say, but the evidence leaves the historian room to wonder. In 1867 a rumor circulated among the Indian nationalists that European powers were about to join a great Mormon army with the purpose of

19. Sampson Folsom to T. Boles, April 9, 1870, LR OIA Choctaw Agency, M 234, R 179, F 003–006.

destroying tribal progressives and saving the traditionalist remnant from its corporate enemies and from the fruits of Indian heterogeneity.[20]

The 1866 treaties as ratified contained rights of way through lands of the major tribes in eastern Indian Territory for two railroad routes, one north to south and one east to west. All but the Cherokees included options to trade some land for stock, though resale was limited to Indians. But Congress did not wait for the final treaty drafts to begin debating to whom the privileges would go, nor did corporate lobbyists find it any longer expedient to maintain low visibility. Four railroads competed for Indian Territory privileges in Washington: the Kansas and Neosho Valley (later Missouri River, Fort Scott and Gulf); the Leavenworth, Lawrence, and Galveston; the Union Pacific, Southern Branch (later Missouri, Kansas and Texas); and the Atlantic and Pacific. The first three were planned as trunk lines from Kansas to the Gulf of Mexico, while the A&P would connect St. Louis with San Francisco along the thirty-fifth parallel route.[21]

It was later officially stated by the Interior Department that the 1866 treaties and the railway charter and land-grant bills that passed the Congress in the same year were "part of the same transaction," designed to establish railroads upon Indian lands. However, the de-

20. James McDaniel et al., *Reply of the Delegates of the Cherokee Nation to the Demands of the Commissioner of Indian Affairs* (Washington, D.C., 1866), Hargrett Indian Pamphlet Collection, Gilcrease. The catalog to the important collection has been published as *The Gilcrease Hargrett catalogue of Imprints. . . .* (Norman: University of Oklahoma Press, 1972). Transcript of meeting, March 30, 1866, Documents accompanying ratified treaties, T 494, R 7, F 0383–95. W. A. Phillips to J. D. Cox, May 7, 1870, package 127, L&RR. W. L. G. Miller to Commissioner of Indian Affairs, Oct. 2, 1867, LR OIA Cherokee Agency, M 234, R 101, F 0455–58.

21. Kappler, *Indian Affairs*, vol. 2., pp. 912, 920, 934, 945. For railroad background, see V. V. Masterson, *The Katy Railroad and the Last Frontier*; Miner, *St. Louis-San Francisco*; Craig Miner, "The Border Tier Line: A History of the Missouri River, Ft. Scott and Gulf Railroad, 1865–1870."

bates in Congress were brief and concentrated little more upon the way in which Indian rights would be influenced by this scheme than had those concerning a policy similarly momentous for the tribes during the 1854 Kansas-Nebraska bill controversy.[22] During the debate upon whether to grant the Atlantic and Pacific 50 million acres of land, including twenty sections per mile across the Indian Territory, tribal delegations in the hall outside asked a senator how this would be done since the United States controlled no land in Indian Territory. The answer was that Indian title, to use the wording of the bill, would be "extinguished as rapidly as may be consistent with public policy and the welfare of the Indians." The grant was contingent upon Indian consent, though no one on the floor that day predicted that that consent would be as difficult to obtain as it turned out to be. It seemed safe to make promises to both corporations and Indians, assuming that the Indian would yield to pressure.[23] Bills for the aid of the three Kansas roads also passed almost without comment, though again a concession was made to the tribes that became troublesome to businessmen. Knowing that treaty negotiators were considering allowing only one north-south line, the bills provided for a competition between the K&NV, the UPSB, and the LL&G. The first to reach the southern border of Kansas would receive the sole right to build through Indian Territory.[24] Perhaps this bit of ethics was a piece of economic planning cloaked in the garb of Indian policy by a government that was not ready to regulate economic enterprise openly. Traffic from Kansas to the Gulf would, in 1866, support only one line profitably. As shall be seen, when traffic increased in the next decade, Congress passed legislation void-

22. S. J. Kirkwood to Commissioner of Indian Affairs, March 31, 1882, LS ID, M 606, R 28, F 0114. The opinion was first expressed in a letter of Secretary Cox, May 21, 1870.

23. *Congressional Globe*, 39th Cong., 1st sess., XXVI, 1100–1103. This phrase about extinguishing Indian title was not in the UPSB bill, and this became the topic for much future discussion.

24. An account of the race is in Masterson, *Katy*, pp. 26–38.

ing the 1866 limitations on railroads in the Indian Territory and granting to itself power to authorize any number of railroads through the region without tribal consent.

Some in the Congress did protest. Sen. Lyman Trumbull of Illinois objected to making railroad land grants through Indian Territory lands when there was no treaty authorization for it and said that, "contingent" or no, the United States was in effect obligating itself to get the Indians out of the way. During the discussion of the Kansas and Neosho Valley charter, Sen. Thomas Hendricks of Indiana, who was just beginning to make his reputation as a land reformer, made the suggestion that it might be well to delay congressional action until the 1866 treaties with the tribes were actually signed. The Congress was giving grants of land when as yet no treaty existed authorizing these railroads to pass through tribal lands. Hendricks's motion lost 16 to 12 and left the Cherokees with the arguing point that the charters of the railroads entering their lands had been signed before the treaties authorizing that entry during the haste of a postwar July. Aaron Cragin of New Hampshire said that these charters opened the way for corporate corruption of tribal governments and thus guaranteed that there would never be an undistorted evaluation of the true Indian attitude toward railroads. But then Cragin was from New England.[25]

Despite an evident corporate victory, railroad officials complained that the treaty was not generous enough. Kersey Coates, president of the K&NV, wrote Indian Commissioner Cooley that he was upset the Cherokee treaty was "different in form from what was expected when Gen. Blunt [James Blunt, his colobbyist] and myself left Washington." The Cherokee legislature had consented to a treaty provision allowing the K&NV to buy an 800,000-acre tract in Kansas. Though the line was able to buy the land for one dollar an acre before public advertisement, the fact that this stipulation was not in the treaty indicates again the restraining influence of the Indian Office. That department was to enforce treaty pro-

25. *Congressional Globe*, 39th Cong., 1st sess., XXXVI, 3125–26; William A. Phillips to J. D. Cox [c. 1870], package 127, L&RR.

visions concerning the race of the three railroads to the border, despite massive pressure, and did not, during the entire period of tribal sovereignty in Indian Territory, actually grant to the railroads the lands promised in the 1866 charters. Rights of way had been obtained. Even the tribes that had been moved into Indian Territory from Kansas and the plains to the west found they were subject to these stipulations, whether or not specific clauses pertaining to the matter were in their treaties. For the moment, the government would not force Indians to yield to white pressure beyond that point.[26]

It was, however, difficult for the humanitarians in Congress to maintain limits on corporate activity when the tribes appeared to promote it. During the consideration of the railroad bills and before ratification of the 1866 treaties, the Cherokees passed a resolution in their national council not only consenting to railroads on their lands but requesting them. Those in Washington who called the railway charters "an entering edge to a scheme for getting the Indian land . . . ultimately to drive the Indians from this Territory" had to face the fact that the Cherokees had established a board of trade to seek out railway promoters who were willing to trade stock options for land. Promoters of industry were encouraged by what they considered a demonstration that the Cherokees had reached that point of civilization characterized by a strong affinity for economic speculation. The white was not trying to rob the Indian, said John Henderson in Congress, but to make him wealthy. The tribes saw and realized that, far from sealing their doom, cooperation with the corporation was their only hope.[27] Given the Indians' actions, there was no effective counter to that argument. The railroad bills passed.

26. *Congressional Globe*, 39th Cong., 1st sess., XXXVI, 3334–36. K. Coates to D. N. Cooley, Aug. 11, 1866, LR OIA Cherokee Agency, M 234, R 100, F 0355–57. For accounts of the struggle with settlers over transfer of Cherokee and Osage lands to railroads, see Craig Miner, "Border Frontier: The Missouri River, Ft. Scott and Gulf Railroad in the Cherokee Neutral Lands, 1868–1870," and Gates, *Acres*, pp. 194–222. S. J. Kirkwood to Commissioner of Indian Affairs, March 31, 1882, LS ID, M 606, R 28, F 0114.

27. *Congressional Globe*, 39th Cong., 1st sess., XXXVI, 3335–36.

The treaties, with their right of way provisions, were all ratified.

It is sure that the events of 1865 and 1866 were a hinge upon which Indian destiny in relation to the American corporation took an almost unnoticed, but irreversible turn. Study of the events of those years frees no group from blame and serves to even the burden of responsibility. Certainly, the Indians were never united against the corporation, and they were less defiant by far in their economic destitution of 1865–1866 than they were four years later, when many tribal progressives discovered that the implementation of agreements with the Missouri, Kansas and Texas Railroad proved much less appealing than had the abstract negotiations. Members of the tribe then disregarded their own participation in the bargaining and directed their bitterness over the division of industrial spoils back toward the treaty negotiations of 1866, as though this attitude toward industrialization had been a long and consistently held principle. At the time the potential results had been less clear, and Indian attitudes more heavily weighted toward giving acculturation and corporations a better than even chance. It can also be concluded, without denying pressures for outright tribal destruction by some corporate and government officials, that there were white proponents on the side of moderation. The Board of Indian Commissioners advised in its reports of 1868 and 1869 that railroad directors should regard the Indian as a human being, not a wild beast, and take responsibility that employees treat him justly. It deplored thoughts of damaging Indian governments merely to aid corporations and advised that it would be better for the government to send a few squadrons of cavalry to massacre the natives than to vacillate with circumstances in a way fair to the hopes of neither white nor red. One may ignore the role of speculating Indians and humanitarian whites only by passing over considerable evidence in a desire to simplify the situation. All such simplification leads to the kind of racism that is contained in the assumption that certain ethnic groups are imbued with universal characteristics, good or evil, profound or silly, independent of the morals or intelligence of their individual members. The danger in calling all Indians who dealt with corporations traitors, when they were in the majority, was that it became difficult to decide whether to protect that tribe's sovereignty or someone's image of what an Indian should be.[28]

One thing was certain. If the industrialization of the Indian Territory were to occur at all, it must be guided by the establishment of rules that reflected some consistent principle rather than the expedience of changing power blocs. Cherokee chief Lewis Downing was near the mark in 1869 when he wrote that rules must be agreed upon and then adhered to, especially since there was such a vast difference between different Indian tribes and between all Indians and the American businessman "in that industry, habit, and energy of character which is the result of the development of the idea of accumulation." To allow circumstances to develop freely here without restraint of agreed-upon policy would not do. "To us," wrote Downing, "it appears that once cut loose from our treaty moorings, we will roll and tumble upon the tempestuous ocean of American politics and congressional legislation, and shipwreck be our inevitable destination."[29]

When the hand that had moved the parties at Fort Smith and Washington from behind a curtain became more visible, its form, size, and power were found to be more awesome than either its friends or enemies had predicted. In the seventies railroad corporations entered the Indian Territory, and the practice of negotiating formal treaties with Indians ended. Coal corporations were established upon tribal lands, followed in the eighties by cattle corporations, and in the nineties by oil corporations. Indian control of their own affairs declined, and the nature of civilization was increasingly determined by the thoughts of gandy dancers, cowboys, and roughnecks. The consequences of postwar decisions concerning the corporation and the Indian made of Lewis Downing a melancholy prophet.

28. AR CIA, 1868, p. 46; ibid., 1869, pp. 73–74.
29. AR CIA, 1869, Appendix F, p. 99.

CHAPTER II

"THEY TAKE STOCK
IN OUR DESTRUCTION"

So quickly did rail follow rhetoric in the Indian Territory, and so rapidly were objections about ethics laid aside that Sen. Lot Morrill of Maine was led to conclude, "Our civilization . . . has become our master; not only master of the savage, but the master of the Government as well." That civilization had at its core the juggernaut of material interest, sweeping other considerations away. In 1853, the U.S. government thirty-fifth parallel surveying expedition marked out a rail line in Indian Territory. In 1857, Thaddeus Hyatt, presumably in Kansas to promote the antislavery cause, took young Robert S. Stevens with him to Indian Territory to examine possibilities for constructing a railroad. Government reports spoke of a "hardy, daring and determined pioneer population" moving toward the area, some drawn by "a restless spirit of adventure" and others by a "feverish spirit of speculation." None, it was said, could or should be effectively restrained by the Indian Office. A congressman in 1852 said, "The Indian is placed between the upper and nether millstones and must be crushed. . . . Humanity may forbid, but the *interest* of the white man demands their extinction." Col. Richard Hinton, who was with the Hyatt railway survey of 1857, wrote a half century later that the sound of the old Indian names in his ears reminded him only of "the story of the vast movements which since 1850 have made the newer West free and secure to industrial life."[1]

1. *Congressional Globe*, 40th Cong., 1st sess., XXXVIII, 686–87. Col. Richard Hinton, "The Indian Territory—Its Status, Development and Future,"

Reformers, like Morrill, could only gape and remark:

You have driven him [the Indian] into the fastness, and you are asked
to say that you will give him one foot of land on which he can stand and
be safe; and the reply is, 'absorb him'; 'his inevitable doom is extinction'; 'We must want to build a railroad'—God only knows where. The
honorable Senator . . . says we have got large rights . . . railroad rights.
What is humanity?[2]

The Cherokees were the first Indians to react to the treaties of
1866, by suggesting that the tribe was hardly the naive victim of
corporate drive. Instead, the National Council tried to capitalize the
land lost to plains tribes in the treaty in such a way as to make it
support an industrial base for the tribe in the future. On October 31,
1866, the Cherokee council guaranteed a $500,000 stock subscription
by the tribe in the Union Pacific, Southern Branch Railroad, to be
paid for whenever the lands west of ninety-six degrees could be
sold to the United States. They gave themselves an option to take
more stock within three years, up to the amount realized from the
sale of one million acres of their western lands. A bonus equal to/
proceeds from 250,000 acres was proffered to aid in construction,
and the corporation was given the right to take building materials
from the Cherokee domain to be paid for in stock as well as cash. The
chief was authorized to make a similar subscription to any east-west
road "the building of which may be advantageous to the Cherokee
Nation."[3]

This decision represented hope, though not pure joy. It was true
that UPSB lobbyists had spent twenty-two days at Tahlequah, the
Cherokee capital, making sure the tribe understood all the advan-

---

p. 457. HR 61, 42d Cong., 2d sess., May 2, 1872 (Serial 1528), pp. 2–3. *Congressional Globe*, 32d Cong., 1st sess., XXI, 2175. Hinton, "The Indian Territory," p. 451.

2. *Congressional Globe*, 40th Cong., 1st sess., XXXVIII, 687.

3. Act of Oct. 31, 1866, Cherokee Railroad box, OU; N. S. Goss to O. H.
Browning, Jan. 3, 1867, LR OIA (see "Abbreviations in Footnotes," p. vii)
Cherokee Agency, M 234, R 101, F 0283–90.

tages of allowing the railroad to pass through their lands, and no doubt handing out bribes. Also diluting the argument that the Indians were entirely taken in by the corporations were the clauses contained in the bill that carefully protected Cherokee control of the railroad. The company was required to start construction in one year and work continuously. In exchange for their subscription, the Cherokees would be entitled to representation by two directors on the railroad board, a stipulation that would have guaranteed them warning of policy changes. The Cherokee National Council claimed the right to regulate freight and passenger rates on the new line, specifying that they should not be higher than rates in Kansas. Also, it must be recognized that the bill granted no lands then held by Cherokees, only the proceeds from land that, according to the new treaty, they were committed to sell anyway.[4]

Still, the railroad was not the only investment the tribe was considering for this money. Their immediate moves to protect their rights to mine salt, gypsum, iron, coal, and petroleum in the outlet, either by subleasing to American corporations or forming their own corporations, strongly indicates a firm hope of accommodation to, and even profit from, the economic changes on the horizon. The Creeks granted more liberal provisions to railroads in their 1866 treaty than did the Cherokees and the same year passed an act allowing the sale to the UPSB of a wide strip of land along its proposed route through their domain.[5]

The Cherokees showed no signs of animosity toward the 1867 UPSB surveying party. G. M. Walker and S. P. Heddon saw Cherokee chief William Ross in October and reported that he gave them information and assistance. Others were friendly to the degree of pointing out coal outcrops, which the surveyors marked for future reference. "All with whom we conversed," they wrote, "either at

4. V. V. Masterson, *The Katy Railroad*, p. 16. N. S. Goss to O. H. Browning, Jan. 3, 1867, LR OIA Cherokee Agency, M 234, R 101, F 0283–90.

5. Richard Fields, W. P. Adair, J. A. Scales to N. C. Taylor, April 15, 1867, LR OIA Cherokee Agency, M 234, R 101, F 0224–26. James D. Morrison, "The Union Pacific, Southern Branch," p. 181.

Ft. Gibson or along the route expressed themselves very friendly to this enterprise and anxious for its early completion." The question is why three years later the Atlantic and Pacific railroad survey team was forcibly removed from the Creek Nation, while the directors of that road, seeking stock and bond subscriptions of the type given the UPSB earlier, met with a curt denial? Why, by 1870, was William Ross himself writing bitter pamphlets protesting that the railroad-territorial scheme was the grossest exploitation? The answer is that events proved to many Indians that the hope of accommodation between corporate ambition and tribal sovereignty was a delusion. Some came to believe that actions, which in 1866 they had regarded as merely practical, were in fact unpatriotic.[6]

Many events of the period immediately after the treaty was signed confirmed the negativism within the tribes. For example, a census taker among the Cherokees spent the year 1868, not taking a census, but lobbying for railroads at the Creek council, for which he was paid two thousand dollars by outside interests. The UPSB acted in such unexpected ways that in April 1868 the Cherokees cancelled their generous stock subscription contract. The chief reported letters from the company that were "calculated to mislead" and of the patent failure of the company to live up to the terms of the council action. In 1869, the Cherokees elected as chief Lewis Downing, a spokesman for anticorporate forces, and passed a law declaring it a penal offense for any tribal citizen to advocate individual ownership of land or to sell land to anyone not a tribal citizen.[7]

The disillusionment with their ability to control outside cor-

6. G. M. Walker to N. S. Goss, Nov. 21, 1867, Cherokee Railroad File (Tahlequah acquisition), IAD. H. Craig Miner, "The Struggle for an East-West Railway into the Indian Territory, 1870–1882," pp. 560–61; for William Ross's biography, with a representative sample of speeches, see *The Life and Times of Honorable William P. Ross* (Fort Smith, 1893), Gilcrease.

7. H. Tompkins to N. G. Taylor, Feb. 29, 1868, LR OIA Cherokee Agency, M 234, R 101, F 1382–86. W. L. G. Miller to P. B. Mascon, April 13, 1868, Cherokee Railroad File (Tahlequah acquisition), IAD. I. N. Parker to E. S. Parker, Oct. 14, 1869, LR OIA Southern Superintendency, M 234, R 838, F 0786–89.

porations led the Indian nations to try chartering their own railways. This was the logical outgrowth of a progressive mentality and the clauses in several of the 1866 treaties stipulating that a unified tribal government (later known as the Okmulgee government) would have the power to charter internal improvement corporations. Had the goal of the United States been merely to guarantee movement of traffic, with no concomitant design to destroy tribal governments, native-run railways would have provided a healing compromise. It was shocking to the tribes that these projects were never given a chance to try and fail but were nipped in the bud by the Indian Office on grounds that introduced fears where hopes had reigned.

The idea for native railroads grew out of a division within the Choctaw tribe. Most wanted railroads, but some feared introducing outside corporations. Action was further complicated because the Choctaws could not agree with the Chickasaws, who by treaty shared their land rights, upon the desirability of granting lands to railroads. The Choctaw council passed a bill in 1869 granting a right of way to any railroad that could enter, on the provision that the tribe could hold stock in it by giving land in exchange. The Chickasaws, however, did not agree. The Chickasaws were in a constant quarrel with the Choctaws because the latter often did not pay to them the one-fourth of all revenues from the jointly held land to which they were entitled. Since the smaller tribe would have less railway mileage than the Choctaws, they feared that the latter, acting as collecting agent for damages paid by U.S. corporations, would add to the list of financial grievances between the tribes. In an attempt at compromise, the Choctaws chartered two Indian railroad corporations: the Choctaw and Chickasaw Central Railway Company and the Choctaw and Chickasaw Thirty-Fifth Parallel Railway Company.[8]

The latter company, chartered in 1870 to build along the east-west route, was a most interesting combination of white and Indian

8. Act of Chickasaws, Sept. 19, 1869, LR OIA Choctaw Agency, M 234, R 178, F 0174–76. For the joint tenancy situation, see A. M. Gibson, *The Chickasaws*, passim.

initiative. According to the charter, the railroad—under the corporate name in the Choctaw language *Palelil 35 Chahta Chikasha Itatuklo Chata Oka*—was allotted a capital stock of $7 million. Six directors were to be of the Choctaw or Chickasaw tribes, and the principal chiefs of both tribes were to be permanent members of the board, thus insuring an Indian majority. But the expertise of whites was recognized. The president was Dudley Jones of Little Rock, Arkansas, and the general agent and chief attorney were also white men. Alternate sections of land on each side of the line were to be given in consideration of construction and issuance of stock.[9] Was this simply a blind used by "invisible" white promoters to bypass treaty stipulations and federal regulations? Was it a genuine and viable attempt at white-native industrial cooperation? No test is available to give us answers, for two familiar specters, tribal division and discouragement by the Indian Office, combined to kill the Choctaw railroads before they were fairly born.

The Thirty-Fifth Parallel Company, about which most information survives, applied to the secretary of the interior in July 1870 for permission to make a survey. The secretary replied to general agent D. H. Barnes of Kalamazoo, Michigan, that he could not recognize the right of the Choctaw council to grant privileges without corresponding action by the "proper authorities" of the United States. This statement was an important qualification upon Indian sovereignty. Added to this, the Chickasaws, remembering intratribal suspicions long predating the industrial age, refused to support the new railroad. Therefore the government could shift a part of the blame for destroying the native railroad to the Indians themselves. Had the tribes been unified, the result might have been the same, but the moral burden would have been more precisely placed.[10]

The Cherokees also chartered a railroad even offering Congress

9. *Charter of the Choctaw and Chickasaw Thirty-Fifth Parallel Railroad Company* (Little Rock, 1870), Hargrett Collection, Gilcrease.

10. J. D. Cox to J. H. Barnes, July 29, 1870, LR OIA Choctaw Agency, M 234, R 179, F 0100. Charles Mix to J. D. Cox, July 11, 1870, package 129, L&RR.

the right to create and regulate the company, so long as it was owned by Cherokee citizens. The instructions given by the Cherokee council to its Washington delegation in 1870 emphasized that permission for the tribe to build its own railroads was of "vital importance" to its future welfare. According to instructions:

> They are assured, that the possession and ownership of a most valuable tract or belt of land through the heart of their country by any corporation of citizens of the United States or foreign countries—capitalists and strangers, who have no sympathy for Indians or their peculiarities, who would desire the lands along their Road brought into market and opened to immigration as speedily as possible—who would only look upon their Nation and perhaps their existence and presence in any form as an encumberance and a nuisance—could only result in the disruption of their Nationality and the ruin of their people.

Tribal leaders explained that they wanted to build their own railroad "for reasons above all pecuniary consideration." They were primarily interested in the role it would play in their continued progress toward "Christian civilization" while maintaining something of their Indian culture and tribal rights.[11]

The response from Washington in this case indicated even more exactly federal attitudes toward Indian sovereignty. In January 1870 Ely S. Parker, himself a mixed-blood Seneca Indian and the first Indian commissioner of Indian affairs, recommended denying the Cherokee request. He explained in a letter to Secretary of the Interior J. D. Cox that it was known that the work could be carried on only by persons "qualified by nature and experience" and that federal aid and supervision was no substitute for the actions of men "who will be governed by motives of self-interest." Parker admitted that the entry of outside corporations might destroy Indian nationality, but he claimed it would not be "good policy to encourage any measures that look to the perpetuation of semi-civilized customs and forms of society, to the detriment of public interest." The institution of the tribe

11. Cherokee delegation to E. S. Parker, Jan. 18, 1870, LR OIA Cherokee Agency, M 234, R 103, F 0496–97.

should be destroyed and its members become U.S. citizens. The Cherokees' request for a native railroad was rejected. The Creeks also applied for permission to build their own railroad, saying their very existence, "which is as dear to them as it is to the people of the United States," depended on the transit arrangements through their country. The request was denied. While Parker has been portrayed in some histories as a persecuted hero to his race, a look at this and later actions in regard to corporations points to the conclusion that his views were little different from those of the whites around him. His position must have disillusioned many persons in Indian Territory.[12]

Facing immediate grading in their lands and chastened by moves discouraging to their industrial and political hopes, in 1870 intratribal division concerning the corporate issue was more evident than ever. Even within the factions that had agreed to railroads in 1866, there were now divisions on strategy. Some, like I. N. Parker, an adopted Cherokee citizen by marriage, assured Washington that unfriendly tribal legislation had been pushed by the "ignorant" traditionalist classes against the better judgment of the Indian intellectuals and that the federal government should intervene. Parker stated the view of one Cherokee faction in saying that, while the railroad would bring ills, tribal resistance to it would more quickly destroy them than trying to adapt. Intransigence would leave noble sentiments, remembered "in verse and prose," but no substance. Other memorialists—white attorneys for the Cherokee Indian delegations—while not opposing rail links per se, were frightened deeply for tribal sovereignty and wanted firm guarantees assuring it before the railroad built a foot of line.[13]

The latter position emerged as native stock options and intratribal

12. E. S. Parker to J. D. Cox, Jan. 24, 1870, LR ID, box 25, RG 48, NA. Cherokee delegation to E. S. Parker, April 14, 1870, LR OIA, Cherokee Agency, M 234, R 103, F 0537–39. G. W. Stidham and Creek delegation to J. D. Cox, April 19, 1870, package 127, L&RR.

13. I. N. Parker to E. S. Parker, Oct. 18, 1869, LR OIA, Southern Superintendency, M 234, R 838, F 0786–89. I. N. Parker to James Bell, Dec. 1, 1869, Cherokee Railroad Box, OU.

corporations failed at the same time that bills were introduced in Congress to create a U.S. territory and to open the country to immigrants who would require transportation by rail. Consequently rhetoric became so intense that it might have been considered typical anti-white Indian eloquence had not a great deal of it been composed by whites, acting as attorneys for mixed-blood factions.

> The advancing hosts have already passed the summit of Pisgah, and are about to descend into Canaan. Stay, or stay your footsteps, ye seekers of wealth. . . . Let not the last footfall of the Red man, as he steps over the boundary of time, echo back to the white man that he is fleeing from his tyranny and oppression into eternity as his last refuge and hope.[14]

Pitchlynn, for the Choctaws, cried that if public opinion did not concern itself for once "with the wrongs done by power to the defenseless," the Indian Territory would be "given away to foreign adventurers and financial rogues." He asked Congress to protect Indians against "those who desire and hunger by crooked means and seemingly just legislation, to possess themselves of their lands." The Cherokee delegation noted that the railroads had aims that were invisible when the 1866 treaties were negotiated, "If the guarantees of the government are to be respected we are entitled at least to existence— leaving out all questions of prosperity and advancement." The railroads claimed too much, "They take stock in our destruction and in the dishonor of the government." The Creek delegation and the Choctaw-Chickasaw delegation agreed that to people "to whom the whole railway subject is a novelty" continued existence depended upon its careful regulation. The Congress, wrote William Phillips for the Cherokees, could no more grant a corporation powers in Indian Territory than the New York legislature could grant one of its corporations powers in Istanbul or Peking. The demands of railroads were in advance of real need, he said, and such "artificial and forcing

---

14. Isaac N. Morris, *Argument of Honorable Isaac N. Morris of Illinois, Of Counsel for the Cherokee Indians, Before the House Committee on Indian Affairs, Against the Bill Proposing to Establish a Territorial Government Over the Indians.* . . . (Washington, D.C., 1870), Indian Pamphlets, Vol. 9, KSHS.

efforts" were inconsistent with the government's duty to give the tribes time to adjust their institutions slowly to new conditions. A memorial signed by four tribes in May 1870, a month before a railroad entered the Cherokee lands from the north, concluded that the action of railroads was designed to precipitate a crisis. This crisis "would lead to a war upon our poor and weak people which would result in their ruin, their utter destruction, and the possession of their lands by railroad speculators and political adventurers—who care as little for their country's honor and good name as they do for an Indian's rights." The invisible hand was now writing on the wall, and the stakes becoming clear. The delegation said that in light of the "astounding facts" that had come to its attention, it must "beg" the federal government "for mercy's sake, and the sake of humanity, to keep its plighted faith." Yet the question of Lot Morrill, some years earlier, remained. When civilization was defined as railroad building, what, to the age of enterprise, was humanity?[15]

Meanwhile, the Kansas railroads had taken on new names and new ambitions. The Kansas and Neosho Valley railroad became, in 1868, the Missouri River, Fort Scott and Gulf. The Union Pacific, Southern Branch, changed its name in March 1870 to Missouri, Kansas and Texas. The management of both roads engaged in a frantic building competition, sometimes by the light of kerosene lamps, which admitted little philosophizing, though in this attitude were highly significant indications of the ultimate destiny of the Indian.

At the end of March 1870 the MRFtS&G struck the southern border of Kansas, just north of the Quapaw reserve. It was reported that ten minutes after that news reached the border town of Baxter Springs a prominent city official was drunk, that in one hour fifty men were drunk, and in two hours one hundred. On May 2 general manager James Joy wired his lobbyist that he had beaten the MK&T by fifty

15. SMD 90, 41st Cong., 2d sess., March 18, 1870 (Serial 1408). Cherokee delegation to J. D. Cox, April 19, 1870; Creek delegation to J. D. Cox, April 19, 1870; W. A. Phillips to J. D. Cox, n.d. (internal evidence would place this letter about the same time as the two above, surely in 1870); Combined delegations to J. D. Cox, May 6, 1870, package 127, L&RR.

miles and that "our Missouri River, Fort Scott and Gulf Road opens today through the Indian country with our business trains." At Baxter, railroad officials celebrated by watching an Indian dance, while William Ross of the Cherokee composed a letter to President Grant, asking for protection against "the ambition of aspiring men, the cupidity of souless corporations and combinations of whatever name, or the mistaken philanthropy of the uninformed."[16]

As Ross wrote, and the Quapaws and Senecas, bedecked in costume jewelry and cavalry sabers, danced for a drunken crowd at Baxter Springs, the MK&T was laying rail by day and night. Since its competitor had reached the border elsewhere than above the Cherokee Nation, where the right of way was, MK&T officials believed that Joy's road would not be recognized by Washington as winner of the privilege to cross Indian Territory. On June 8, Levi Parsons, representing the MK&T, wired the secretary of the interior to confirm that the "Katy," as the road was nicknamed, had reached the Cherokee Nation. The first spike in the Indian Territory was driven by E. C. Boudinot, leader of the Cherokee southern faction, who said that he had no fear of a railroad that would make his people wealthy and bind them to the federal government. R. S. Stevens, who had been with Hyatt on the 1857 survey, had speculated in Indian lands in Kansas, and was now manager of the MK&T, made a more sweeping statement:[17]

It is with feelings of no ordinary interest that we meet on this spot considered by many as on the verge of civilization—on the line which divides the red man from the white man. This gathering augurs that the two civilization which meet and commingle here today are to be blended into one and that line which separates them to be blotted out. . . . Nor

16. *Wyandotte Gazette*, March 31, 1870. J. F. Joy to James Craig (telegram), May 2, 1870, package 127, L&RR. *Wyandotte Gazette*, May 19, 1870; William Ross to U. S. Grant, June 6, 1870, LR OIA Southern Superintendency, M 234, R 839, F 0200–0205.

17. Levi Parsons to J. D. Cox (telegram), June 8, 1870, LR OIA, Southern Superintendency, M 234, R 839, F 403. *Emporia News*, June 17, 1870.

shall we stop here. . . . We shall not pause . . . till our engine stands panting in the palaces of the Montezumas and the halls of the Aztecs.[18]

Comment in Kansas was more threatening yet to any hope that tribal sovereignty and railroads might coexist. The *Emporia News,* located at the regional headquarters for the MK&T, editorialized that it was not a "sugar and plum" Indian policy that had cleared Kansas Indian reserves for railroads, and bullets might likewise be necessary to the south:

> If the Indians in demanding their rights did not thus . . . block the wheels of the car of progress, then their requests would be entitled to some consideration. But if what they asked for should be granted, then the pioneer must be restricted to certain well-defined bounds, the development of mines must not be extended beyond such and such limits, and the building of railroads with the tide of teeming multitudes of busy, active men they carry with them must be checked. But the fact is, this state of things can not come to pass. . . . Red Cloud and Spotted Tail must either take hold and help the white man develop the great West, constructing railroads, working mines, and building towns, or they must be removed to new hunting grounds. Extermination is a terrible word; but finally, we fear, they will come to know fully its bitter meaning, unless they subdue their wild restless natures and consent to engage in the peaceful pursuits of civilization.

The *News* considered the line of railroad cars "the greatest of all medicines" and the whistle of the steam engine the death knell of the Indian race.[19]

The rival Kansas corporations moved forward with great confidence. By July 1870 white settlers were staking claims in the Cherokee country along the rail survey, arguing that the federal government was unwilling or unable to stop them. MK&T officials wrote the Indian Office that since the Cherokee council supported it, and individual Cherokees were competing for tie and coal contracts, the

18. Masterson, *Katy,* p. 72.
19. *Emporia News,* June 24, Sept. 16, 1870.

corporation did not expect that its designs would be questioned by "our own government." MRFtS&G employees built cattle pens in the Quapaw lands, observing that if its rival could continue building without obtaining specific permission through further legislation, it intended to do the same. Ironically, the most serious struggle of the year 1870 was not between railroads and Indians, but between these two railroads for the north-south franchise. Indians stood helplessly in the wings, clutching memorials and protests and learning new things about their future as viewed by the American body corporate.[20]

There was real danger at this juncture that treaty guarantees might be abandoned altogether and arguments among corporations might be settled by allowing them all to build into Indian country. The secretary of the interior must be credited for preserving the right-of-way limitations in the treaties despite these odds. For example, when a Cherokee delegation argued that the MK&T had left gaps in their line in Kansas and was therefore not entitled to grade in Indian Territory, Ely Parker, the Seneca commissioner of Indian affairs, defended the railroad.[21] Secretary J. D. Cox disagreed and demanded a meeting at Washington of all interested railroad and Indian delegations. He also set in motion a field investigation to determine quality of construction upon the two potential north-south lines through Indian Territory. Cox said that the negotiation for removal of small tribes to Indian Territory had been based upon federal assurance that it would not be opened to wholesale railroad building and that therefore good faith required that pressure from corporations be resisted.[22]

20. W. L. S. Miller, Maxwell Chambers to James Vann, July 26, 1870, LR OIA, Cherokee Agency, M 234, R 103, F 0326–29. Levi Parsons to J. D. Cox, April 15, 1870; J. E. McKeighan to George Mitchell, April 17, 1870, package 127, L&RR; Masterson, *Katy*, pp. 52, 58.

21. E. S. Parker to J. D. Cox, May 12, 1870, package 127, L&RR.

22. J. D. Cox to President, May 21, 1870, LR OIA, Southern Superintendency, M 234, R 839, F 0363–96. Cox, in this long letter, consistently agreed with the Indian delegations in deprecating "any course which may throw them into closer contact or more direct competition with our own people, than absolutely necessary."

The Little Rock and Fort Smith railroad had obtained a land grant from the Choctaws, but the Chickasaws would not go along. The railroad was asking the Indian Office to intervene.[23] Cox believed that compromising on such an issue would subject the dignity of government to a most unreliable circumstantial pressure. He therefore validated the victory of the MK&T, based on a technicality as it was, and ignored the plea of his investigating team that the MRFtS&G be allowed access also, lest numerous stockholders be ruined and the economy suffer. He also made distinctions when it came to evaluating Indian opinion.[24] He knew that Joy was doubtless correct when he said he could get the consent of the Quapaws to railroad building through the liberal use of money, since, in Joy's words, "We have found when money is in question the Indian will bargain for it—covets it—is willing to trade for it, quite as clearly and earnestly as his white neighbor."[25] Yet he decided not to allow unsupervised corporate lobbying to encourage the rapacious elements within the tribes. He respected a Cherokee argument that the MK&T not be allowed to build a line to Fort Smith, planned as a boost for sagging finances, but should be required by the government to cleave to the original north-south route to Texas.[26]

Cox's attitude here romanticized neither the corporation nor the Indian and is a model of appropriate action in a difficult situation by a practical, but also mildly courageous official. It was men in the midst of the compromises of power, like Cox—not the New England intel-

23. C. W. Huntington to J. D. Cox, May 24, 1870, package 127, L&RR.

24. Enoch Hoag and W. B. Hazen to E. S. Parker, June 13, 1870, LR OIA, Southern Superintendency, M 234, R 839, F 0266–70.

25. James Joy to James Craig, June 2, 1870, ibid., F 0292–305.

26. W. A. Phillips to the President, June 14, 1870, LR OIA, Cherokee Agency, M 234, R 103, F 1023–25; to J. D. Cox, June 21, 1870, package 128, L&RR; to J. D. Cox, July (?), package 129, ibid. Cox's deliberations and decision are detailed in: William F. Cady to J. D. Cox, June 29, 1870, package 128, L&RR; J. D. Cox to Commissioner of Indian Affairs, July 2, 1870, LR OIA, Southern Superintendency, M 234, R 839, F 0405–11; J. D. Cox to President, July 12, 1870, package 129, L&RR.

lectuals nor the isolated full blood—who were in a position to influence
the nature of the meeting between Indian and corporation. Had it not
been for a few like him, in federal and tribal government and on corporate boards, the destruction of the tribes' power would have come
sooner. Had there been more, it need not have come at all.

The MK&T was not a huge corporation, however soulless it
might have been. In July 1870 it owned 15 locomotives, 6 baggage cars,
50 stock cars, 118 flat cars, 58 box cars, and 9 hand trucks. But to the
Cherokees, it looked awesome, not so much because of its size as
because of its influence in stirring the spirit of the whites on the border. Chief Downing asked that Indians be allowed to air their objections at a U.S. court hearing before trains began to run, and Enoch
Hoag, a Quaker Indian superintendent, admitted that the railroad
situation was bound to upset President U. S. Grant's newly instituted
Indian "Peace Policy." To the Indian, Hoag wrote, "the signs of the
time in the influx of immigration, the tone of the public press, the
boldness of adventurers rushing down upon the Indian lands, the
rapid extension of railroads, with their treasurer purchasing lands
and influence, are alarming signs of impending evil." William Adair,
a native Cherokee delegate in Washington, went on a speaking tour
of the east coast in the fall of 1870, with the theme that "the innate
genius of the Indian race was radically different from the white one;
that the two races were, therefore, by nature antagonistic to each
other, and could not be *forced* into an immediate commingling . . .
without a '*war of races*,' which could have but one logical result,
vis., the *deterioration* and *destruction* of the weaker party, the Indians." Adair hoped that education of the public to the true interest of
the Indian would cut off the corporate threat. He agreed with Peter
Pitchlynn that any breach in the old guarantees would let in a tide
to inundate those Indians who thought to make a tiny rift to slake
their thirst "and foolishly imagine it will grow no wider and
deeper."[27]

The progressive factions, especially after the failure of the move-

27. Levi Parsons certificate, July 5, 1870, package 129, L&RR. Lewis
Downing to J. D. Cox, Aug. 1, 1879, package 130, L&RR. AR CIA, 1870, p. 260.

ment to establish railways run by tribes, lost ground in all tribes. A bill introduced by them in the Choctaw council of 1870 for individual allotment of lands was defeated, and the sense of the debate was that railroad building was a thing to be feared. The Cherokees began framing legislation to limit taking of timber by corporations and asked their agent for troops to regulate the disorder around railroad construction camps. That agent, John Craig, recognized, with only fifteen miles of line built, that the railroad was eroding tribal sovereignty. The question was, he wrote, whether these lands were to be used to enrich railways or to be the abiding place of a nation. "In the world's history no dependent nation has been denied the privilege of living under their peculiar laws and institutions, unless when its destruction was intended." Yet, the Indians were being asked to compromise most of their economic institutions, including common landholding. Craig wrote that railroads and settlers "shoulder each other to the press" to print accounts of the way the land should be taken.[28]

While progressives were restive at the introduction of railroads, full bloods were unnerved. One Choctaw of this class expressed his fears thus:

I have ridden on those railroads east of the Mississippi. They have little houses on wheels—whole strings of them. One string can carry several hundred people. These little houses can be shut up and the doors locked. If we allow the railroads to come, the white men will give a picnic some time by the side of the iron road and will invite all the fullbloods to attend. They will get the men to play ball off a piece. Then they will get our women to go into the little houses on wheels and will lock them up

---

Letter of W. P. Adair, Cherokee Delegate, Addressed to His People (Washington, D.C., 1870), Foreman Collection, Gilcrease. *Letter of P. P. Pitchlynn to the People of the Choctaw and Chickasaw Nations Upon the Question of Sectionizing and Dividing Their Lands in Severalty,* Hargrett Collection, Gilcrease.

28. AR CIA, 1870, p. 292. John Craig to Commissioner of Indian Affairs, Sept. 15, 1870, LR OIA, Cherokee Agency, M 234, R 103, F 0379–82. AR CIA, 1870, pp. 286–87.

and run off with them into Texas or Missouri. Then what will we do for women?[29]

Coleman Cole, later chief of the Choctaws, thought that the railroad would "gobble" the executive branches of the Indian nations. "I am afraid," he told an investigating committee, "I might get into a greasy pot or something and come out and be muddy black and that I would be gone." Inquiring further what he meant, the committee recorded this exchange:

Q. You don't like Mr. [Robert S.] Stevens much now?
A. I don't like the steam that was burning there.
Q. The steam that was burning there?
A. On the Railroad.
Q. You don't like the Railroad now?
A. The way it smells.
Q. You were afraid you would get boiled up in a pot of grease if you took a ride with him?
A. Yes, Sir, if he had got me away in Texas there.[30]

Surely, there was little attempt here to meet the white man upon his own cultural ground or to match him at games of interpretation at which he was skilled. There was only a blanketed Indian, well in the minority within his own tribe, forming vague pictures of a belching steam monster, about which the words of attorneys were flying.

On June 6, 1870, at noon, an MK&T 4–4–0 locomotive "uttered its premonitory shriek of progress" and crossed the border into the Indian Territory. One of the thirty-five people there recollected later that it had come "whistlin', snortin', and chuggin' with a big noise," and all were afraid it would not stop or would jump the track, and so ran into the timber. When it did stop, the people returned slowly to look it over.[31]

In a way, this is what happened to the Indian nations at large.

29. Morrison, "Union Pacific, Southern Branch," p. 176.
30. Testimony of Coleman Cole, July 7, 1877, irregularly shaped papers, file 310, shelf 4, RG 75, NA.
31. The account of the crossing is in a loose-leaf file marked "Railroads" in the library of the Oklahoma Historical Society.

They had, in the sixties, been resigned to, if not eager for, the railroad. When it came steaming into their territory with its lobbyists and its demands for land and new political forms, however, they became frightened at these unexpected noisy aspects. Then, slowly, the progressives returned to give the real thing a looking over, and to estimate what of their interest they could salvage. As tribes, if not as a race, the Indian attitude toward railroad building was not far from that of contemporary small-town whites, who vigorously promoted a railroad into their town and then complained of its abuses once it arrived.[32] The *Vindicator*, published at Atoka, Choctaw Nation, expressed well the sense of shock, recognition, and shattering of illusion, that moved the tribes in the seventies:

> Hitherto they have taken no thought for themselves, but have listened to the syren song of that sweet delusion that whispered in their ears a perfect tranquility, and a guarantee of undisturbed repose beneath the umbrage of their own forrests [*sic*] But the puff and blow of the steam car, sweeping to and fro, through the very heart of the country, has falsified the promise, and warned them to be up and doing.[33]

The corporation was in the field, its strength was gauged, and the battle was joined.

32. For an account of this pattern see H. Craig Miner, "Hopes and Fears: Ambivalence in the Anti-Railroad Movement at Springfield, Missouri, 1870–1880," *Missouri Historical Society Bulletin*, XXVII (Jan. 1971), 129–46.

33. *Vindicator*, July 11, 1872.

CHAPTER **III**

CAPITALISTS AND STRANGERS

The Missouri, Kansas and Texas railroad claimed in Washington that not only did it have no intention of violating Indian rights during its construction period but it also feared "even to injure their sensibilities." Nevertheless Cherokee agent John Craig requested in September 1870 that U.S. troops be dispatched to stop timber cutting by the railroad, since no timber contracts had been submitted by the corporation for approval by himself or clerks in the East. He also complained of the illegal liquor traffic that was fostered by railroad work gangs. Ironically, Craig was not granted the use of troops, while the railroad corporation did get a contingent of frontier regulars to protect its gandy dancers against possible violence from the tribes. Railroad officers argued that "any informality which may have occurred in our proceeding . . . has been entirely unintentional" and noted that liquor stores were outside their area of responsibility. If anyone was being exploited, wrote rail official Levi Parsons, it was the corporation. Stone was being sold to it at one dollar a yard when it was provided free in the states in return for opening quarries. Also Indian and federal legislation was unspecific as to whether the railroad should pay individual claimants or the tribe for timber used, with the result that the tribe sometimes asked for payment even after receipts to individuals had been produced by the railroad. Parsons found it necessary to suspend operations in the middle of October to go to the Territory and personally supervise matters.[1]

1. Levi Parsons to J. D. Cox, Oct. 12, 1870, box 130, L&RR (for "Abbreviations in Footnotes," see p. vii). John Craig to Commissioner of Indian Affairs, Sept. 26, 1870, LR OIA Cherokee Agency, M 234, R 103, F 0396–98. H. R. Clum to W. T. Otto, Oct. 4, 1870, box 130, L&RR. George Denison to

One Indian whose sensibilities *were* injured was Choctaw Peter Pitchlynn. He emphasized that the MK&T was yet claiming a land grant and was willing to lobby in Congress for a territorial government in order to get it. The points in the new railroad bills that were circulating in Washington gave the strong impression that "not even a decent regard was paid to the faith of treaties, or to common honesty, or to the public opinion of mankind." If the Indian were to sacrifice tribal sovereignty, Pitchlynn believed that he should at least exact a price for it, a position for which he could not be accused of idealism. There was an element of sour grapes in his complaint that the new rail bills did not allow the tribe to subscribe stock in land, but only in cash, and that new laws extended U.S. revenue regulations ("annoying, vexatious, odious and absurd") to the manufacture of tobacco and spirits in the Indian Territory. Yet his writing showed a subtle understanding of the process by which the tribes would lose power to the corporation. Indians should, he wrote to his peers, take a militant attitude toward any who assented to the "hideous and dishonorable" doctrine that treaties were not binding. Humble words and "honeyed phrases," "deprecating remonstrances," and "meek expostulations," were not acceptable, "Although the weak cannot resist the strong, nor vindicate their rights by arms, they lose all when they beg for favors and acts of grace, instead of insisting on them as rights." Such begging strengthened the aggressor. If the Indians stood united and made no accommodation, they would have at least a moral power, "which the strongest Empires must respect."[2]

That sort of talk led the railroad to compromise. Late in October it applied to the Cherokee Nation to buy land on both sides of its track, rather than waiting for it to come free by the destruction of

W. T. Otto, Oct. 6, 1870, LR OIA Cherokee Agency, M 234, R 103, F 0811–13. Levi Parsons to J. D. Cox, Oct. 12, 1870; Levi Parsons to Lewis Downing, Sept. 20, 1870; Levi Parsons to Britton and Gray, Oct. 19, 1870, box 130, L&RR.

2. *Report of P. P. Pitchlynn to His Excellency the Principal Chief and General Council of the Choctaw Nation. . . .* (Washington, D.C., 1870), 17653, Choctaw-Federal Relations File, IAD. An excellent biography is W. David Baird, *Peter Pitchlynn: Chief of the Choctaws.*

the tribes. "If no more lands are acquired," Parsons wrote to Commissioner of Indian Affairs Ely Parker, "it places all of the people doing business with the Railroad in the position of committing trespass constantly upon the lands of the Indians, which will be a constant source of difficulty and differences not only between the Indians and the Railroad Company, but also between the Indians and the public at large." Parsons recognized well enough that the whistle on the iron horse would fall upon vacant ground unless it was accompanied by the shouts of townsite lot speculators arguing over where best to put the depot and the hotel. It had entered the country with the intention, as was universal in western railroading at the time, of making up through land speculation the income statement deficits that might result from sparse traffic in the early years of a pioneer enterprise. The company also asked permission to buy land around depot sites and to be considered first if the Indian Territory grazing land west of ninety-six degrees were ever opened for private bids.[3]

It might be argued that this was an attempt, given the circumstances, to be fair and to protect Indian financial interests, if not political rights. The Cherokees, however, unequivocally refused. Evidence indicates that the reason for their refusal was not that they intended to prevent townsite development along the railroad but that they estimated they would profit more by the development of the townsites themselves, through their newly appointed townsite commissioners, than by sale of blocks of land to the railroad. Also, and this was the reason most broadly advertised, there was a fear that any land negotiation with the corporation was only a "preliminary formality," to be followed by the forced taking of their lands by a corporate-government cadre. "If parcels of their lands should go into the possession of a railroad company," wrote John Craig, "the corporation, with its adverse and conflicting interests, would inevitably become the too powerful master of the Cherokee Nation." If the mere presence of whites among them, he continued, had been enough

3. Levi Parsons to E. S. Parker, Oct. 31, 1870, LR OIA Cherokee Agency, M 234, R 103, F 1043–45. Levi Parsons to [E. S.] Parker, Nov. 18, 1870, LR OIA Cherokee Agency, M 234, R 103, F 1053.

to justify removing the Cherokees from their homes in the Southeast, how were they to estimate the dangers of locating a land-owning corporation in their midst? The tribe decided that if the railroad were to come, it would not own any land except a two-hundred-foot right of way and minimal station and switching grounds.[4]

Having reached that impasse on landholding, the parties wrangled over use of the land's products. The Cherokees passed a tie law on December 14, which for the first time defined the procedure for taking timber. The principal chief was to grant licenses to individual Cherokee citizens to provide ties to the railroad, and these contracts were to be approved by the National Council and the Indian Office. To prevent monopoly among Indian enterpreneurs the act limited the extent of a contract that could be made by any individual Indian or company of Indians to ten thousand ties. The tribe was to be paid a royalty of five cents per tie, fifteen cents per cubic yard of stone, and fifteen per cent of actual cash value for timber taken for bridges, depots, and cars. Through this legislation the tribe recognized the right of its individual citizens to "preempt" lands in the common domain along the proposed line of the railroad, and so to act like communists as regarded purchase of the land and like capitalists when it came to collection for the ties cut from it.[5]

Railroad officials were upset with this arrangement, as were some members of the tribe. Chief Downing asked whether the agent in the field might represent the Indian office in Washington in approving tie contracts. Levi Parsons thought that the tie law, passed in response to a company request for permission to purchase from individuals, created a bureaucratic procedure that would damage the corporation. In the interest of continued rapid construction, Parsons asked officials at Washington to allow the railroad to delay filing copies of tie contracts "because if we first have to make our contracts with the Chero-

4. John Craig to Commissioner of Indian Affairs, Nov. 30, 1870, LR OIA Cherokee Agency, M 234, R 103, F 0485–92.

5. Act of Dec. 10, 1870, Cherokee railroad file, OU; Lewis Downing to E. S. Parker, Dec. 16, 1870, LR OIA Cherokee Agency, M 234, R 104, F 1155–56.

kee citizens and send them to Tahlequah, their Capital, to be ratified
by the proper Chief, and then to Washington to be ratified by the
Department before we can commence under such contracts to get our
ties, it will use up all the time from this to the first of April, and we
can build our Road and have it running before we can get through
the several formalities required by this bill." While the tie law was
often violated, it was not modified. When the attorney for the Atlantic
and Pacific railroad advised the tribe in 1871 that his line was about to
enter the Cherokee Nation from the east, the tie plan, with all its
complications, was described to him.[6]

F. S. Hodges made the A&P survey in 1870–1871. Meeting a less
friendly reception than had the MK&T surveyors before him, Hodges
was once ordered out of the Territory by the Indian Office for meddling in areas he was not authorized to deal with. All delays, however,
were a matter of days. Hodges, after passing the Creek village of
"Tulsey Town" (later Tulsa, Oklahoma), crossed the Arkansas
River and headed west, his goal to mark a line toward Albuquerque
through the domain of the plains tribes then being moved into
western Indian Territory. He did so despite a snow storm and surveyed sixteen hundred miles of potential A&P line that winter, from
Missouri to California. In an epic effort, he covered three thousand
miles by wagon, losing five of his thirteen men to exposure.[7]

The Indians in the western region, however, were less impressed
by Hodges's dedication than surprised that he should be there at all.
They responded not with legal briefs but with physical threats. The
army officers waiting for Hodges at the Cheyenne and Arapaho
agency learned that a full-scale attack upon the surveyors was planned.
The surveying party was once attacked by Lone Wolf and seventy-
five Kiowa Indians, who harrassed them for twenty-four hours and

6. Lewis Downing to E. S. Parker, Dec. 16, 1870, ibid.; Levi Parsons to
Columbus Delano, Dec. 28, 1870, box 130, L&RR. C. J. Hillyer to E. S. Parker,
Jan. 14, 1871, LR OIA Cherokee Agency, M 234, R 104, F 0579–84. A copy
of the tie law is included in this letter.

7. F. S. Hodges, "Report of Survey for the Atlantic and Pacific R.R. Co.
Missouri to Arizona, 1870 and 1871," Library, Oklahoma Historical Society.

stole some equipment.[8] It is well to note that the MK&T did complete its north-south line through the region of the "civilized" tribes laden with progressive elements, while the A&P was never able to penetrate the western region with rail. While it would be an oversimplification to attribute the A&P's problems solely to the stubbornness of the western tribes, this fact does suggest that tribes with a stronger full-blood faction and a more "primitive" attitude toward corporate benefits were able to resist more effectively. Awareness of some of the attractions of civilization also seems to have left tribes more vulnerable to its abuses.

The railroad activity on two fronts, as it saddened the native hunters, made the boomer glad. In January 1871 the Office of Indian Affairs received a request from the Western Refrigerator Car Company to erect a slaughterhouse at the proposed crossing of the two new Indian Territory railroads. The MK&T continued to ask, now from the Creeks, that it be allowed to buy Indian land in order to create industry and was encouraged when officials of the federal government hinted that they wished it were possible, though they dared not authorize it. The A&P had to buy its right of way through the small domains of the Shawnees and Wyandottes, east of the Cherokees, paying the former $25 and the latter $15 an acre. But to a writer for the *Missouri Democrat* such a small concession was worthwhile, for it allowed him to stand at Seneca, Missouri, watch A&P crews build the Grand River bridge into the Indian Territory, and gaze out "over the grand Deer Park, reserved by good old Uncle Samuel for his festive wards, the 'noble red man.'" Thomas Fletcher, a former governor of Missouri and an A&P director, held Indian "pow-wows" with great success. Sunday school groups from St. Louis rode the rail to the border to wage, with their lunch baskets, what journalists called "the wars of the Pic-nics." Katy superintendent Stevens toured the BIT (Beautiful Indian Territory) in his private car "Prairie Queen," while a traveler lodging at Chouteau, I.T., in a makeshift railway car hotel, thought he heard in a dream "the sound of that advancing multitude which comes from all these deserts." This

8. Ibid.; Robert C. Carriker, *Fort Supply, Indian Territory*, p. 60.

smiling entourage staged only a mock attack with its ice cream and ginger snap outings, its grand tours, and its wakeful dreaming. But concealed therein was something real—the acquisitive spirit of these crowds and their unimpeachable assumptions about that abstraction that full stomachs daily thanked, "Progress." And Progress too must be fed.[9]

In the fall of 1871, the first Indian Territory railroad boom town was laid out where the two lines were to cross. E. C. Boudinot, cooperating for the moment with the MK&T, exercised his rights as a tribal citizen by fencing one thousand acres of land and dubbing it "Vinita" after the young sculptress Vinnie Ream. The A&P, sensing the profit in this, hired another group of Indian citizens to lay out an alternate townsite, Downingville. Boudinot was wooed by the A&P with an offer of one-third of the proceeds and changed sides, taking his town name, Vinita, with him. The struggle for position resulted in fist fights between grading crews and lawsuits against Boudinot by the MK&T, which claimed that his hotel and restaurant were so close to their line that it obstructed the view of engineers. There were meetings aimed at resolving differences, but a representative of the MK&T could say only that, in his view, his counterpart from the A&P spoke in the manner of "an insane man, or a man mad with passion, rather than . . . a gentleman representing a respectable Railroad corporation." To spite each other, the two corporations made no attempt to coordinate train schedules. Even an attorney for one of the companies admitted that the affair was "childish."[10] It revealed

9. D. W. Douldin to (?), Jan. 28, 1871, LR OIA Cherokee Agency, M 234, R 104, F 0158–59. Levi Parsons to Columbus Delano, March 4, 1871; H. R. Clum to Delano, March 25, 1871, box 131, L&RR. E. S. Parker to Columbus Delano, March 14, 1871, Report Books OIA, M 348, R 20, F 0115–16. *Missouri Democrat*, Feb. 12, 1871; H. Craig Miner, *St. Louis-San Francisco Transcontinental Railroad: The Thirty-Fifth Parallel Project, 1853–1890*, p. 79. *Emporia News*, May 26, Aug. 18, 1871; *Missouri Democrat*, Nov. 20, 1871.

10. The best account of the remarkable events at the Vinita crossing is a fifty-page letter Frank Bond to George Denison, Jan. 6, 1872, box 133, L&RR. See also James Baker to M. Hilton, Dec. 4, 1871, ibid.; Masterson, *Katy*, pp. 127–30.

the slashing style of corporations when set against each other and caused the tribes to wonder what waited for them once the internal fray ended.

No better example than Boudinot exists of the usefulness to corporations of a tribal progressive. He claimed his association with railroads was merely a business relationship and that he was loyal to his tribe.[11] The opposing Cherokee faction, however, regarded the results of his actions as anything but neutral. So dangerous did they consider his Vinita hotel, which he rented to a white man, that they tore it down in 1879. Boudinot told members of Congress that he could not return home for fear of assassination. His attempts to collect damages from his tribe for the destruction of his hotel dragged on in the courts until 1882 and aired the dirty linen of Indian disunity as railroad actions at Vinita had done for corporate struggles.[12] People like Boudinot could and did introduce settlers into the country under the pretense that they were employees of a tribal citizen. Failing to profit as railroad pawns in townsiting (as did Boudinot, and J. M. Bryan at Chouteau), they could turn to lobbying for territorial government. And they were always ready for the first chance. In 1879, Boudinot wrote his aunt that he was using inside information on the building plans of railroads to make a killing in land claimed along the line. He asked the Congress to force the Cherokees to change their own tribal laws regarding landholding by Indians so he could make more profit at townsiting. Far from regarding him as a loyal tribesman with unusually advanced views, some members of the tribe said he was "a self exiled renegade taking up his residence

11. A summary of Boudinot's defenses is *Speech of E. C. Boudinot of the Cherokee Nation, Delivered at Vinita, Indian Territory. . . .* (St. Louis, 1874), bound in Speeches of E. C. Boudinot, Gilcrease.

12. D. W. Bushyhead to Hiram Price, Aug. 15, 1882, Cherokee Townsite File (Tahlequah Acquisition), IAD. The documentation on the Boudinot hotel case is very extensive, much of it peripheral to the study of the corporation, but fascinating. The manuscript sources for it are SC # 51, RG 75, NA; the Cherokee Townsite File (Tahlequah Acquisition), IAD; and Cherokee Nation Papers, OU. Of the last, a large number are typescript copies of Boudinot's personal papers.

wherever free lunches and dead head passes could be had." While most congressmen agreed that this mixed-blood Cherokee was "the most courtly gentleman through whose veins courses Indian blood" they had ever met, a congressional committee dryly noted that his "personal greed . . . seems to overleap his love of his own people."[13]

The man was surely a new type that historians must take account of in their assessment of the range of "Indian" behavior. Faced with the option that Boudinot was "either a designing knave or a contemptible fool," most chose the former interpretation. Hundreds of his letters now at the University of Oklahoma reveal in their tone and language a man almost distastefully aggressive, garrulous, violently colorful, and possessed of a collection of ambitions that put him in closer proximity to Jay Gould than Red Cloud. In 1879, in response to an insult, he took Cherokee delegate John Adair "out from the presence of the ladies" and beat him with a stick, reporting that "he is marked badly. I got off without a scratch." His reaction to an unfavorable editorial was to walk into the offices of the *Tahlequah Telephone* and shoot the editor to death where he sat. This purely arrogant man was a contender for the governorship of Kansas in the 1870s, and in 1885 it was widely rumored that he would be appointed Commissioner of Indian Affairs. Many considered that his success had less to do with his hardly ingratiating style than with the support of the corporations with which he associated. It was the corporation, it was said, that was responsible for such a freak of evolution of a tribal citizen as the character of Elias C. Boudinot.[14]

The evidence indicates that, while the full bloods may have fled

13. E. C. Boudinot to Mrs. Sarah Watie, Oct. 12, 1879, box 3, Cherokee Nation Papers, OU. HR 98, 42d Cong., 3d sess., 1873 (S 1578), p. 183. L. B. Bell, mss. brief, n.d., SC 51, NA. *Congressional Globe*, 42d Cong., 3d sess., XLVI, 612–19. HR 98, 42d Cong., 3d sess., 1873 (S 1578), p. 183.

14. L. B. Bell, brief, SC 51, NA. E. C. Boudinot to J. M. Bell, Jan. 4, 1879, box 3, Cherokee Nation Papers, OU. *Tahlequah Telephone*, Oct. 28, 1887. Stephen T. Cormier, "Land, Currency, Cherokees and William Addison Phillips: A Study in Contradiction," p. 17. H. Craig Miner, "The Struggle for an East-West Railway into Indian Territory, 1870–1882," pp. 567–72.

for the hills to get away from the smell of railroad smoke, a large number of tribal citizens took something closer to Boudinot's tack. The reams of paper in the government files on claims arbitrations for the thirty-four miles of A&P construction from Missouri to Vinita strongly indicate that many speculated with the tribal land-holding rules in just the way white men stretched the intent of the Homestead Law. They cut marks on trees, put up bogus improvements, sold timber to the railroad, and then placed remarkably high evaluations upon land to which they might have the most tenuous of claims. Neither Indian nor railroad was satisfied with the decisions of the arbitration commissions, which had to be appointed when there was disagreement upon the extent of damages caused by railroad buildings to nearly every farm along the track. The champion of the claims business was Cherokee James Andrain. He once estimated damage to a corn field at $400, while the railroad offered $2.50. Claims for stock killed were usually paid by A&P stock agent Charles Rogers in the interest of peace, though he wrote to his superiors that they were far higher than the reasonable cash value of the animals. Still there was a limit. When, some years later, Irishman Patrick Shanahan set up a fort across the survey and held off workmen with a shotgun, A&P officers went to Washington to demonstrate that he was not even a tribal citizen. Claims in general were less easily paid when the financial panic of 1873 sent both Indian Territory railroads to the receivers, with their sharp pencils. Attorneys flocked into the region, and with them another aspect of industrial civilization: endless and vexatious litigation—a constant preoccupation with the value of things as these things changed hands rapidly or were consumed.[15]

The western tribes continued to be most adamant in questioning the need for the very existence of corporations. In June 1871 a group of Cheyenne, Arapaho, and Wichita chiefs visited New York and Boston under the sponsorship of the Board of Indian Commissioners. Stone Calf, a Cheyenne, remarked at the Cooper Institute in New York that the idea was to teach the Indian agriculture, yet railroad building interfered:

15. Miner, *St. Louis-San Francisco*, p. 130.

Before they ever ploughed or planted an acre of corn for us they com-
menced to build railroads through our country. What use have we for
railroads in our country? What have we to transport from other nations?
Nothing. We are living wild, really living on the prairies as we have in
former times.[16]

Complaints mounted that railroads hurt the Indian freighting business. Finally, in March 1873 A&P surveying crews were attacked,
several men were killed, and the equipment used to mark the route
destroyed.[17]

The Five Tribes felt as threatened, though their reaction was not
as direct nor their rhetoric unique. In 1871, it became clear that the
Indian Territory railhead towns were becoming violent places and
that newspapers, encouraged by the railroads, played up the violence
in order to show that the tribal governments were ineffective. Cherokee Agent Jones noted that since his wards did not hold their lands
in severalty and so could not sell it, the "boom" did not benefit them
financially but only denuded the country of timber as it went on to
roadbeds and into telegraph poles. Traffickers in illegal liquor threatened death to those who would testify against them.[18]

So as issues defined themselves, they were met by Indians with
feelings ranging from violence to despair, with techniques varying
from war club to claims adjustment, and with governments from
camp fire gathering to bicameral legislature. The residents of the
Indian Territory met specific case after specific case with no more
than the usual combination of principle and avarice, but with an
occasional logic and nobility that made the business of dislodging
them a long and, at least historically, educational process.

One instrument for unification of Indian opinion was the tribal
newspaper. Yet these newspapers reflected the ambivalence toward
the corporation characteristic of their readers, so much so that some

16. AR CIA, 1871, pp. 30–37.
17. Carriker, *Fort Supply*, pp. 76–77.
18. J. H. Beadle, *The Undeveloped West; or Five Years in the Territories,*
pp. 369–71. AR CIA, 1871, p. 982.

ardent nationalists charged that they were all in the control of white corporations. Most were not involved (as was E. C. Boudinot's paper *Indian Progress*) in open promotion of settler and railroad schemes, but the balance was toward accommodation. The *Cherokee Advocate,* official organ of the tribe, reported in the fall of 1871 that a debate had taken place among young Cherokee men about whether railroads should be introduced into the country, and the question was decided in the negative. Foolishness, said *Advocate* editor William Boudinot, with only slightly less zeal than his brother. Every corporation the tribe faced was more powerful than the tribal government, and only a reasoned approach would prevent a collision that would destroy everything Indian. The *Advocate* was against allotment in severalty because that might confirm the railroad's contingent land grant, and it was hardly naive about the fact that both rail lines had sold land-grant bonds based upon their lands throughout Europe. Yet it did not take a consistent stand against the creation of a U.S. Territory, which the corporations so much desired that representatives said bluntly that they would give up all claims to land in exchange for the great economic boom that would come from taking the land from the tribal governments and opening it to white settlers.[19] One looks in vain for any Indian newspaper in this period that would take the kind of anti-corporate stand that the *Vinita Chieftain* did in the 1880s while fighting the Cherokee Strip Live Stock Association. The *Vindicator* at Atoka, Choctaw Nation, and the *Indian Citizen* at Muskogee, Creek Nation, did not differ significantly from the *Advocate*. The former approved plans in 1872 to allow the Little Rock and Fort Smith railway into the Territory, despite lack of any treaty provision. Its comment had the familiar tone of irony and resignation, but also of practical consent:

> Do not think that Railroads will pass quietly through the country without affecting you; it is the death blow to all Old Fogyism, and will soon call where you will have no voice for the opening of the whole country, and

19. *Cherokee Advocate*, Oct. 21, Dec. 9, 1871.

we need not say it will be heard. Then, while it is yet time, look up your advantages and secure them. Be liberal in your views for Civilization must move on and you have only one alternative, and that, to move with it.[20]

The same month, the *Advocate* printed without comment a letter from Fort Sill expressing joy and the progress of the A&P and hoping that Congress would get rid of Indian titles. "What a wanton, wicked waste of domain is this Indian Territory," the writer mused, "Thank God these barbarians of the continent are wasting away."[21]

Accepting the layered reality of the corporate-Indian situation, it is not surprising to find that white men were to be found speaking as meaningfully against the corporate invasion as any Indian. In this group was tribal attorney William A. Phillips, who acted no more than any other from unmixed motives but provided withal some of the most eloquent defenses against corporate abuse Indians could have asked for. At the Arlington House in Washington, appearing before the Board of Indian Commissioners in January 1872, Phillips was in his medium. The Cherokees, he said, had a fee simple title to their lands, given as compensation for their removal. If there was anything imperfect in the title, it was the fault of the U.S., which had granted it, and it should be made good not taken advantage of— "Anything else is mere violence." To think of granting Indian lands to a railroad company and to propose such schemes for developing their lands as were current was as absurd, Phillips said, as granting a twenty-mile wide strip between Washington and New York to a corporation and then taking it all, no matter what its true worth, at $1.25 an acre. Phillips mockingly asked if we did not have an Indian policy. Is this policy not to keep Indian Territory for Indians? Is this policy consistent with granting a forty-mile wide strip through the region to railroads and filling it with white people, living under no law, and setting up "grogshops" all along? "Shall there be a lawless belt, or shall we be forced to destroy Indian governments and Indian

20. *Choctaw Vindicator*, March 16, 1872.
21. *Cherokee Advocate*, March 2, 1872.

civilization; to revolutionize our so-called Indian policy, and blast it, at its very inception, in order that great corporations may make money through our bad faith out of lands that neither belong to them or to the United States?" To do that would be to repeat what had happened in Kansas before the remnants of the tribes, whose sovereignty there was destroyed by corporate ambition, had even made their way to their promised new homes in the center of the next target. Phillips was confident and fluent; sure of his ground. "We [should] not permit," he said, "our wish, that they be civilized like us, to run away with our judgement."[22]

Phillips was a strong advocate because he lived in a sense in two worlds. He had been a land speculator and political promoter in Salina, Kansas. He had been an officer in the Civil War. He had known the world of corporate interest as an insider. He was in 1872 a newly elected congressman. Yet, he was an alien in thought, an economic radical who was never fully converted to the capitalist ethic—who, while favoring economic growth, never assumed that civilization was the same thing as enterprise. He shared many of the ideas of Henry George, and wrote a book, *Land, Labor and Law*, in 1885, which appeared on socialist reading lists.[23]

Phillips was not alone among white men in his views about the danger to Indian rights represented by the railroads. James Harlan of the Senate Committee on Indian Affairs went so far as to advise the suspension of A&P construction for a season, in order that the Congress might investigate the effects of introducing thousands of laborers "outside the usual restraints of civilized society" into the red man's midst.[24] The entering wedge idea held by the quiet railroad lobbyists at the Fort Smith conference was proving true. Almost no issue discussed as a cause for a change in the status of Indian Territory tribes in the seventies was unrelated to the introduction of railroads.

For evidence of the effects, there was no need to read broad-gauged memorials. For one thing, tribal progressives were finding

22. AR CIA, 1871, pp. 184–85.
23. See Cormier, "Land, Currency, Cherokees," passim.
24. James Harlan to C. Delano, June 10, 1872, box 12, L&RR.

that profiting along with the railroad was all but impossible. The MK&T charged twelve cents a mile for passengers in the Cherokee Nation (vs. three to four cents in Missouri and Kansas) and similarly high freight rates, dashing forever the Indian hope that they were trading their privacy for the "conveniences, privileges and profits" the railroad would provide. Even if the tribes paid the rates, they complained that the company refused to receive their freight along its line, would not erect warehouse facilities, and, in short, did everything possible to bolster its case in Congress that, as long as the tribes remained, profitable corporate enterprise was impossible. Trains refused to stop at Vinita even to exchange U.S. mail. The stage line to outlying districts, the Overland Transit Company, was owned by the Katy. Chief Cyrus Harris of the Chickasaws thought that these practices came with ill grace from a company that made such exertions to get the sole right of way through the Indian country. It was, he said, nothing more than extortion by a monopoly.[25] The solution to that, unfortunately for tribes already so shaken by corporate intrusion, was to introduce more railroads so as to provide competition.

The Choctaws did more than complain. In 1876, they appointed a revenue collector and began to exercise their right as a sovereign nation to tax the MK&T one and one-half per cent a year on the cash valuation of all its property. The tribe argued, with fine logic, that if the railroad did not give them any consideration in rates, there was no reason why it should be freed of the taxes it paid in other areas. This was a delicate gesture, for it turned directly upon the extent of tribal sovereignty. It was a test, and, though railroad officials asked the federal government to suspend these laws, they held. The Indian spokesmen claimed that if the Choctaws had the power to grant rights of way to railroads, they had the power to tax them. It was a brilliant move. Wrote the Choctaw tax collector, "The association of railroads and Indian rights is a new subject and the Choctaws are just

25. Pleasant Porter et al., memorial, in T. A. Walker to Secretary of Interior, Dec. 23, 1871, box 132, L&RR; Cyrus Harris to President, Jan. 23, 1873, LR OIA Choctaw Agency, M 234, R 180, F 0429–33.

now brought to a proper comprehension of it."[26] The new strategy resulted from a recognition of the real issue at hand, corporate power versus Indian sovereignty. The time had come to meet fire with fire.

Even those who ignored railroad rate discriminations and tried to be accommodating, like Choctaw Allen Wright, could not help but complain about the "offscourings of the earth" that gathered around the stations in railroad towns. Railroad physicians introduced liquor there "for medicinal purposes," and one of them, Dr. D. M. Hailey, got into the Choctaw coal business on the side. These doctors in turn did a lively business in treating venereal disease spread by such lovelies as Maggie Mitchell, head of a ring of Muskogee prostitutes. Storekeepers imported to supply railroad employees and contractors traded illegally with the Indians, while agents looked on mildly or participated. They simply accepted the word of mouth report that the owners of all these stores were Indians. There was much violence. The 1872 shotgun battle between U.S. marshals and a Cherokee jury, known as the Going Snake Affray, was caused by competition between Indian and federal courts about jurisdiction over criminally inclined railroad employees. It seemed for awhile that no one was in control in the towns. Cherokee chief William Ross said that the rowdies in Fort Gibson carried weapons and were absolutely disdainful of any law, white or Indian. When troops that were sent to control Katy construction towns in 1872 were removed, agent Griffith estimated that "no one will be safe from here to the end of track."[27]

26. J. S. Standley to Z. Chandler, May 12, 1876, LR OIA Choctaw Agency, M 234, R 183, F 0170–73.

27. HR 98, 42d Cong., 3d sess., 1873, (S. 1578), p. 565. T. D. Griffith to F. A. Walker, Aug. 14, 1872, LR OIA Choctaw Agency, M 234, R 180, F 0136. S. W. Marston to E. A. Hayt, May 30, 1878, LR OIA Union Agency, M 234, R 870, F 0960. Logan Roots to George Williams, May 7, 1872, LR OIA Cherokee Agency, M 234, R 105, F 0433–41. William Ross to C. Delano, March 18, 1874, Cherokee Townsite File (Tahlequah Acquisition), IAD. T. D. Griffith to C. Delano (telegram), June 24, 1872, LR OIA Choctaw Agency, M 234, R 180, F 0101.

Railroad towns, in concentrating economic affairs in new locations, profoundly and inadvertently influenced the tribal way of life. Since Indians were not properly vaccinated, smallpox among the tribes could be devastating. With the coming of the railroad, the problem of epidemic was greatly exaggerated. The Cherokee agent said that Indians were exposed to the disease by people moving through on trains when they gathered to collect freight and mail at the stations; there were frightful results in the backcountry. In addition to this new fear, the concentration of life at railroad stations changed routes of public travel and made it difficult for Indian agents to reach the full bloods in the backcountry, or for that matter even the tribal capitals, which were located off the lines. Albert Parsons, a Choctaw agent, said that in 1873 it took him nine days to travel 260 miles to see an Indian. Many of the old stagecoach lines went out of existence with the coming of the railroad, and Indian highways, never a model of maintenance, deteriorated further.[28]

Agency locations were influenced by the activity at railroad towns, and, when they were moved to the railroad, a gap was created between the meeting places of native legislatures and the offices of federal agents. The move of the Choctaw-Chickasaw agency from Boggy Depot to Atoka, the latter on the railroad, created quite a controversy. Atoka City had a newspaper (the *Vindicator*), four saw mills, a lumber yard, and even a bookstore. When the biweekly stagecoach serving the Choctaw capital, Boggy Depot, was discontinued in July, 1873, it was little wonder that agent Parsons asked that his office be moved to the more progressive railroad town. Parsons argued that the Indians had a natural curiosity to visit the railroad and that coming to Atoka to do business with him would give them a healthy contact with civilization. Soon, however, Indians protested that they had wished the agency removed from its former location at Fort Sill to its present one at Boggy Depot because the soldiers at Fort Sill had interfered with them and insulted their women and children. That

28. John Jones to F. A. Walker, March 1, 1872, LR OIA Cherokee Agency, M 234, R 105, F 0312–13. Albert Parsons to E. P. Smith, n.d. (1873), May 17, 1873, LR OIA Choctaw Agency, M 234, R 180, F 0640–42, 0652–57.

situation would be worse at Atoka, they said, "where desperadoes congregate free from all control" and would prevent the agent from conducting his business without outside pressures. Parsons responded that Atoka was a "moral place," and the Choctaws and Chickasaws were intelligent enough to handle themselves with the sharpest of traders. He wrote that the protest was not really an expression of moral outrage but only a front for factional self-interest. Former agent D. H. Cooper had wished to keep the agency at Boggy Depot until he could sell his property there before news of a move damaged values. He had shared the action with a few Indians, who had then written the memorial. This confusion of villains and victims muddied the issue for a time, and in that time the agency was moved to the rail town. A not untypical circumstance; and a not untypical result.[29]

The MK&T completed its line to Texas in January 1873 rolling, in the language of a magazine writer, "with the rattle and rush of carwheels; by the sites of ghost-ridden terminus towns, where fierce little hells of gambling and murder flourished for a few short weeks . . . ; among the swart, fierce Cherokees, Choctaws, Creeks and Chickasaws, bringing momentary progress into their quaint, superstition-laden villages." It spawned an industrial revolution. In 1872, a corporation was formed in the Chickasaw Nation by a group of men from Suffolk, Virginia, encouraged by the entry of the railroad to begin drilling for oil. The A&P requested withdrawal of "public lands" in Indian Territory for a branch to Fort Smith, causing the Cherokees to wonder just where these "public lands" might be. In 1874, a bill was introduced in the Congress to allow any five men to form a corporation and build a railroad through Indian lands without tribal consent.[30]

29. *Choctaw Vindicator*, Sept. 14, 1872. A. Parsons to Edward Smith, July 26, 1873, F 0713–18; Cyrus Harris to Commissioner of Indian Affairs, Oct. 7, 1872, F 0201–2; Albert Parsons to Edward Smith, Aug. 9, 1873, F 0723–25, LR OIA Choctaw Agency, M 234, R 180.

30. "The Great South: The New Route to the Gulf," p. 259. *Cherokee Advocate*, March 2, 1872. C. J. Hillyer to Columbus Delano; Cherokee delegation to R. R. Cown, May 14, 1872, package 12, L&RR.

Though the 1874 bill failed, there was little doubt that Indian doom was accelerated by the laying of rails. One member of Congress perceived that it now seemed that a treaty was only a treaty when it suited the purpose of the United States. Opposition to the bill to allow free access to Indian Territory by corporations was based not on the grounds that it was immoral but that it might touch off an expensive Indian war. Said one member with supreme irony:

> The higher law of Piegan massacres is being constantly applied. . . . The world was not made in a day, and something ought to be left for future Credit Mobiliers to accomplish. Of course, human life is of no consideration in the eye of that civilization of the highest character of which a railway is the symbol, but is there not land enough for the locomotive to snort through belonging to us white and black people that railroad monopolists can steal without getting up more expensive Indian massacres? We do not mind being robbed ourselves, and have already lost 200,000,000 acres or so, besides paying the thieves for building the roads through them; but it costs so much to kill an Indian that we would like to postpone the operation of the higher law awhile until the finances get in better condition.[31]

Wrote the commissioner of Indian affairs, "This case differs from others recorded in history only in this—that never was an evil so gigantic environed, invaded, devoured by forces so tremendous, so appalling in the celerity and the certainty of their advance." This, he said, was the beginning of the end for aboriginal America.[32]

The image of the Indian that came from the image-making department of the "lofty, spacious and beautifully furnished" offices of the MK&T railroad in Sedalia or from the walnut cubicles of the A&P in St. Louis was not favorable. Being practitioners of the "science of system" and followers of the rule that there was a time and place for everything, railroad officers contended that it was time that the Indian be put in his place—and that place was not the fertile country that he claimed. The MK&T emphasized that it had reached Texas

31. *Cherokee Advocate*, May 9, 1874.
32. AR CIA, 1872, p. 8.

only "after a struggle that has no parallel in the history of railroad building" and that reports from the field had described full-blood Indians as a "degraded, shabby, do nothing set, filthy to nausea [*sic*]."[33] That they should inherit such a beautiful land was, according to a *Scribners* correspondent "a constant source of torment to the brave white men of the border, in whom the spirit of speculation is very strong." The long grasses bent in the wind, the timber stood against the sky, and in the background the steam engine whistled through sleepy little Indian towns. It could not be. The boomer would not let it. "He aches to be admitted to the territory. . . . He is crazed with visions of far-spreading, flower-bespangled prairies, the fertile foot-hills, the rich quarries, mines and valley lands."[34] Rhetoric had not slowed the leading edge of boom civilization, the corporation; physical threats had not slowed it; the hiring of white attorneys had not slowed it; attempts to satiate it cheaply or to change its direction had failed. Once started, it was like a car rolling downhill, gaining momentum, using all in its way as fuel. It remained only to try to derail it by placing tiny splinters, such as an Indian might find, across the track.

33. *Sedalia Democrat*, Oct. 27, 1874, Dec. 5, 1872.
34. "The Great South," p. 276.

CHAPTER IV

COAL AND TIES
THE CONFRONTATION

Railroad building brought with it a rush for the mines. Thomas Nuttall noticed coal outcrops in the Indian Territory on his visit there in 1819, and the Pacific Railway Surveys of the fifties had observed Indians making use of the coal from their lands in their blacksmith shops. As early as 1851 there was sale and trading of coal claims among Indian citizens, and in 1869 the Cherokees, soon followed by the Choctaws and Creeks, passed legislation regulating leasing of coal claims to individuals or companies of Indians upon payment of royalty to the tribe. These laws were not designed for corporate activity but were directed at Kansans crossing the border to take coal for Arkansas City, Wichita, and Coffeyville furnaces.[1]

Corporations, however, came to dominate mining in a way that tested tribal institutions. In June 1872 Joshua Pusley and other Choctaws leased a mining tract in the Choctaw Nation to the Osage Coal and Mining Company. The site was near McAlester station on the MK&T and was in an area of rich veins that required mechanized techniques, and some capital, to exploit. The Katy built a branch to the mine, and many of the mine's directors were also MK&T directors. Yet the railroad company here used the time-tested legalistic device of claiming that the coal company was a separate operation, despite interlocking directorates. The issue was delicate in that it

1. Gene Aldrich, "A History of the Coal Industry in Oklahoma to 1907," pp. 3, 5, 9. H. Craig Miner, "The Cherokee Oil and Gas Co., 1889–1902: Indian Sovereignty and Economic Change," p. 51. Hueston Smith to D. W. Bushyhead, Dec. 28, 1875, Cherokee Mineral File (Tahlequah acquisition), IAD (for "Abbreviations in Footnotes," see p. vii).

involved the regulation of a railroad that was perhaps in collusion with a supplier that had no treaty rights to operate at all. It was of utmost importance to corporate development, not only because of railroads' need for subsidiary coal and timber operations but also due to early signs of the magnificent potential for the oil industry in Indian Territory. The Chickasaw Oil Company, formed by a group of Virginians in 1872, failed because of the investors' concern about the status of Indian leases. But in 1874 the Oklahoma Mining Company bored a four-hundred-foot oil well. Would the corporation stop at two railroad routes providing minimal communication across tribal lands when there was an empire at stake?[2]

The Osage Coal and Mining Company lease was controversial in the extreme. For one thing, no royalty was paid to the tribe but only to the individual Indians in the leasing cartel. Many U.S. officials regarded this as a violation of a February 1872 Indian Office ruling that no contract between an individual Indian and whites would be regarded as binding. The Choctaw Nation tried to collect. It created the office of National Agent in 1871 to gather a tribal royalty (the railroad called it a tax) on coal, stone, and timber. This law, however, was declared unconstitutional by the Choctaw Supreme Court in 1872, just as the Osage Coal contracts were drawn. The grounds were that the Chickasaws were not properly provided for—the old feud. A similar law was passed in 1873, struck down by the same tribal court in 1875, and then reenacted in virtually the same form. Again the corporation was allowed to slip through the haze of factional bickering with a wide smile of innocence.[3]

In the confusion, the coal company had obtained permission from the Choctaw agent to pay royalties to individuals and could argue that to pass a law changing this was unfair to its vested interest.

2. Aldrich, "Coal Industry," pp. 11–13. J. H. Moore, *The Political Condition of the Indians and the Resources of the Indian Territory*, pp. 55–56.

3. Columbus Delano to H. R. Clum, March 3, 1873, LR OIA Choctaw Agency, M 234, R 180, F 0548–51. SR 744, 45th Cong., 3d sess., 1879 (S 1839), p. 13; MK&T 1877 hearings, ISP file 310, shelf 4 (SC 136), pp. 59, 67, 96–97; H. T. Lemist to G. W. Ingalls, Nov. 16, 1875, SC 84.

Robert Stevens of the MK&T said that the royalty paid to the individuals was very high and that the new national law was "clearly in the nature of 'blackmail,' so to speak." But when he asked the Office of Indian Affairs to intervene to stop collection of the national royalty, the secretary of the interior replied that if the employees of the coal company were not employees of the railroad, they had no right to be in Indian Territory, as there was no treaty provision for coal leases.[4]

Washington officials were here on strong legal ground, and it became a question of whether economic interest or legal abstraction would prevail. In 1875 the federal government, responding to requests from the Choctaw chief, stopped all shipments of coal from the McAlester mines until the Choctaws could devise clear legislation governing the payment of royalties. Though the MK&T claimed to have no interest in the mines, it was the MK&T engines that were thus denied inexpensive coal, and it was the MK&T officers who responded. The railroad made it clear that the U.S. economy was terribly dependent upon its Kansas-to-Texas trunk line, carrying about one-half the supplies for the territory west of the Mississippi adjoining the gulf. If the McAlester lines closed, the closest supply of coal was Fort Scott, Kansas, and that source was already supplying most of the Missouri Valley. The general superintendent of the railroad, A. B. Garner, wrote that if coal shipments were stopped, all deliveries to southwestern forts, for which the Katy had most of the contracts, would stop, as would mails for the entire region. The Osage mines were then shipping out twenty to thirty twelve-ton carloads of coal a day, employed two hundred men, and had a capital investment of $100,000. It was an interest difficult to tamper with. The government backed down, allowing the mine to operate and putting pressure upon the Indians to frame satisfactory legislation. The federal government's lack of moral forti-

4. R. S. Stevens to F. A. Walker, Feb. 12, 1873, F 0837–39; Columbus Delano to Commissioner of Indian Affairs, March 3, 1873, F 0545–46, LR OIA Choctaw Agency, M 234, R 180.

tude in the face of economic blackmail resulted in political cost to the Indian.[5]

There were, in addition, the progressives to contend with. In the Choctaw Nation coal business, the equivalents of E. C. Boudinot were J. J. McAlester and Robert L. Ream. Both had interests in the Osage company, though, like Boudinot, they loudly proclaimed their Indianness and denied that a prudent investment made them corporate lackeys. Ream, a white man who was a citizen by intermarriage, had been in the civil engineering and steamboating business before going to the Indian Territory and said that tribal authorities originally encouraged his operating a ferry, building a toll bridge, and speculating in coal claims, objecting only after the coming of the railroad.[6]

The manipulations of men like Ream might seem trivial enough, but the fact that they were thorns in the side of first government, then corporate interests, and then the tribes led to more fundamental questions regarding the suitability of such men to operate in the garb of Indian citizens under the protection of tribal sovereignty. In 1874, for example, Ream instituted charges against Agent Albert Parsons in connection with a claim for some damages to a toll bridge. In order to collect a few more dollars, Ream charged Parsons, who thought the settlement was just, with being in the pay of the railroad company, thereby arousing all sorts of sleeping animosity. He said that George Reynolds, former Seminole agent, was employed by the Katy railroad to manipulate the Office of Indian Affairs in the interest of the corporation and that poor wards of the government like himself were helpless because, with dual sovereignty, neither tribal nor U.S. courts assumed jurisdiction over disputes between In-

5. Z. Chandler to Commissioner of Indian Affairs, Dec. 10, 1875; A. B. Garner to J. J. Upham, Jan. 16, 1876; H. T. Lemist to G. W. Ingalls, Nov. 16, 1875, SC 84. *Indian Journal* (Muskogee), Aug. 10, 1876.

6. ISP file 310, shelf 4 (SC 136), pp. 221–26. A good summary of favorable Choctaw attitudes toward McAlester and Ream is *Indian Journal*, Aug. 10, 1876, May 24, Sept. 8, 1877.

dians and railroads. Ream again clogged administrative machinery in the late seventies in a long dispute with D. M. Hailey, a white McAlester physician, over ownership of certain coal claims. This time Ream went to the tribal courts. He got a favorable judgment at the Tobucksy County Court, but when the tribal supreme court reversed this decision, he charged that that body had been corrupted by the Choctaw chief, Green McCurtain, because the executive officer of the tribe had himself been speculating in the mines in question. While he appealed the decision in Washington, officials of the Atoka Coal and Mining Company, which was leasing the mines at issue between Ream and Hailey, were confused about whom to pay and so paid no one.[7]

The potentials of threats to Indian sovereignty were completely exposed as a result of the implications of these activities. Chief McCurtain in 1882 instructed the Atoka Company to pay Hailey, as ordered by the tribal court, and argued that neither the commissioner of Indian affairs nor the secretary of the interior had any power to order otherwise regarding the internal affairs of the tribe. At the same time Secretary of the Interior Henry Teller wrote the coal corporation that it was the federal government's view that Ream was the rightful owner. McCurtain told the company that if it did not pay Hailey, he would have its lease revoked. Teller told it that if it did not pay Ream, the Indian Office would have its employees declared intruders in Indian Territory and have its machinery removed. Teller said that the Choctaws were sovereign only so long as their actions did not conflict with the U.S. Constitution, and in this case they did. The corporation deserves the sympathy here and cannot be blamed for picking the stronger of the two adversaries, paying Ream, and then asking the federal government to protect it against the resolve of the Choctaw government to close the mine. Agent John Tufts so warned the Choctaws that if they moved against the

7. R. L. Ream to P. P. Pitchlynn and Choctaw delegation, Jan. 5, 1874, SC 136, tray 1; R. L. Ream to Z. Chandler, April 21, 1876, LR OIA Choctaw Agency, M 234, R 183, F 0148–49. [Henry] Teller to Commissioner of Indian Affairs, June 16, 1882, SC 119.

lease or destroyed company property they would face military action by the United States. Thus was tribal independence diminished.[8]

Once someone like Ream lashed out and introduced internal feuds into the Washington bureaucracy, misunderstanding was inevitable. In the case of the Ream-Hailey argument, the Choctaws tried to explain that they wished to invalidate the lease because a white man named G. S. Williford, agent for the Texas Central railroad, was involved in the transfers, and according to Choctaw law any transfer to a noncitizen invalidated a lease. In addition there was evidence that Mrs. Ream was romantically involved with Williford. Teller's correspondence indicates that he misunderstood this point completely, thinking the Indians were calling the Reams noncitizens. Tribal representatives asked if it mattered anyway. They admitted their court process was slow but wondered that this should be an excuse for taking their judicial power. "The failure or delay of justice," went their memorial, "in a given case, would not work a forfeiture of jurisdiction any more than does such delay in the cases of countless claims which, year after year, cumber calenders of the American congress, transfer jurisdiction of such cases to foreign powers."[9] Whether the Choctaw Supreme Court made a just decision was not a question for an outside power to determine.

The federal government's response to this was intransigent, reflecting its disposition toward destruction of Indian sovereignty in order to regularize corporate leaseholds. One analyst who had been to the Territory reported to Washington that Mrs. Ream was an intelligent, able woman, while the tribal judiciary was "corrupt

8. J. F. McCurtain to Atoka Coal and Mining Co., June 28, 1882; [Henry] Teller to Commissioner of Indian Affairs, June 16, 1882; Teller to Commissioner of Indian Affairs, July 28, 1882; John Tufts to Hiram Price, Aug. 29, 1882, ibid.

9. *Memorial of the Choctaw and Chickasaw Nations . . . Relating to Their Jurisdiction . . . Under the Treaty of . . . 1855* (Washington, D.C., 1883), pp. 21–22, 33–34. This important pamphlet contains a reprint of testimony in the Ream case at the back. See also J. H. McCurtain to Secretary of Interior, Jan. 16, 1882. Both documents are in SC 119.

and ignorant." Van H. Manning, arguing before the Interior Department on behalf of the Reams, said that the case illustrated that the U.S. government should never have entered into treaty stipulations with the Indians but since it had, it should not let these promises interfere with the correction of evident outrages. The only solution, said Manning, was for the federal government to assume direct control of the Indians, and thus stop repeating "the disgraceful chapter written and re-written, and which makes us blush everytime we turn to the book."[10]

The liberality of the Indians toward intermarried citizens, which was based upon a tradition of matriarchal property rights, combined with the immense profits to be gained by leasing to corporations to make the relatively trivial financial interest of "white Indians" like Ream a major device for the destruction of the tribal system which created them. Like Boudinot, Ream was extreme in everything. In 1876 he was involved in a gun battle in McAlester, caused by a combination of drunkeness and a quarrel over coal rights, and killed the county sheriff. In 1877, during hearings over coal royalties, Chief Coleman Cole had to have Ream arrested in order to force him to testify. He escaped a Choctaw jail and fled to Parsons, Kansas, where finally he was apprehended. His excuse was that Indian public feeling against leasing coal claims to corporations was so high that he feared physical violence were he to testify.[11]

As was the case with building railroads, the Indians were not unwilling for their resources to be developed and searched for ways that this could be done without a compromise of their political power. The *Vindicator* advised in an 1875 editorial that native-run corporations, so unsuccessful in heading off railroads, be tried in the coal fields. Surely, it stated, there were enough "men of tact" among the tribes to man large-scale mining corporations, especially if the peo-

10. D. H. Armstrong to Henry Teller, April 17, 1882; Van H. Manning to Hiram Price, April 25, 1882, SC 119.

11. SR 744, 45th Cong., 3d sess., 1879 (S 1839), p. 173. *Indian Journal*, Sept. 8, 1877.

ple of the United States were allowed to provide the capital. This sort of experience would be useful to young Indians in adjusting to industrial civilization and would stimulate the energy of all in the service enterprises it would produce. The suggestion was not taken up. Things were moving too easily and too powerfully in other channels. In 1901, there were thirty-nine U.S. coal corporations operating in the Choctaw Nation, employing 4,600 noncitizen miners and mining almost one and one-half million tons of coal a year. In 1907, the Choctaw Nation was gone.[12]

These new problems did not, however, displace the older ones, particularly the nagging issue of the amount railways should compensate the tribes for timber taken in construction. In arguing their case, the Indians were forced for the first time carefully to define the nature of their communal landholding system and to spell out in legal phrases a system that had existed on the basis of mutual trust, in the absence of pressure from civilized development. The central question was whether the Indians should benefit as individuals, or as a tribe, or both. Since the Cherokees early defined by legislation that individuals must take tie licenses and pay royalties to the tribe, the bulk of the difficulty centered in the Choctaw country.

The tie compensation issue paralleled the coal controversy in its raising hard questions regarding sovereignty. The Choctaw National Agent, appointed in 1871, failed to file bond, so the Choctaw chief asked U.S. Agent Theophilus Griffith to act, for a time, as a collection agent for the five-cent-a-tie royalty for the tribe. Griffith accepted, thinking this the best way to insure justice for the Choctaws and Chickasaws until they could agree upon their own machinery. However, John P. C. Shanks, a member of Congress visiting the Indian Territory to investigate frauds, charged in 1872 that Griffith, in so doing, was meddling in a matter that was none of his affair. Indians took up the cry, charging that Griffith was in the pay of the railroad and overlooked ties being shipped out of the Nation for use upon the Creek lands, where timber was scarce. Griffith was

12. *Choctaw Vindicator*, April 3, 1875. Aldrich, "Coal Industry," p. 18.

called before a House committee to explain, bringing with him knowledge of many of the tribe's questionable dealings.[13]

Griffith confessed that he had tried to influence and advise the Choctaw government about tie royalties for their own benefit, as he perceived it. The original act called for a seven and one-half cent royalty, five cents for the Nation and two and one-half cents for the salary of the National Agent. Griffith had told the chief that, since Stevens of the Katy had been getting ties in the Cherokee Nation for five cents, the road would be reluctant to pay more. He also told the chief that, because there were no stipulations in the act for the Chickasaw's share, it was a violation of the 1866 treaty and would never be upheld by the federal government. Therefore, when the tribal collector failed on his bond, the chief asked Griffith to take over the duty for five cents total, no salary for himself, and informally to give the Chickasaws one-fourth, thus satisfying legality without losing face. Griffith said he had gotten permission to do this from the tribal legislature and that it was agreeable to the railroad. The House committee, however, upbraided him for presuming to advise the Choctaws and charged him with having forced the Choctaw National Agent to resign. Griffith was astounded and could say only that he would be happy to be barred by the Department from the business of tie claims, as it would relieve him of "a great deal of perplexing work" for which he was not paid.[14]

Griffith's successor, Albert Parsons, could not give testimony concerning Griffith's behavior but could attest there was pressure on the agent to involve himself in irregular practices in collusion with corporations. He charged that the Katy railroad was practicing a "farce" in connection with tie compensation. Railroad-tie contractors would find some pliant Choctaw and pay him a small sum to make a claim. The contractor then cut off the timber, and the "settler" gave him a receipt for a five-cent-a-tie royalty. The Indian was prob-

13. T. D. Griffith to F. A. Walker, July 11, 1872; William Bryant to C. Delano, Dec. 21, 1872, SC 136, tray 1.

14. HR 98, 42d Cong., 3d sess., 1872 (S 1578), pp. 669–73.

ably never paid the five cents but was on a salary from the railroad. He moved on, settled another claim, and the process was repeated. The receipts went by the bushel to the agent, who, not having time to investigate, signed and forwarded them to Washington.[15] There they were approved, all in due form, which was, according to the ironic comment of an Indian attorney, as follows:

> his
> Big-Company X man
> mark
> Witness: Truthful James, the contractor
> Approved: Parsons, Indian Agent[16]

Parsons believed the procedure would have been fine, had there been any tribal or federal authority for individual sales, or if allotments had taken place so that Indian claimants had a firm title to individual holdings.[17] But there was not such authority. The commissioner of Indian affairs asked in 1873 that no timber be shipped out without a written contract approved by him, but the railroad ignored him. When Parsons asked R. S. Stevens about it, the latter responded: "Well what are [you] going to do if we continue to ship ties, &c. How are you going to prevent it. You cannot stop us. We have bought these ties and paid for them, and we are going to ship them. We do not care whether we bought them of the men who owned them or not." Parsons said that Stevens offered him money for attending strictly to duty and making no independent investigations. The agent thought that the U.S. government must intervene, demanding that royalty be paid to the Nation for all ties, whether claimed by individuals or not. This would interfere with tribal sovereignty, but the tribe was powerless to protect itself. Wrote Parsons:

15. Albert Parsons to Edward P. Smith, June 28, 1873, SC 136, tray 1.
16. *The Choctaw and Chickasaw Nations of Indians . . . vs. Missouri, Kansas and Texas Railroad Co. . . . Concluding Argument for Complainants* (Washington, D.C., [1882]), pp. 19, 45, copy in ibid.
17. Albert Parsons to Edward P. Smith, June 28, 1873, SC 136, tray 1.

To call upon the National authorities here to prevent it would amount to nothing. The R.R. would laugh at them. The R.R. co. must be taught that it cannot move in this matter without any regard to these nations whatever or by authority purchased of U.S. agents or dishonest Choctaws.[18]

The railroad had its own version of this. Stevens said that he had written federal authorities regularly explaining the method of paying for ties, and there had been no objection. It was the railroad's understanding that the Choctaw National Agent was to collect royalties for ties taken from land unoccupied by individual Indians, and upon claimed land, payment was to be made to individuals. Stevens wrote that he had a meeting with Choctaw National Agent D. F. Harkins in January 1874 with a view toward settling all past differences. It was agreed then that the railroad would pay the tribe $448.97 in full satisfaction of money owed for ties on unoccupied lands prior to that date and thereafter would pay Harkins's royalty regularly. When this sum was paid, and an additional payment of $1,505 made with great ceremony before the Choctaw legislature, Stevens considered the matter closed.[19]

Stevens was willing to sanction a good deal more flexibility than Parsons regarding field matters. He said he bought lumber from Choctaw-run sawmills and used it for bridges in Texas and that he paid Indians for ties with goods from company stores set up for railroad employees without speculating whether this might be a violation of the trade and intercourse acts. He had simply wished to build a railroad and did it as best he could in the absence of consistent rulings. Parsons was positive that the Choctaw Nation had never authorized its citizens to cut or sell ties as individuals, but he confessed that Stevens might have honestly believed that it had, since there were plenty of Choctaws, wishing to sell ties, to tell him so. Stevens thought the whole idea of individual entrepreneurship among Indians was healthy and could not understand why the Indian Office should have any objection to these men "trading and trafficking, manning

18. Ibid., July 5, 1873.
19. Affidavit of Robert Stevens, May 14, 1881, SC 136, tray 1.

their mills, disposing of their lumber, and gradually adopting the habits of civilization."[20]

Harkins and the Choctaws had a third explanation. Harkins, in a sharp letter to Stevens, challenged the story of the payment of $448.00. True, he said, such a payment was made, but there was no understanding that it covered all tie-royalty claims. For one thing, it had nothing to do with the major Choctaw contract with J. G. Lindsay for thirty thousand ties. Harkins went on:

> When I first visited your office I supposed I would have a gentleman to deal fairly and on the square, but I find you are disposed to cheat and swindle the Choctaw people. . . . You have trampled over our lands long enough. You have now come to the point you must stop.

The national agent argued that out of courtesy he had allowed the Osage Coal Company to use timber to prop its banks without paying royalty but that since relations had become strained, he now demanded payment, and the Choctaws would resist additional cutting for mine shafts by force of arms. Harkins went so far as to travel to Washington to expose the "perfect swindle" on the tie royalties. "Old Stevens treated me like a dog," he wrote to a friend. "The last time I seen him he would not speak to me. I have heard of that rascal Reynolds and Parsons riding up and down the road singing territorial times."[21]

The railroad men did not change their story conceding only that, since no railroad official spoke Choctaw, it was a bit difficult to determine whether the tribe had any objections to the $1,505 payment made in full council.[22] The federal government was forced to step in as arbiter, holding extensive hearings upon the tie and coal compensation question in 1877. When it did intervene, tribal authority was again diminished, though the tribal treasury may have gained.

20. R. S. Stevens to E. P. Smith, June 9, 1873; A. Parsons to E. P. Smith, Sept. 12, 1873, ibid. R. S. Stevens to H. R. Clum, Sept. 25, 1873, LR OIA Choctaw Agency, M 234, R 180, F 0865–68.

21. D. F. Harkins to R. S. Stevens, July 28, 1874, ISP file 310, shelf 4 (SC 136). D. F. Harkins to "Capt.," April 6, 1874, SC 136, tray 1.

22. ISP file 310, shelf 4 (SC 136), p. 179.

The first hearing was held in July 1877 under the supervision of S. W. Marston, agent for the new agency of the combined Five Tribes known as the Union Agency. The Choctaws protested that the railroad would be represented by the best legal minds available and asked that the government provide them with similar counsel. Marston recommended that their request be fulfilled and that free transportation be provided to all Indians wishing to be present. The agent, in addition, drew up careful rules to insure fairness. Both railroad and Indians were to have the chance to obtain written depositions.[23]

No sooner were these rules formulated than they were aborted. An oral hearing with no written depositions was set, apparently upon instructions from Washington. It was done with so little warning that the railroad complained its key witnesses (Stevens, Lindsay, Griffith, Parsons) were unavailable. No attorney was provided for the Indians. They used B. F. Grafton, who had often represented them, to oppose rail attorneys B. C. Foster and T. C. Sears as the stenographer took notes of testimony lasting from July 7 to 9. Briefs were submitted by both parties through the rest of the year, and in January 1878 Marston made his report, concluding that the railway had made a fair settlement and that there was no collusion between the MK&T railroad and the Osage Coal and Mining Company.[24]

The Indians demanded a new hearing, and one was held in 1881, climaxing another battle of briefs. Among those deposed in 1881 was Jay Gould, new boss of the Katy, who said that the whole Indian claim was an "afterthought" that the railroad was in no financial condition to honor.[25] In November 1882 more awards were made, still unsatisfactory to the Indians, who submitted still more

23. Coleman Cole to U. S. Grant, Feb. 19, 1877, Choctaw Railroad File, IAD. S. W. Marston to J. Q. Smith, March 19, 1877; J. S. Stanley, D. F. Harkins to J. Q. Smith, April 18, 1877, SC 136, tray 1.

24. ISP file 310, shelf 4, pp. 1, 243. Marston report, Jan. 3, 1878, SC 136, tray 1.

25. T. C. Sears to Wm. Leeds, May 16, 1878, LR OIA Union Agency, M 234, R 870, F 0791; Gould deposition, May 26, 1881, SC 136, tray 3.

arguments in protest. It was a long and tiring process, but one that was strikingly revealing, in the language and approach of both sides, of the political and economic stakes of corporate intrusion. Tribal citizens in attendance began to see the interconnections of the different corporations with which they were dealing. One wrote to the *Indian Journal* that those people getting on and off MK&T trains with the care of the industrial struggle etched in their faces would make the few remaining Indian reservations into Indian burial places:

> . . . unless we can bring our minds to adopt their modes of life and aggression. These threads of iron laying there so still gleaming in the sunlight, are part of the network of veins that reach to the centers of trade and commerce—. . . . which are but an aggregation of strugglers for life and wealth, not in the main by producing of wealth, but simply pulling it up in every possible form, then each striking for a share by shrewd bargain and sale.[26]

B. F. Grafton was eloquent for the Choctaws in these hearings. He scoffed at the railroad argument that since the line increased the value of Choctaw lands, it need pay no damages. The market in Indian Territory, he said, was a local one, and necessities brought from the states were as cheap before the railroad as they were now. Who was to estimate the damage from horse thieves, counterfeiters, and murderers brought in by the cars? How much was the expense to the Choctaws of maintaining delegations in Washington to fight attempts by the railroads to push through a territorial government and collect their contingent land grants? All witnesses from the tribe appearing for the railroad were, Grafton observed, progressives in favor of taking the power to govern out of the hands of the tribe and therefore casting it "to the railroad company as clay in the hands of the potter."[27]

26. *Indian Journal*, July 26, 1877.

27. B. F. Grafton, *The Choctaw and Chickasaw Nations Complainants vs. The Missouri, Kansas and Texas Railway Company, and Its Assignees, The Union Trust Co. of New York, Respondents. Complainants' Brief.* (Washington, D.C.[1877]), pp. 6–8, 15–17, 24, 30, copy in SC 136, tray 2.

T. C. Sears responded for the railway. He said that the Indian nations should not have been represented at all at the hearings because they made an unconditional grant of right of way and building materials in the 1866 treaty; the only people affected were individual claimants. The United States should not have been there either, nor should "complaints for alleged injuries against the National authority of either" have been discussed in a situation that was purely business. He cited *U.S.* vs *Cook,* an 1873 U.S. Supreme Court case which concluded that the Indian tribes as tribes had no right to sell timber because the ultimate fee title to their lands rested with the U.S. He neglected to mention that the Five Tribes claimed to have a fee simple title, granted on removal, unlike other tribes. Sears concluded that the bureaucratic procedure provided for approving tie contracts was impractical and that Indian complaints did not represent the tribe at large, but only "a small ring that has for years used the Indian name to enrich its members by extortions from Railway companies and others."[28]

Grafton found this approach arrogant in the extreme. Why should the company get all this without compensation?

> Are the men and methods of this railway company so different from the men and methods of other railway companies . . . that it should be blasphemy to suggest a doubt whether the value of their presence or of their disinterested efforts to evangelize the Indians, will warrent them taking from the red man without compensation what they cannot take from the white man without compensation? Is the Missouri, Kansas and Texas railway company a missionary society or an eleemosynary institution, that it should obtain for nothing that which the Baltimore and Ohio railway company . . . must pay its money? . . . Does this company pay in benevolence for what other companies pay in cash?

The Indian attorney called Sears's appeal a "fish market" argument and reminded that the tribes were not "carpet-baggers on this west-

28. T. C. Sears, *Commissioner of Indian Affairs. The Choctaw and Chickasaw Nations, Etc. vs. The Missouri, Kansas & Texas Railway Company. Argument for Railway Company Upon Confirmation of the Award.* (Sedalia, Mo., 1878), pp. 14, 29, 70, copy in ISP file 310, shelf 4 (SC 136).

ern continent, indebted for accommodation to the white race, indigenous to the soil." If the railroad men wished to remind how enthusiastic the Indians signing the 1855 treaties were for railroads, it might be well to warn them that those Indians also could use the scalping knife, and maybe should again, on their enemies.[29]

Final arguments were submitted for the railway in 1881 by the well-respected railway attorneys Britton and Gray. Their point was that no complaints had come from the Indians until years after the alleged damage and came at a time when the Katy was in receivership and most of the individuals who had been employed during the construction period scattered and unavailable. While the tribe might make vague claims, no amount of hair-splitting could obscure the fact that the company had a receipt given by the Choctaw legislature in October of 1873, in satisfaction of the entire amount due the tribe.[30]

The Indian Office, in making a final decision upon this controversy, had also before it the testimony heard by the Patterson committee of 1878. The subcommittee of the Senate Committee on Territories, headed by John Patterson, was thought by some, as shall be seen, to be a tool of the railroads. At least, it seemed that all testimony given before it had a decided prorailroad slant.

In November 1882 the commissioner of Indian affairs made a final decision very unsatisfactory to the Choctaws, as it granted them nearly nothing. After the 1877 hearings, the government had agreed to a figure of $89,000. The Indians felt the testimony in the reopened case justified a larger award and finally compromised on $98,000. Much of this, however, was disallowed in the 1882 awards. All claims for large timbers were rejected on the grounds that there were not supposed to be any Indian-run sawmills to cut them. Claims on stone quarrying were disallowed on the ground that

29. B. F. Grafton, *Reply to Argument for Respondents. . . .* (Washington, D.C., n.d.), pp. 2, 7, 24, copy in SC 136, tray 1.

30. Britton & Gray, attorneys, *In the Matter of the Choctaw and Chickasaw Nations Against the Missouri, Kansas and Texas Ry. Co. Argument for the Respondent* (Washington, D.C., 1881), 4, 45, copy in SC 136, tray 1.

stone had no value, and the tie claims were thrown out because individuals had already been paid.[31]

The corporations' argument in the tie case, while technically
successful, seems weak in several areas. First, it is difficult to believe
that the corporation did not suspect the Choctaw Nation would
ask a royalty, particularly in light of the precedent for this in the
Cherokee Nation and the passage of several Choctaw laws to that
effect, which were struck down by the tribal courts. Choctaw law
allowed individuals to claim land and use timber for improvements, but there was no provision for them to sell timber as individuals. The implication was that the Nation alone had that right.
If the rail company believed, as Sears argued, that the tribes had
given up their right to collect in the 1866 treaties, why did it agree to
pay the Cherokees? and why did it pay the Choctaws $2,000 a
year and the Chickasaws $1,200 a year in royalties after 1876? By
1897, $1.2 million had been paid by coal companies to the Choctaw
and Chickasaw governments and $800,000 to individual Indian citi-
zens.[32] Also, the company's failure to comply with the terms of its
bond regarding procedure for the approval of contracts, a lapse that
all company officials admitted, is questionable policy, especially in
light of charges against the Choctaw agents. On the other hand,
the tribes failed to prevent their members from selling timber, and
evidence in the tribal archives fails to contradict the railroad point
that there was little Indian complaint at the time the timber was
taken.

The coal and tie question made it clearer than ever that somehow
the Indian economic system was an obstacle to the United States,
which was moving to destroy it. Tribal thinkers asked why it could

31. Shellenbarger & Wilson, *Before the Hon. Commissioner of Indian
Affairs. The Choctaw and Chickasaw Nations of Indians Complainant v.
Missouri, Kansas and Texas Railroad Co., Respondent. Concluding Argument
for Complainants* (Washington, D.C., [1882]), pp. 1–3, 7–8, 18, 58, copy in
ISP file 310, shelf 4 (SC 136).

32. Aldrich, "Coal Industry," pp. 13–14.

not exist as an *"imperium in imperio"* as had some parts of the Roman empire, but they recognized well enough that "those in the West or East who live by land speculation, railroad companies, and others, are in arms against it." To destroy common land tenure was viewed as the necessary preliminary to civilization, as confident industrialists defined it—industrial civilization, which nineteenth-century white men so loved that they could not share Indian doubts about the future of "the United States land system, which makes the earth a chattel."[33] William Ross of the Cherokees saw it best of all:

Railroads, aye railroads! Eminent domain!! Government sovereignty!!!. . . . I am aware that railroads and telegraph lines are a great and growing fact in the present age of the world and that if it were possible to arrest their construction, to stay the revolution of their wheels, to darken their headlights and to lull the electric spark which bears with lightning speed its mysterious language along valleys, over mountains and under the depths of great oceans, it would bring chaos and ruin and stop the advancement of human progress. But . . . there is no humiliation more degrading, no bondage more absolute, no mastery more insolent than such as result from irresponsible wealth hedged in, protected and made defiant by law that places it above and beyond all local law and sentiment over those upon whom it operates . . . It means simply at no distant day, the control of the legislation of our national councils, the corruption or disregard of officials, the possession of our mines, the dequestration of our lands, the subjugation of our people. . . . Omens of evil portent hurtle in the passing breeze and flash athwart gathering clouds within the circle of our own horizon.[34]

The only defense for the Indian, said Ross, was to educate himself not to be the instrument of his own ruin by the development of cultured minds capable of rising above economic interest. "We need

33. W. P. Adair, Daniel Ross, W. A. Phillips, *Brief on Behalf of the Cherokee Nation on the Question Touching Her Jurisdiction* (n.p., n.d.), pp. 3, 12, Gilcrease.

34. *The Life and Times of Hon. William P. Ross* (Fort Smith, 1893), 149, copy at Gilcrease.

sharp men but no sharpers, operators not bosses, proficients not pretenders, workers not shysters."[35]

For all that, the loud and the shallow were abroad in force. Within and without the tribes, at the Indian capitals, and at the lobby chambers in Washington, friends of industrial civilization were, through the seventies, eschewing involvement in the myriad specifics at issue between the corporation and the Indian and driving directly at the source of business frustration—Indian sovereignty itself.

35. Ibid., p. 154.

CHAPTER V

THE TERRITORIAL RING

Corporations operating in Indian Territory functioned on two levels in dealing with this unique political and economic situation. There were the immediate difficulties, such as the struggle over compensation for coal and ties. But the solutions to these problems were each determined discretely, and there was no continuity to point to an ultimate general policy. The compromises on technicalities might lead to profit for corporations, or more or less royalties for Indians, but they did not coalesce into a system that would assure similar results in the future. The companies therefore accompanied their technical holding action in the Territory with a strategy of more basic political import. They all contributed to the drive for creating a U.S. territorial government in the region, thus eliminating dual sovereignty once and for all and opening the region to white settlement. The corporate lobby pressing for this was known popularly as the Territorial Ring, and it should take its place beside the Tweed Ring, the Whiskey Ring, and the Gas Ring among the mysterious tokens of Gilded Age transformation of the world.

It cannot be said that Congress was immediately amenable to territorialization of the tribal domain. It was rather a process of slow slippage that finally burst into a tide of promotion. A New England senator was shocked by the idea in 1865:

> It changes I believe, very materially and radically our whole Indian policy. It violates our treaties. . . . and worse than all, it will be a stain upon the national honor. . . . Let us pause before we drive these Cherokees from their last earthly resting place—for they have now reached it—

to gratify the insatiable desire for land, which, like an evil spirit, seems to possess the minds of our people.[1]

Yet by 1871, the balance was tipping. Levi Parsons in that year sent the Interior Department a territorial bill of his own composition, which he recommended be sent directly to the floor of Congress to avoid much committee work. Newspapers in the West editorialized against the formation of a united Indian government or anything else that might tend to preserve or strengthen Indian sovereignty.[2]

The Indian delegations, in making plans to defend against territorialization, had doubts that its moral arguments would carry weight when contrasted to the "insatiate rapacity of organized land pirates ... whose capacity for absorbing the soil is one of the marvels of Western civilization." Especially discouraging was the observable fact that those who had the most direct economic interest in extinction of Indian sovereignty were the very men who had most influence in determining Indian policy in Washington.[3] The Ring included western congressmen (like Sidney Clarke), who claimed a superior practical knowledge of affairs on the border. Corporations had excellent political connections, and for the time being the potential settler, a powerful voting bloc, supported the corporations' territorial goals.

Not only those with direct interests in inhabiting or doing business in the Indian Territory led the Indians to despair of the special political status they desired, there was a consensus among the public about the prerogatives of progress. When C. J. Hillyer, attorney for the A&P railroad, wrote in 1871 a pamphlet entitled *Atlantic and Pacific Railroad and the Indian Territory*, his hymn to the corporation conformed with the prejudices both of the congressmen to whom it was distributed and a large proportion of the general public.

1. *Congressional Globe*, 38th Cong., 2d sess., XXXV, 1304.
2. Levi Parsons to C. Delano, Nov. 3, 1871, box 132, L&RR. *Missouri Democrat*, Jan. 13, 1871.
3. Lewis Downing et al., *Protest of the Cherokee Nation Against a Territorial Government* (Washington, D.C., 1871), Gilcrease.

Unable to collect its land grant, the A&P was stalled at Vinita and in financial difficulty. For this, Hillyer blamed the present Indian policy. The road had been honestly managed, he said. There had been no "Credit Mobilier" scandal. It had plans grand enough: a branch to Memphis and a line crossing the Arizona and New Mexico desert to connect St. Louis with San Francisco. To accomplish this goal it needed income from trade. Hillyer was expressing no more than the obvious conclusion that "a railroad and a wilderness are incompatible things, and cannot long co-exist." The A&P, he pointed out, might as well "for all business purposes, build a road for three hundred miles through a tunnel or a desert, as through the fertile Indian country in its present condition." Under laws permitting tribal control, the corporate representatives could see no chance that the region would develop appropriate industry, nor a much greater population than the forty-five thousand people who now inhabited its seventy thousand square miles. Hillyer argued that Congress had promised to extinguish the Indian title in the railroad's land grant, and he asked in addition that the country be opened to settlement. The A&P would not be the only party to benefit, he remarked in the pamphlet, but general economic well-being would be promoted. His statement was not a singular testimony but a benchmark in industrial destiny.[4]

The philosophy of Hillyer's pamphlet was that the government should "without *practical* injustice to the Indian" (italics added) promote first "the general welfare and prosperity of our own citizens." It was assumed that welfare and prosperity were essentially the same and that "practical" injustice was the only kind worth considering. Abstract moral considerations might be ignored. Wrote Hillyer, "There is no such sacredness in a treaty stipulation made years ago with an Indian tribe as to require or permit it to obstruct the national growth." Since the treaty-making system had been ended by Congress in 1871, railroad officials felt that the sense of Congress should now be dominant in Indian affairs. Any suffering the Indians

4. C. J. Hillyer, *Atlantic and Pacific Railroad and the Indian Territory*, pp. 1–6, 8.

underwent was caused by their refusal to conform to the habits of their betters. "They have insisted the country remain a wilderness because they prefer to live in a wilderness. . . . They have insisted that their own habits, notions and sentiments in this regard shall be respected, regardless of its effects upon the wants and necessities of the human race." The railroad was not interested in cultural anthropology. The Indians would benefit financially from the coming of the railroad, and financial prosperity was the mania of the age. He could no longer be treated as a martyr, this Indian, as a child or a wild beast, but must take his chance with others in the economic struggle that would measure the fitness of his race by the profits it generated. Attention need no longer be paid to arguments that "it offends his prejudices, wounds his vanity, and makes impossible his indolence." For the corporation was coming, and the Indian was going, "Whether one Indian or five thousand be killed in the operation, the result must be obtained." The Congress would give the railroad a land grant and traffic: the railroad would give the government a new state and immense gains in taxable property. To condemn this sort of exchange, this devotion to the future and carelessness of the past was "to pronounce false and fallacious the universally accepted American idea of what constitutes human progress and achievement."[5]

Hillyer's pamphlet was remarkable only for its honesty not for the quality of opinions it contained. Most Americans could not face the fact that in the moral sphere as much as the economic, someone always must pay. Those very people who were now deploring the inhumanity of their ancestors were, Hillyer pointed out, enjoying the fruits of those old cruelties without compunction of conscience—nor would they give them up for the principle they now espoused. New conditions gave rise to new wants and new necessities. Said the attorney:

However the Indians may regard this quest [for land], we, as American citizens cannot turn our backs upon our own civilization. We can neither

5. Ibid., pp. 14, 26, 28, 30, 36–37, 39, 42, 52, 61.

deny its superior excellence, nor refuse to follow the dictates of its necessities. We must determine our duties and rights from our own standpoint of intelligence.[6]

No more perfect expression of nineteenth-century ethnocentrism is likely to be found. Hillyer's *Atlantic and Pacific Railroad and the Indian Territory* is one of the most revealing documents of the Territorial Ring.

While Indian newspapers branded the corporation as the most dangerous threat to Indian existence because it was "the most powerful, the most interested in, and the most *actively* clamorous for the destruction of the Indian governments," natives saved their most caustic invective for such Indian members of the Territorial Ring as E. C. Boudinot. Lewis Downing wrote, "He uses the name of the Cherokees for the purpose of robbing and crushing the Cherokee people. He prostitutes his Indian blood to these base purposes for the sake of money." Boudinot's worst act, thought Downing, was to leave the impression that the Cherokees were divided on the question, that because of Boudinot's verbosity it was believed his view was more widely held than a careful survey of the tribe would indicate.[7]

Boudinot felt that territorial government was only part of a system of practical accommodation by the Indian to the corporation. Indians must adjust, as there was no longer any place to move them out of the way, leaving them to face physical extermination if they did not cooperate. "The waves of commerce and trade are dashing against our borders," Boudinot intoned. "Shall we flourish the broken sceptre of our treaties, and like Canute, bid them subside? ... Can you not hear the mutterings of the storm? Can you not see the lightnings flash?" Boudinot had personal experience with the futility of resistance. He had a tobacco factory once in Indian Territory that was confiscated by the United States for failure to pay an American revenue tax. Maybe if the "scantily clad brethren

6. Ibid., pp. 36, 38.

7. *Choctaw Vindicator*, June 28, 1873. Lewis Downing to John Jones, Feb. 12, 1872, LR OIA Cherokee Agency, M 234, R 105, F 0269–74 (for "Abbreviations in Footnotes," see p. vii).

of the plains" ever stopped his "frothing steed" long enough to try to go into business, as eventually he must, he would come to accept Boudinot's point of view. "He would be more fortunate than I," the progressive wailed, "if he saved his frothing steed and quiver of arrows from a decree of forfeiture." To resist change at last was out of the question. As Choctaw Chief Allen Wright put it, "It is idle to talk of things remaining as they were."[8]

In addition to speaking of the inevitability of corporate development, Boudinot harped upon the possibility of controlling it for the economic benefit of the Indian. Those critics who talked about the secret ring of schemers meeting in corporate board rooms and hatching plots for the ruin of the tribes were, according to Boudinot, the victims of "Munchausen tendencies." He tried hard to minimize the extent of land that might be taken by railroads if the contingent land grants were given, reducing the estimate from the 23 million acres then reported in newspapers to 2.5 million. His estimate was as inaccurate on the low side as the other was high. He did make the point that the railroads were willing to give up all claims to land grants in return for a territorial government. That argument seems unconvincing to the historian who knows that as late as 1903 the Katy was involved in court proceedings to claim its grant, but it was the official line of the companies then. Boudinot was especially upset with those who advertised that if Indian lands were allotted to individual owners, the Indian domain would automatically revert to railroads on the theory that the "tribal title" was gone. He regarded the Indian nationalists as ignorant, if well meaning. They would deny the intelligent Indian the chance of a sure title to a princely estate as well as a possible place of influence on a board of directors in order to work themselves into an antique fury over

---

8. E. C. Boudinot, *The Matters, Customs, Traditions and Present Condition of the Civilized Indians of the Indian Territory* (n.p., [1872]) p. 1, Gilcrease. *Speech of Elias C. Boudinot, A Cherokee Indian, Delivered before the House Committee on Territories . . . in Reply to Wm. P. Ross. . . .* (Washington, D.C., 1872), pp. 18, 23, 27, Hargrett, Gilcrease. *Missouri Patriot*, Feb. 8, 1872.

an invasion they were powerless to resist.[9] "We cannot silence the white man's axe; we cannot check the advancing multitudes; we cannot resurrect the canoe: but we can join the resistless army of civilization and progress, and thus save our people from destruction."[10] It was a poetically phrased, nonracial version of Hillyer's argument.

Despite this advice, there were many in the Indian Territory who were preparing for political war. Territorial bills were being regularly tabled, but the pressure remained. Finally, one would pass. Wrote the normally moderate *Advocate*:

> If it were only possible to choke each honorable schemer, with the instrument of his cruel designs against our country as he presents it. But no. We must face them all [the territorial bills] the best way we may. We must examine them, expose them, denounce them, defeat them, if we can.... The bane of this and the other nations of this Territory is— railroads.... We cheerfully gave them the right of way.... But we expected the engine to go through quietly and civilly like a decent vehicle. ... The railroads have made *themselves* the bane of this country.[11]

Why, asked the editor, could a citizen of the United States not find something better to do with his time than "blaming people for acting differently from the way he thinks they ought to act, or from the way he would act if he were only in their place."[12]

A member of the Ring closer to the center than Boudinot was J. P. C. Shanks of Indiana, head of the House Committee on Indian Affairs. While warning Indians not to trust those who wanted to be friends merely to achieve their own ends, Shanks was guilty of a little

9. *Oklahoma. Argument of Col. E. C. Boudinot Before the Committee on Territories, Jan. 29, 1878* (Alexandria, Va., 1878), pp. 27, 30–32, Frank Phillips Collection, OU.

10. *Speech of Elias C. Boudinot of the Cherokee Nation Delivered Before the House Committee on Territories, March 5, 1872...In Reply to the Second Argument of the Indian Delegates* (Washington, D.C., 1872), p. 16, Hargrett, Gilcrease.

11. *Cherokee Advocate*, Aug. 21, 1872.

12. Ibid., May 4, 1872.

corporate booming of his own. In the summer of 1872, he visited the Indian Territory on a fact-finding tour and wrote a long letter to the *New York Herald*, using his official findings as commercial propaganda for corporate interests. Shanks wrote from Boggy Depot, Choctaw Nation, that the railroad would soon change everything there for the better. It would make the trade and intercourse laws a "dead letter," would hasten the elimination of the common landholding system, and would create towns where now there were none. Either the Indians or the railroad must give way, Shanks wrote, and it clearly would not, and should not, be the railroad:

> It may be hard for the government, which has pledged its solemn faith to these people, to find itself compelled to violate that pledge. But EVEN GOVERNMENTS CANNOT STAND IN THE WAY OF PROGRESS. The laws of trade are more powerful than those of Congress. . . . the thing is inevitable.

Economics would dictate politics, Shanks thought, and would result in the destruction of the "shams and farces" that served as tribal governments. The *Vindicator* commented that given the kind of rhetoric in Shanks's letter, "It is no use to talk about this or that Congressman being friends to the Indian, for the Past has conclusively shown us that there are really no true friends of the Indians— in the light of an isolated Nationality."[13]

The press, which had long warmed to talking about the final solution to the Indian question, became hot over the territorial issue. Newspaper reporters found laughable the antics of Bull Eagle, a Sioux Indian, who during a conference to sign railroad agreements, rushed up to a congressman and tore the papers to bits saying all white men were liars.[14] The visit to St. Louis of Spotted Tail and his attempts to order dinner in a fancy restaurant were satirized in the daily newspapers.[15] In some, like the *Missouri Democrat*, President Grant's Indian Peace Policy was criticized because the need for St. Louis to

13. Ibid., July 20, 1872; *Choctaw Vindicator*, Aug. 24, 1872.
14. *Missouri Democrat*, Aug. 3, 1872.
15. *Cheyenne Leader* quoting *St. Louis Globe Democrat*, Sept. 14, 1872.

obtain a railway outlet across Indian Territory justified outright extermination of the tribes standing in the way. In an article in the *Democrat* it was stated that self-government was a comedy for such brutes as the Indians, and extermination was not so much barbarity as simple necessity. "The world in its onward progress must crush somebody, and humanity cannot invariably afford to be humanitarian in excess." The paper went on to suggest that government distilleries be established and offer a ten-gallon whiskey bounty for every Indian scalp brought in, setting the Indians against each other:

> The result would be agreeable to the Indians, who enjoy nothing so much as killing other people, and getting drunk themselves. . . . many moons would not have elapsed when the last of the Mohicans could be seen, in the very last throe of the jim-jams, breathing an atmosphere and treading a hemisphere of snakes, approaching Fort Bourbon, scalping himself, and handing over the trophy, to fall lifeless on the eight gallons of whiskey which he has thus dearly purchased.[16]

When significant numbers of people found amusement in that sort of writing, there was no need for special conspiracies on the part of the Territorial Ring.

The tribal delegations and attorneys in Washington, however, were not ready to steal away, and they made a strong stand during the congressional debates upon an 1872 bill to repeal the contingent land grants to Indian Territory railroads. Some who argued for this bill were perhaps more enemies of the railroad than friends to the Indians, but articulate attacks on corporate pretensions were made.

Daniel Finn of Arkansas asked the House Committee on Indian Affairs whether the United States was not hiding from its moral responsibilities by allowing railroads, seeking land grants, to coerce the Indians into changing their lives? Were not these grants the cause of the swarm of lobbyists, all working for railroads, who were seen about the Capitol promoting territorial bills. Finn called the Ring a "far reaching and deeply plotted scheme," which he said began during the Civil War when certain men gathered wealth while com-

16. *Missouri Democrat*, Sept. 23, 1872.

manding troops or acting as government contractors. They had planned the 1866 treaties and railroad bills and pressed them through at the end of a session. "The design was so covert as to be hardly noticed. . . . but now the design is too patent to be covered up, even by putting on an air of injured innocence." Finn thought there were four ways the Indian could lose his sovereignty: by extinguishing tribal relations, by abandoning the country, by selling to the United States, and by the mere force of the stronger, regardless of justice. It was in this fourth direction that the railroads were tending. Was not the choice clear? Was it not between the *contingent privileges* of the railroads, and the *rights* of the Indians?[17]

The committee heard a similar argument from W. R. Laughlin of Kansas. Laughlin said that he was in Washington only to help a neighbor who had fallen among thieves. Really he was there representing Kansas settlers who did not wish Indian lands to fall into the hands of the railroad, lest farmers be denied a chance to get them cheaply. These railroad schemers, he said, were giving the settlers a bad name. It was the Ring that was sinister, and the corporations were behind the Ring. "They have reduced to an *Infernal science* the processes by which they plunder the Government, the settlers and the Indians." The method the corporations used, he explained, was to promote, *sub rosa*, internal dissent within the tribes, set factions at each others throats, and then move in behind the corporate steamroller to restore order. The United States had used this method in its imperial adventures, why not private concerns? "Dissention will be industriously sown," Laughlin concluded, "Deception, fear, fraud, and every base intrigue will be used without scruple in the frantic strife to secure the vast prize." Laughlin sat down.[18] The bill to repeal land grants was defeated in committee.

Cherokee Chief William Ross was another vocal influence for

17. *Argument of Daniel C. Finn of Arkansas on House Resolution 1132* (Washington, D.C., 1872), pp. 11, 14–19, 22–23, Indian Pamphlets Collection, Vol. 5, KSHS.

18. *Argument of W. R. Laughlin of Kansas on House Resolution 1132. . . .* (Washington, D.C., 1872), pp. 2, 11, ibid.

the position against assigning territorial status. In numerous briefs and pamphlets, he repeated that the single key to all territorial bills was industrial opportunity for the corporation and that all other reasons given were hypocritical. He made the point that he doubted if much support could be generated for a territorial bill that omitted all reference to Indian lands, ignored contingent rail grants, and prohibited the territorial legislature from chartering railroad corporations. "Nor do I concede for a moment that the subject of legislation for the organization of the Indian Territory is a question of expediency alone. . . . When physically applied it is true: when legally and morally it is false." If it happened, the poverty-bound full bloods, for whose "protection" the bills were ostensibly designed, would be driven into flint hills and narrow gorges so that railroad companies and claims speculators might settle comfortably upon the fertile plain. The only people from whom Indians needed protection, thought Ross, were those reformers who were framing bills to make their lands a U.S. territory. The tribes were self-sustaining and happy with their economic life.[19]

Ross with his appeals to Congress mounted a campaign of education and unification among his own people. Before the death of John Ross in 1872, William Ross reemphasized the dangers of which the old chief had warned in the fifties. "When huge cables stretch across the great ocean and railroads across a great continent, from the rising to the setting sun; when the blood of the most restless and enterprising and greedy population on the face of the earth is mantling and flowing all around us . . . there is not time for the children of the country to grow up in idleness and ignorance." Ross wrote a series of articles in the *Advocate* in 1874 in which he made the point that not every change is an improvement, and Indians must learn to discriminate between the false and true promises of corporate capitalism. When Katy excursion trains loaded up Indian leaders, wined and dined them, took them to the company shops at Sedalia, along with congressmen, it reminded Ross of the scenes just before the enforced removal of the tribes from their lands east of the Mississippi. The corporations

19. *The Life and Times of Hon. William P. Ross*, pp. 43, 50.

were, he said, using all devices "so available to capital and cunning" to create public sentiment for the destruction of the tribes. If the railroads had made a bad bargain in the treaty guarantees, their own homily—"business is business"—should be thrown back at them. Surely the Indian was no apostle of any form of civilization that resorted to "a breach of faith which even barbarians abhor" and should not be tempted by promises of civilization to give up his rights "in order that corporations may be enriched and railroad stocks advanced in Wall Street." Corporations everywhere inundated the Indians with arguments and demands. "I am no alarmist," said Ross, "but be ye not deceived."[20]

The Ring was active to be sure. Thomas Fitch, member of Congess from Nevada, spoke at the Mercantile Library Hall in St. Louis upon the theme of territorial government. He alluded to the "Chinese policy" of the tribes of the West, which were lobbying against railroads "for fear the whistle of the locomotive might scare the game of the noble Choctaw," and he criticized Indian spokesmen like Ross for themselves being the biggest land speculators in the United States. Why should American civilization pen up thousands in factories and tenements in order that the Indians might enjoy the free air of their beautiful country? Government aid to the tribes, which was costing more than if each were given a suite of rooms at the Astor House, should be cut off and the aborigines forced to work or starve. "If he will be a drone, let him meet the drone's fate. . . . If he will not mount the car of progress, or get out of the way, let him be crushed." John Conner of Texas said in Congress that the Indian nations had "not a single attribute of sovereignty." Governor Woodson of Missouri spoke of the Indian Territory as though it were already public domain.[21]

It would be unfair to say that the Indian nations had no friends in their fight. Why else should a campaign for territorialization that began in 1866 be not even partially successful until the creation of Oklahoma Territory in 1889, and not then include the area of the Five

20. Ibid., p. 57. *Cherokee Advocate*, Oct. 17, 1874.
21. *Missouri Democrat*, Nov. 13, 1872. *Congressional Globe*, 42d Cong., 3d sess., XLVI, 617, 619. *Cherokee Advocate*, Jan. 17, 1874.

Tribes? The historian can differentiate between individual scoundrels, which according to evidence existed on both sides, and races of scoundrels (or for that matter heroes), which it did not. For example, George McKee of Mississippi suggested in Congress that the United States should "cease kicking these Indians before us as a foot-ball." He said that E. C. Boudinot's faction periodically lost in tribal elections, indicating a majority of Cherokees that did not like his policy could at times be mustered. The Indian Territory corporations were only "villainous heirs seeking to compass the death of the parent in order to come more quickly into their inheritance." Surely, McKee thought, the United States had not become so hard "as to wish to see the blood of the red man coined by huckstering traders into dollars and the honor of this Government bartered for its greenback promises to pay."[22]

The argument by proponents of territorialization, however, ultimately convinced more. It turned upon the idea of "protection." The Indians were wards of the white man and had been allowed to play at self-governance only so long as they did not hurt themselves. When they got out of line, the guardian must intervene for their own good. Choctaw Agent Albert Parsons wrote Washington in 1874, that the Indian governments were too weak to prevent crime, and it was unfair to leave them on their own against desperadoes, white and red. The Indian, if he would not do it on his own, should be forced to prefer civilization and education to the grogshop, no matter if it should conflict with the financial interest of certain Choctaw and congressional leaders.[23]

The Osage delegation disagreed sharply in 1875. It contended that crime in the Indian Territory was the result of the failure of the United States to enforce trade laws or to allow the Indian governments the military power to do it themselves rather than to any intrinsic weakness of Indian governments. The real question was not whether the Osages were Christians but whether the whites were Christian. Why

22. *Congressional Globe*, 42d Cong., 3d sess., XLVI, 648, 651–52, 655.
23. A. Parsons to E. P. Smith, March 28, 1874, LR OIA Choctaw Agency, M 234, R 181, F 0472–75; Parsons to Smith, April 21, 1874, SC 136, tray 1.

should it be expected that a territorial government would suddenly civilize the Osages when it took the Anglo-Saxon eighteen hundred years to evolve from primitive Briton to his present state? Or was that really the object? Maybe Congress should pay more attention to railroad conditional land grants and notice that one of the leading members of the Board of Indian Commissioners, organized to advise on policy, was the vice-president of the Atlantic and Pacific railroad. The Osage delegation claimed that the first conditional land grant on record was when Satan took Jesus up to a high mountain and showed him the kingdoms of the world.[24] That scene had been repeated many times since and was ultimately the issue in Indian Territory.

By the centennial year, 1876, the Indians were very tired of resisting territorial bills buried in measures for protection or attached to appropriation bills. Since 1866, fifty territorial bills for the Indian Territory had been brought before Congress. Yet, they returned in new dress. One tribal delegate expressed it thus:

> That you may, without disgust, take to your arms the deformed babe which was first dropped as a bastard in your midst about eight years ago, and which since has been shoved from one committee to another all over your Capitol, its friends now present it to you fresh from cunning fingers directed by the most fastidious taste newly washed, powdered, perfumed, and dressed. Nevertheless its identity is easily traced. No . . . new christening can make it other than it has ever been . . . a cheat, a fraud.[25]

The Indians complained that their remonstrances were given to a clerk in the Indian office and purposefully lost. Unless the government compensated the railroads somehow for the promise of land grants, territorial legislation would be like the fabled serpent that grew two heads each time one was lopped off.[26]

24. SMD 72, 42d Cong., 2d sess., 1875 (S 1630), *passim*.

25. Daniel Ross et al., *Remonstrance of the Cherokee, Creek, Choctaw and Seminole Delegations Against the Organization of the Indian Territory....* (Washington, D.C., 1876), pp. 3–4, Hargrett, Gilcrease.

26. *Cherokee Advocate*, May 6, 1876.

In the mid-seventies, E. C. Boudinot created a journalistic forum for his views, a newspaper at Muskogee, Creek Nation, called *Indian Progress*. This paper supported a group of resolutions adopted at Caddo, I.T., which were mild, but requested a U.S. court and left the door open for territorial government. Many believed the newspaper was supported by railroad money, and the Creek government tried to close it on the grounds that managing editor E. Poe Harris had never applied to the Creek government for a license. Owner Boudinot and editor Harris replied that they had permission from the U.S. agent, again raising the issue of dual sovereignty. The Creeks reacted by confiscating the newspaper building, an act Boudinot characterized as "stupid impertinence." The pair besieged government offices with the argument that this only proved that free speech and a free press could not operate as long as the Indian governments remained.[27]

In addition to this indirect slight, the railroad interest made itself unpopular through the statements of MK&T attorney Gardiner C. Hubbard. In February 1876 Hubbard made a speech on the territorial question that was widely regarded as an *ex cathedra* statement by the Territorial Ring. He said that the 1866 treaties were not ordinary treaties, since they in effect included the railway land-grant acts as part of the same transaction. The railroad and Paris and Amsterdam holders of bonds issued by the A&P and MK&T based upon Indian Territory lands had a vested interest in these lands. The Indian, trying to deal through his government with the corporation, was only meddling in "matters which he did not comprehend, the value of which he could not appreciate."[28]

The Indian delegations, thinking it was odd that two hundred railroad incorporaters should each benefit to the extent of $1,150,000

27. The story of the newspaper may be found in the following: E. C. Boudinot to Samuel Checote, Oct. 12, 1875; to G. W. Ingalls, Oct. 4, Oct. 25, 1875; G. W. Ingalls to E. P. Smith, Oct. 27, 1875; John Shanks to E. P. Smith, Oct. 30, 1875, all in Creek Newspaper File, sec. X, IAD; *Choctaw Vindicator*, Nov. 10, 1875.

28. *Cherokee Advocate*, April 29, 1876.

from the sale of 23 million acres of land, continued the fight.[29] They were somewhat encouraged, not by great success, but by the enormity of disaster avoided. The Cherokee delegation reported that it had resisted fourteen territorial bills in the 1876 session and defeated land-grant bills for several railroads wishing to enter the Territory. It was hoped that in the wake of the Grant administration scandals the public would take a more critical stance toward the Indian Territory schemes.[30] But the A&P, when reorganized in 1876 as the St. Louis and San Francisco Railway Company, was like a dangerous snake shedding its skin and approaching from the rear while attackers blasted away at a shell. James Brown, MK&T passenger agent, did not show much evidence of change of direction either:

> Large as life you will see him with an open book in his hand looking innocent and virtuous and happy. In the open book it is written "Free Guide to Texas, M.K.&T." On the other page it goes on to say, "The only route through the beautiful Indian Territory, enter Texas at the gate city Denison," while on his valise is printed in letters that he who runs at thirty miles may read: "Check me over the M.K.&T. Railway."[31]

One of the first things the St. Louis and San Francisco (Frisco) company did was to make a more determined effort than ever to collect the A&P land grant. It was disappointed in October 1877 when J. A. Williamson, commissioner of the General Land Office, wrote the opinion that he would not withdraw lands for the company in the Indian Territory because under the treaty the corporation had no claim to such lands without Indian consent.[32] This decision, more than any other single event, turned all efforts of the corporations toward creating a territorial government, since there no longer seemed to be a chance of carving out an empire for themselves as long as tribal governments were there to resist. The blow dealt their hopes for a land grant by the Land Office was fresh when the Patterson

29. *Indian Journal*, June 1, 1876.
30. Ibid., Sept. 7, 1876.
31. *Atoka Independent*, May 31, 1876.
32. H. Craig Miner, *The St. Louis-San Francisco Transcontinental Railroad*, p. 104.

investigating committee went to Indian Territory to study matters there in 1878.

James Baker, president of the Frisco, was first to testify before the committee. He told the senators that there should be at least a U.S. court in the region with authority to foreclose mortgages. Due to the confused situation concerning sovereignty, land-grant bonds for his company's Central Division (Indian Territory) were selling for five cents on the dollar. He admitted, in response to questions from Cherokee attorney William Adair, that he personally had written several of the territorial bills then before Congress but denied Adair's charge that he had distributed bonds among influential Indians to cultivate influence. Baker's statement that he thought a territorial bill would provide the Indians with a better government than they ever had provoked a violent exchange with Adair. Had Baker ever read the constitution and laws of the Cherokee Nation? Did he know how long they had had a written form of government? Baker, after several clumsy responses, became vindictive and called the Cherokee government "an absolute mockery." The two had to be quieted by the chairman and the session temporarily halted.[33]

B. F. Grafton tried to outline to the committee the legal and philosophic justifications for tribal sovereignty. He was listened to politely, and the senators admitted that there was a "certain degree of poetical justice" in what he said. But, they told him, the federal government as a practical matter would never recognize the complete sovereignty of the tribes. The committee concluded that the tribes had a "quasi independence" but that the tribal court system should be immediately replaced by U.S. courts in which "the rights of property shall be adequately protected." Indian lands should be alloted, and all Indians should be made U.S. citizens.[34]

Soon after the appearance of the Patterson committee report, there were charges of fraud. The *New York Tribune* wrote that the railroad companies, whose affairs were presumably being investigated, exercised a large and illegitimate influence over the committee.

33. SR 744, 45th Cong., 3d sess., 1879 (S 1839), pp. 2–6.
34. Ibid., pp. 68 ff.; pp. i–v, 485.

The *Tribune* staff reported the effects on the stock market while the committee was in the Indian Territory. On February 4, 1879, when the group met to consider the testimony, 700 shares of MK&T stock sold at six dollars a share. On the fifth, when the conclusions were published in New York papers, sales were 3,500 shares at six and seven-eighths. The reporters also checked the committee's expense account. They found people on the payroll who did no work, and unusual amounts paid to the MK&T railroad for transportation and lodging. More was paid for seven people than had been paid for a previous committee of ten that traveled to the Pacific coast. A Washington lobbyist for the Katy was paid $173 for summoning witnesses and $123 for being a witness himself. The manuscript copy of the testimony revealed that T. C. Sears, Katy attorney, had been allowed to do much of the questioning, though his name was removed from the committee's printed report. The *Tribune* concluded that this "jovial junketing party" had been a fraud upon the Indians and the taxpayers, and an attempt to whitewash a shameful situation.[35]

Indian analysts were even less kind. They reported that Gardiner Hubbard of the Katy had objected to any Indian delegates appearing to participate in the questioning. The investigation was a surprise to the Indians, while the railroad had been warned well in advance.[36] The committee never left the railroad line, even when invited to Tahlequah, the Cherokee capital, to see the council in session. Most of the antirailroad tribal faction lived in the backcountry, away from the railroad, so that this policy automatically resulted in a prorailroad bias.[37] J. Elliot Condict, a druggist from Philadelphia who had traveled in Indian Territory as a gentleman of leisure was called upon for expert testimony on the state of the tribal governments. Condict privately handed out six-shooters and sets of harness to influential Indians while in the area testifying and told the Choctaw chief that he

35. *New York Tribune*, Feb. 13, March 22, April 23, 1879.
36. *Atoka Independent*, May 31, 1878.
37. Charles Thompson, petition, Dec. 5, 1878, LR OIA Union Agency, M 234, R 871, F 0018.

hoped to get a nice position on the railroad.[38] Few Indians were interviewed, and the bulk of the testimony was taken outside the Territory proper. Peter Pitchlynn said that full bloods whose testimony was included did not really testify at all, but proterritorial statements were written out for them by Union Agent S. W. Marston.[39] Wrote B. F. Grafton:

> I know that the long roll had been sounded in the camp of certain railway jobbers and land-grabbers—the enemies of these people—and that they have gathered in this our Capitol from the money centers of the Old World and from our own 'Wall Street,' and hover about this building as birds of prey. I know they hope and believe they will succeed in this unholy cause, but let me warn them they cannot accomplish their wicked purpose with *stocks* and *bonds*. The price of these lands will be paid in human blood. Who, among those Indians is so lost to love of country, home, and little ones as not to lay down his life in defense of them.[40]

E. C. Boudinot reported in early 1879 that he was up at 6:00 A.M. and worked until 3:00 A.M. fighting Adair, Ross, and Grafton before the committee. "I am worn out and half sick."[41]

Ultimately, the Territorial Ring gained its power from the inability of the American people to abide enclaves of significant cultural or economic variation, from the Mormons through the rest of the spectrum. It should not have been necessary to establish that Indians were ideal beings, or that tribal governments were advanced institutions capable of dealing efficiently with all contingencies, only that they operated as cleanly, though differently, than most human institutions. Sen. George McKee concluded during an 1873 territorial bill

38. *Argument of B. F. Grafton, Delivered January 24, 1879, Before the Committee on Territories of the United States Senate* (n.p., n.d.), p. 3, Frank Phillips Collection, OU.

39. HMD 13, 46th Cong., 1st sess., 1879 (S 1876), p. 6.

40. *Argument of B. F. Grafton, Delivered January 24, 1879. . . .* p. 30.

41. E. C. Boudinot to Mrs. Sarah Watie, Jan. 29, 1879, box 3, Cherokee Nation Papers, OU.

debate that the Indian's only crime seemed to be living where and how it suited him to live:

> The great argument, reiterated over and over, is that the territory as it now stands, is an anomaly. Wondrous word; an anomaly! What a potent argument! Because, forsooth, it is not exactly like the other territories, it is an 'anomaly' and must be abolished. Why do they not say at once that the Indian himself is an 'anomaly' and therefore ought to be abolished.[42]

The territorial sentiment, as it developed in the seventies, was not at all far from that last conclusion. Most knew, as Indian Commissioner Francis Walker put it in 1873: "We may have no fear that the dying curse of the red man, outcast and homeless by our fault, will bring bareness upon the soil that once was his, or dry the streams of the beautiful land that, through so much of evil and of good, has become our patrimony."[43] The weapons the Indians had were rhetoric, dreams, abstractions. They were as grass to be mown by the hard headed of that generation, by whose bombast the little voices of the sensitive were stilled.

42. *Congressional Globe*, 42d Cong., 3d sess., XLVI, 650.
43. F. A. Walker, "The Indian Question," p. 388.

CHAPTER VI

"THE PHILISTINES ARE UPON US"

At the turn of the decade of the eighties, it was clear
that the pragmatic weight of numbers would operate more powerfully to diminish tribal sovereignty in Indian Territory than a carload
of petitions and legal briefs. Most fearsome was the alliance between
corporations and settler organizations (some of them also corporations) urging to open the territory to settlement, and thus using mass
agitation to break the Indian hold. Reporters for Indian newspapers
noticed "many a greedy covetous eye . . . through the windows of the
passing trains, as the iron horse swiftly hurries them by."[1]

There was much evidence of an alliance of convenience between
settlers and corporations. It was widely believed that boomer newspapers, such as the *Kansas City Times*, were subsidized by rail corporations with interest in Indian Territory. Although colonization societies might severely criticize railroad monopolies in their speeches,
the societies sometimes met in railroad offices. C. C. Carpenter, who
had been active in promoting an invasion of miners into the Black
Hills in 1876, driving the Sioux before them, found a new field in
which to agitate against the sovereignty of Indian Territory, with
the financial support, it was said, of the Missouri, Kansas and Texas.
David L. Payne, the best known of the boomers, was assumed to represent the Atlantic and Pacific-Frisco system, and Judge James Baker, a
Frisco officer, defended Payne at his trial for illegal settlement in 1881.
The Leavenworth, Lawrence and Galveston railroad was charged
with giving Payne $500. Sen. George Vest of Missouri, active in Con-

1. *Indian Journal*, Aug. 19, 1880.

gress for the settler interest, was a former MK&T attorney and was thought by the Cherokees to be still in the pay of the company and of the "emigration conspiracy" generally. Katy chief attorney T. C. Sears made no secret of the fact that he worked closely with E. C. Boudinot to advise settler groups of legal loopholes that might allow them to penetrate the "Chinese Wall." E. C. Boudinot had known David Payne when the latter was doorkeeper at the House of Representatives, and they had plotted boomer schemes together. C. C. Carpenter's organization at Kansas City had a Vinita branch under the leadership of prominent Cherokee citizens, including Superintendent of Schools S. S. Stephens, who themselves wanted to settle and develop the Cherokee Outlet and even form a native corporation to sublease oil rights.[2]

The tone taken by the "civilizers" became much more direct in the 1880s. The Board of Indian Commissioners wrote in its 1879 report that, however much people moralized over the natural rights of the Indian, those rights had to be limited, and the limit was that 12 million acres of land, fertile and rich in ore, could not long "be kept simply as a park, in which wild beasts are hunted by wilder men."[3] Wrote a *New York Tribune* reporter from the Choctaw Nation:

> We have snivelled over the wrongs of the red man for the past hundred years, spoiling him by sentimental sympathy and coddling, while we tried to compromise with our morbid consciences by pretending to suffer remorse without making restitution. . . . I know of no subject upon which so much cant has been delivered as on the treatment of Indians.[4]

2. John O'Neill to E. A. Hayt, May 4, May 6, 1879, SC 111, tray 1. Carl C. Rister, *Land Hunger: David L. Payne and the Oklahoma Boomers*, p. 94; *Indian Journal*, March 3, 1880; Jan. 6, 1881; March 11, 1880. W. P. Adair et al. to E. A. Hayt, April 16, 1879, SC 111, tray 11 (for "Abbreviations in Footnotes," see p. vii). Rister, *Land Hunger*, p. 47. W. P. Adair to E. A. Hayt, April 19, 1879; E. C. Boudinot to Augustus Albert, March 31, 1879, SC 111, tray 1.

3. Loring B. Priest, *Uncle Sam's Stepchildren: The Reformation of United States Indian Policy, 1865–1887*, p. 219.

4. *New York Tribune*, Jan. 11, 1879.

It seemed that the time for hypocrisy was over and that the corporation was ready to emerge fully from its "invisible" position, and, with
confidence in public support, to follow the direct line of C. J. Hillyer's
pamphlet. "These railroad men," the *Advocate* observed, "having
doubtless become proselyted to the Beecher 'latter day' doctrine that
there is no 'hell,' seem to have picked up courage, and now dare to
say, that their talk about religion, and 'the better protection of life' &c.
was all 'stuff,' and that the great motive power 'behind the scenes,' in
this 'Oklahoma' job, is their railroad bonds." While tribal citizens
protested that whatever civilization they had come from, the Christian religion rather than railroads, prominent ministers, like Washington Gladden, were writing that a true understanding of Christianity was impossible without active participation in the ritual of
accumulation. The corporation was not wholly responsible for creating this public sentiment, but it confidently thrived in it.[5]

It seemed that every threat to the Indian involved the corporation directly or indirectly. Marshall Murdock wrote in the *Wichita
Eagle* in 1879 that the A&P and MK&T railroads had for years been
lobbying in conjunction with commercial interests from Kansas City
and St. Louis for the opening of the Indian Territory. When Murdock served in the Kansas state senate, Robert Stevens took all state
government officials of Kansas to the heart of Indian Territory on a
special train, where they were plied with food and drink and advised
of the railroad's views on the status of the region. Murdock was
against opening the region because he feared it would result in the
depopulation of Kansas, but men like David Payne were able to use
corporate arguments for their own ends. In an 1879 pamphlet, Payne
argued that a federal law passed in 1878 stated that anywhere there
was a railroad grant, homestead and preemption laws would apply
and that therefore it was in the settlers' interest to support railroad claims. Land Commissioner Williamson's strong 1877 decision

5. *Cherokee Advocate*, April 20, 1878. Washington Gladden, "Christianity
and Wealth," p. 904; W. P. Adair, et al., *Memorial of the Indian Delegates
from the Indian Country....* (n.p., n.d.) Frank Phillips Collection, OU.

against the right of the A&P to a land grant was qualified by the attorney general less than two years later. Williamson himself went to work for the Frisco railroad.[6]

One of the most surprising patterns to emerge at this time is the documentable conclusion that corporations were the real driving powers on both sides of the debate over Indian sovereignty. It may be said that the long survival of Indian governments in the face of pressure was due mostly to the fact that some corporations found it in their interest temporarily to preserve Indian sovereignty, or protect some Indian right, and therefore threw their power against the corporate despoilers. A single company could change sides as its interest demanded, or even be on both sides at once. A good example is the Frisco railway. Before 1882, the Frisco bought more than five thousand shares in David Payne's colonization corporation. However, in that year an interest in the company was bought by Jay Could. Gould already controlled the MK&T, and all other roads from the Mississippi Valley into Texas. Therefore, in the interest of preventing other lines from getting privileges there, he often acted as "friend" to the Indian. So Frisco policy changed. The *Wichita Eagle*, however, suggested that, for all this public stance, the Frisco still supported Payne privately because settlement of the Indian Territory would cut off the cattle drive north to Kansas and force cattle shipments onto the Gould roads in Indian Territory and Texas. The cattle corporations of the eighties also supported Indians' rights because they had not been granted leases on Indian lands and did not wish to sacrifice them to competitors or farmers. On the other side were the "out" corporations, especially railroads pleading for rights of way and the oil interests, which maneuvered for franchises throughout the decade. Had corporations not been as divided as the Indians in their interests, the game would have ended quickly. During the eighties a tenuous balance existed between all the various powers external to

6. Rister, *Land Hunger*, pp. 42, 106–7. For Williamson's railroad career see Ch. X of H. Craig Miner, *The St. Louis-San Francisco Transcontinental Railroad*.

and inimical to a true Indian nationalism, but in their struggles with each other they gave that nationalism a new life.[7]

The year 1882 represented a climax in the struggle for Indian sovereignty against railroad intrusion. The congressional decision of that year to grant the Frisco railroad a right of way through the Choctaw Nation on a route not specifically stipulated in a treaty was one of the most significant watersheds in the post–Civil War history of Indian policy. The precedent was thereby set that Congress might authorize corporations to exercise privileges upon Indian lands without consulting the tribes. A thing more damaging to the national hopes of the Indians could hardly be imagined.

The pressure for new rights of way, which led to the 1882 debate, kept Indian delegations busy throughout the seventies. The "Fine Arkansas Gentlemen, Close to the Choctaw Line," as a popular song put it, pushed hard to construct the Little Rock and Fort Smith road into the Indian nations. At one time some track was built, but, much to the chagrin of some tribal progressives who had invested in the line, the track was torn up by order of the Office of Indian Affairs. The MK&T very much wanted a Memphis branch to connect Texas with the Southeast, though this route was not provided for in the 1866 treaties. The St. Louis and San Francisco wished to take its time on the A&P route west of Vinita and instead push south through the Choctaw Nation to Texas in order to break Gould's monopoly there. Control of an interest in the Frisco by the Atchison, Topeka and Santa Fe, acquired in 1880, encouraged this policy until Gould's takeover in 1882. No number of failures disqualified the corporate contestant, while the fate of the Indian governments could ride upon a single majority against them on a single bill. In 1879 there was a bill before Congress to allow any railroad company that requested it to build two lines, from Fort Smith to Kansas along the Arkansas River and from Kansas to Texas west of the Arkansas.

7. Rister, *Land Hunger*, p. 107. H. Craig Miner, "The Colonization of the St. Louis and San Francisco Railway Company, 1880–82: A Study of Corporate Diplomacy," pp. 345–62. *Wichita Eagle*, Sept. 28, 1882.

In 1880, the Chicago, Texas and Mexican Central railroad inquired if the consent of the Choctaw Nation was necessary to allow it to build through their country of if Congress could grant a right of way. Gen. U. S. Grant invested a great deal in this line, which could save $2 million on its Mexican route by going through Indian Territory. While the Cherokees were fighting this proposal, officials of the Little Rock and Fort Smith again attempted to lobby at Tahlequah. "We assume," the lobbyists stated, "that our Cherokee neighbors will fall in with the civilization of the age."[8]

The Cherokee chief, Dennis Bushyhead, ordered copies of the Patterson report on railroad rights, as well as two volumes of railroad statistics, in preparation for a long battle. He found it clearly indicated the intent of the 1866 treaty to limit rights of way to two and that building a branch line for the MK&T would not be legally sound. He refused a Katy request that he be polite and approve their Fort Smith line. He wished to be the railroad's friend, he said, but the cost this time was too high. It would "sap the very foundations of our relations with the general government." So the Cherokee government braced for a struggle, with a balance of $97.83 in its tribal treasury and a few "pigeon holes" in ramshackle desks to provide organization to a campaign against some of the most powerful corporations in the world.[9]

8. S. A. Galpin to Joseph Converse, Feb. 23, 1877; J. Q. Smith to Joseph Converse, Dec. 11, 1876, Cherokee Railroad File (Tahlequah acquisition), IAD; *Indian Journal* (Muskogee), Sept. 7, 1876. D. W. Bushyhead to National Council, Nov. 23, 1881, Cherokee Railroad Box, OU. Copies of bills of April 21, 1879 (H.R. 1222) and Dec. 17, 1879 (H.R. 3032) in ibid.; D. W. Bushyhead to National Council, Nov. 10, 1881, Cherokee volume 715–D, IAD. John A. Rudd to D. W. Bushyhead, Aug. 30, 1881, Cherokee Railroad File (Tahlequah acquisition), IAD; C. Schurz to James Simpson, Nov. 13, 1880; William Fishback to D. W. Bushyhead, Oct. 17, 1881, LR OIA Union Agency, M 234, R 874, document I 604.

9. J. A. Sibbald to D. W. Bushyhead, Oct. 28, 1881, Cherokee Railroad File (Tahlequah acquisition), IAD. David Kelse to D. W. Bushyhead, May 7, 1881; Executive Office to Kelso, May 11, 1881, Cherokee Railroad Box, OU;

The little progress that was made in the early eighties was at most temporary. For example, the tribes made an agreement with the Frisco to allow damage claims to be arbitrated by the tribal courts. This boost to Indian sovereignty was, however, withdrawn by Judge I. C. Parker at the Fort Smith federal court. Treaties, he ruled, did not foresee any agreement to submit claims to Indian courts, and the Indians were not competent to make any such agreement. The "hanging judge" concluded: "I admit it is a proposition startling in its character, that the citizens of the Indian country had no remedy in their courts against this railroad company. . . . But courts cannot make the law. They must take it as they find it." Likewise, the complaints of the western tribes merely provided newspaper copy. A Cheyenne chief, Whirlwind, was especially eloquent in pleading with the Great Father "to keep back this Rail Road," which was ruining the Indian freighting business, before "there is any bad talk and any of the young men get foolish." Luckily for the Cheyennes, the railroads were too busy in the south to worry for the moment about the western part of Indian Territory.[10]

Frisco officials decided in 1880 to build a branch from its line in Missouri, south through Arkansas, and, by way of a corner of the Choctaw Nation, into Texas. Its lobbyists had been among the Choctaws and reported that some factions were willing to agree to this route provided the road limited itself strictly to a right of way and did not engage in mining or lumbering. The question was considered by the Choctaw Houses of Warriors and Kings in the fall of 1880 and was an issue in the tribal elections of 1881. The new chief, J. F. McCurtain, recommended that the franchise be given, and in the fall of 1881 representatives from the Frisco and the Chicago,

D. W. Bushyhead to National Council, Nov. 10, 1881, Cherokee volume 715–D, IAD. D. W. Bushyhead to National Council, Dec. 9, 1881, Cherokee volume 715–D, IAD.

10. Undated manuscript decision, St. Louis and San Francisco Railway Company vs. William Henderson, Cherokee Railroad File (Tahlequah acquisition), IAD. John Miles to Office of Indian Affairs, Jan. 3, 1882, SC 102.

Texas and Mexican Central appeared in Indian Territory to compete for the prize.[11]

The federal government was represented at these negotiations by Uri J. Baxter, a law clerk from the Department of the Interior. His role was shadowy, the Indians later charging that he had pressured them. The *New York Times* reported that Baxter was there to aid the Chicago, Texas and Mexican Central. Considering the political clout of that line's investors, such a conclusion cannot be ruled out. The official correspondence with him, however, indicates that he was dispatched to see that no "undue influence" was used by the railroads to force Indian agreement and that any legal documents drawn up were financially equitable.[12]

The corporation men met with Baxter soon after their arrival in Indian Territory and worked out an agreement through which the Chicago, Texas and Mexican Central withdrew from the competition. The Choctaws therefore had no opportunity to play one interest against the other for the best possible arrangement. The public explanation was that the Frisco was more popular among the tribes. More likely, J.&W. Seligman and Company, investment bankers, wished to avoid unpleasantness between the two railroads, both of which were underwritten largely by the firm (which was also Jay Gould's banking house, and a major security holder in the MK&T).[13]

After this private meeting with the railroads, Uri Baxter acted confidently, organizing and presiding over most of the subsequent meetings between the Frisco and the tribe. He called McCurtain "governor," which led some to believe that he already considered the area a U.S. territory. He made motions in the Choctaw Council, which was illegal for a noncitizen, under the Choctaw constitution. He gave several speeches that left the impression that the U.S. government

11. Angie Debo, *The Rise and Fall of the Choctaw Nation*, pp. 121–23.

12. *New York Times*, Jan. 24, 1882, 1–1. Baxter's correspondence is in SED 15, 47th Cong., 1st sess., 1882 (S 1986).

13. *New York Tribune*, Dec. 5, 1881. For Seligman's role, see Miner, *St. Louis-San Francisco*, passim.

was the party urging rail concession. Finally, Baxter placed the right-of-way bill before the Choctaw legislature, despite complaints that changes had been made in the manuscript version that it had approved before it was printed.[14]

The bill was defeated on a tie vote of the council but revived and forwarded to Washington when the tribal attorney general ruled that the Choctaw Speaker of the House had voted twice. Later several members of the U.S. Congress expressed serious doubts about the attorney general's interpretation, but it did not prevent Congress from accepting this proceeding as constituting Indian consent. It could be that the Choctaws felt threatened with worse attacks on their sovereignty if they did not grant this concession. At least, one of them noted, there was "a misapprehension of the real relation of the Government of the United States in the premises," occasioned by Baxter's confusing, and perhaps officially unauthorized, statements and behavior.[15]

The bill was economically fair to the Choctaws. That was not what made it damaging. In fact, the Senate Committee on Indian Affairs, to whom it was referred upon reaching the Capitol, made a number of changes in the tribal version, all designed to provide more compensation and protection for the Indians. The significance was that Congress felt qualified to make changes and to pass the revised bill without again consulting the Indians. Also it decided in the course of debates upon the bill that Indians, like U.S. citizens, should thereafter be subject to eminent domain. Sen. Sam Maxey of Texas said simply that Congress would no longer listen to the "I forbid" of Indians or anyone else in matters of economic expansion. The *New York Tribune* called the new right of way a bald victory for railroad power and commented that there was no state in the Union "none in

14. Testimony Before Senate Committee on Railroads, c. Jan. 1882, #19743, Choctaw Railroad File, IAD.

15. Debo, *Rise and Fall*, p. 122. *Congressional Globe*, 47th Cong., 1st sess., XIII, 2567. *San Francisco Chronicle*, Jan. 11, 1882; SED 44, 47th Cong., 1st sess., 1882 (S 1987), p. 12.

the civilized world that could be persuaded to tolerate a railroad on those terms."[16]

As in the boomer question, the interests of the Indians faded into the background of the right-of-way debate, and the struggle was between the competing interests of corporations. A Chickasaw delegation came to Washington to protest that the Choctaws had again not consulted with them about the new version of the bill. A Choctaw delegation was there arguing that the vote in the Choctaw legislature had been irregular and that the tribe had really not consented. They were quickly accused of being in the pay of Jay Gould, who was interested in stopping the Frisco from attacking his Texas monopoly. Baxter produced a letter from chief McCurtain, which stated that Gould was at the bottom of the "Indian" protests, and further evidence was found in the fact that the Indian delegation left Washington when Gould bought into the Frisco in January 1882.[17] Gould and the monopoly issue were politically popular questions at the time, and attempts to direct the right-of-way debate into the broader, but less timely channel of concern for Indian rights were overwhelmed in the hysteria of the moment's bugaboo. By the time the bill was passed, it is worth remembering, Gould was on the Frisco board, and breaking his monopoly was no longer at issue. In fact, the Gould-dominated Frisco waited years before ever building the line that it had so eagerly sought. Still, the precedent was set. Said one Choctaw: "We find when an Indian is to be robbed, white man unites. I am afraid of them."[18]

C. J. Hillyer's 1871 pamphlet on A&P rights in Indian Territory was distributed to members of Congress in 1882, and there is no indication that many disagreed with its conclusions. Senators argued that

16. *Congressional Record*, 47th Cong., 1st sess., XIII, 503–4. *New York Tribune*, Dec. 5, 1881.

17. J. F. McCurtain to U. J. Baxter, Jan. 3, 1882, SC 97; *Congressional Record*, 47th Cong., 1st sess., XIII, 2576. For more detail on the charges of Indian collusion with Gould, see H. Craig Miner, "The Struggle for an East-West Railway into Indian Territory, 1870–1872," pp. 576–77.

18. Testimony, #19743, Choctaw Railroad File, IAD.

the 1866 treaties were void if they denied the United States the right of eminent domain upon Indian lands, since U.S. sovereignty could never be alienated. The men in Washington brushed aside questions of legal or ethical consistency to offer without shame the gift of economic gain, which had swallowed so much that was once dear to them. The new railroad branch would open the pine lands of the Choctaws to commercial sawmills, yielding the tribe large royalties, at least until the timber was gone. The coal fields would prosper, Texas cotton would find additional markets, and the cattle business would flourish. Augustus Garland of Arkansas said that even Indian deaths and burials were taken care of at government expense, and it was foolish to talk about their consent. George Vest of Missouri, the former MK&T attorney, called the Indians ungrateful for meeting a request for a right of transit with grandiose philosophical musings about a nation of robbers and the doom of a dream. To one House member, it was "prepostrous" that a government able to plow up cemeteries and take down houses to clear the way for commerce in the states should allow its hands to be tied by a band of Indians. Saddest of all, the proponents of corporate progress were able to argue that because of the influence of the progressives within the tribe, any bill resulting from another meeting of the tribal council would reflect the demands of the railroad even more than the current bill.[19]

Although congressmen with another point of view were few and uncertain, their comments at this time should be examined in retrospect. Those who were against the bill were mostly from New England, John Ingalls of Kansas being the only western senator against it, and the vote was more sectional than partisan.[20]

Sen. Joseph Hawley of Connecticut apologized for taking the Senate's time in what he knew to be a fruitless cause, but was concerned that, unless he spoke, "the curious historian manifesting an

19. *Congressional Record*, 47th Cong., 1st sess., XIII, 2519, 2521, 2530, 2570, 2574, 2801–3, 6583, 6586, 6588.

20. For a sectional analysis of the vote, see Loring B. Priest, *Uncle Sam's Stepchildren: The Reformation of United States Indian Policy, 1865–1887*, pp. 221–22.

interest in the Indian race" would find no evidence in the *Congressional Record* that any one man in 1882 recognized that the Congress was about to commit a great wrong. Even the railroads, he said, did not ask that Congress destroy Indian power to regulate railroad rights of way; they had approached the Choctaws first. If Congress had the right to abolish Indian sovereignty because eminent domain could not be alienated, why could not Spain or France, who had once controlled areas in the United States, build railroads there now, or Mexico authorize corporations to operate in Texas? John Ingalls was more blunt still. He said the Senate was like the witches in *Macbeth*, who said one thing and did another. It pretended to overthrow a monopoly by granting a charter to a line that belonged to the very monopolist in question. A few others chimed in, asking whether the United States had ever been serious about Indian sovereignty or had it merely been playacting.[21]

"I shall have done my duty," said Hawley as he rose to speak, "though there may be nobody to listen, and perhaps nobody to read afterward." No one listened. Said George Vest, "All this aesthetic talk and constitutional argument amounts to nothing in the face of the great fact that the people of the United States today are stopped in their imperial course toward the Southwest." Indian talk about the earth being their mother, which could not be scarred by surveyor's chains, was called "poppycock." Said a Texas senator, "We will not be penned up; we will not be hindered."[22]

If congressional opponents of the right-of-way bill were made to look ridiculous, the Indians who spoke against it were mercilessly pilloried. The Arkansas papers endlessly made fun of B. F. Overton and Daniel Ross, a Chickasaw and a Cherokee, who worked in Washington against the Frisco bill. The *Arkansas Sentinel* at Fayetteville, a division point on the railroad's new branch, printed "A True Story for Little Indian Boys," in which Ross and Overton were seen as Irish "Big Injuns" who were secretly paid to lobby until "Uncle Sam he

21. *Congressional Record*, 47th Cong., 1st sess., XIII, 2565–68, 2572, 2765–67.
22. Ibid., pp. 2565, 2570, 2801, 504.

slapped them galliwest and crooked and told them to go home and mind their own business if they had any." Ross's report to the Cherokee Nation on these matters was described as "the funniest document we have seen for many a year," and the antirailroad lobby "a ridiculous movement which none but natural born fools would have thought of." The Arkansas press even made fun of Chief Bushyhead's Thanksgiving proclamation for 1882, in which he prayed that the government might not "drag and thrust the remnant of our race into the abyss." It was claimed in the press that Ross and Overton had by their complaints opened the issue that resulted in the determination of eminent domain. Further opposition by them would bring a territorial government because their stand would be considered an obstacle to Manifest Destiny. Wrote the *Sentinel*: "There was an old man /named Ross. / Of Injuns he thought he was / boss; / He tried hard to kill / 'The right of way bill,' / What a fool was this fellow Ross."[23]

After the 1882 decision a writer for the *Sentinel* concluded that "opposition is now a thing of the past" and that the Indian Territory "must and will be checkered with railroads." The Indian representatives did not agree, and they peppered the nation with new arguments and defenses. William A. Phillips presented oral arguments at the Indian Office off and on for three months in 1882, pointing out that records of the government were being "garbled, erased or destroyed," history was being altered to eliminate reminders of past recognition of tribal powers. Even Spencer Stephens, who had promoted railways, stated that if railways came without allotment of lands, the tribes would be left with an awkward system, half ancient and half modern, which could only do them harm. In the field, the Cherokee National Railway was chartered, reviving the old schemes of the seventies. The stock was equally divided between Cherokee and U.S. citizens, and the line was to run through Tahlequah, the tribal capital. It was never built.[24]

23. *Arkansas Sentinel*, Aug. 30, Dec. 6, Aug. 9, 1882.
24. Ibid., Aug. 2, 1882. W. A. Phillips et al., *Petition to the Honorable Secretary Upon the Grievous Abuse of Intruders in the Cherokee Nation . . .* , Grant Foreman Papers, box 15, Gilcrease. *The Indian Question Discussed by*

Early in 1884, there was a crisis when a number of right-of-way bills were introduced into the Congress, thus for the first time providing a pragmatic test of the 1882 policy. The most significant were on behalf of the Gulf, Colorado and Santa Fe, and the Southern Kansas Railway Company. The former was a Santa Fe subsidiary building north from Houston, Texas, and the latter was a merger of the LL&G and the MRFtS&G, contenders since 1866 for a north-south franchise. In February of 1884 all tribal delegations submitted protests on the grounds that these bills proposed to take Indian property without consulting tribal legislatures and were therefore "entirely subversive, of all law order or peace in the Indian Territory." The delegations were not granted a hearing before the congressional committees. The bills proposed allowing white settlement along the new lines, specified all legal problems connected with them would be heard in U.S. courts, and did not even require the corporations to submit specifications for definite routes in advance.[25]

The committees reported to Congress simply that the Frisco bill was a precedent for congressional control of this sort of thing.[26] Debates centered again on breaking Gould's Texas monopoly, not on Indian rights. The question of submitting anything to the Indian councils was met with lurid descriptions of the way in which these councils were manipulated and corrupted by Gould lobbyists. Everything indicated that the Indian nations were doomed. The members of Congress asked that detailed provisions regulating the new corporations be written into the 1884 bills, as the corporations would last forever, while the political forms then existing in the Indian Territory

---

Spencer S. Stephens of the Cherokee Nation (Titusville, 1882), Cherokee Nation Papers, series V, vol. III, OU. Act to Incorporate Cherokee National Railway, n.d., Cherokee Railroad Box, OU.

25. D. W. Bushyhead et al., *Message of the Cherokee and Creek Delegations to the Congress of the United States, 1884*, Frank Phillips Collection, OU. Debates on the two bills are in *Congressional Globe*, 48th Cong., 1st sess., XV, 5472–75, 4711–26.

26. HR 1356, 49th Cong., 1st sess., 1886 (S 2439); HR 211, 48th Cong., 1st sess., 1884 (Serial 2253).

had a short lease.[27] The bills passed. The tribal delegations were despondent.

One Cherokee, however, was jubilant—E. C. Boudinot. The new Santa Fe line would run very near his ranch, and the new acts gave him a chance to indulge in a round of "I told you sos," while restating his advice on Indian accommodation. The proper attitude toward these acts, he wrote, was to read them carefully and try to improve upon them, instead of protesting. All other bills would be copies of these. Boudinot was sure at this point that his influence in the Congress exceeded that of the official Cherokee delegation. "I've got the thieves by the throat," he rhapsodized, "and I shall not let go until there [sic] thieving official lives are squeezed out of them." Boudinot, in his private letters, gloried in the fact that his old nemesis, Chief Dennis Bushyhead, could do nothing about stopping railroad bills. "Bushy, Phillips & Hooley [L. B. Bell] have no influence here: everybody laughs at them; you can hear on all sides the remark—'What a damn set of fools they are.'" The "foolishness" was Bushyhead's request that tribal governments, if they agreed not to resist progress, be allowed to retain some controls over corporations within their region.[28]

After that, the dike holding back free railroad expression burst. The Frisco in late 1884 began running hunting excursions into Indian Territory from its exclusive resort at Eureka Springs, Arkansas. E. C. Boudinot organized his own railroad, the Pacific and Great Eastern, with plans to connect to the Frisco at Tulsa. "Redbird," a correspondent of the *Vinita Chieftain*, noticed in 1885 that all Cherokees were showing a tendency toward land sales and speculation, which was an invitation to national ruin. He saw the Cherokees' state as a ship going down while scavengers waited to pick through the wreck. Expanding the metaphor, he compared the carefree tribal citizens

27. See note 25 about the location of the debates.
28. E. C. Boudinot to James Bell, June 23, 1884; E. C. Boudinot to James M. Bell, June 28, 1884, Cherokee Railroad Box, OU. *Vinita Chieftain*, Nov. 13, 1884.

to so many mice running around the deck happily picking up crumbs, while "there is a mighty unseen hand upon the helm steering us into the vortex of national ruin." "Redbird" was joined by "Woodpecker," "Sapsucker," "Raven," and an aviary of others in a long newspaper exchange upon land selling. On many points opinions varied but all agreed: "There is a buzzing. If our people are going to save their lands they must get together.... The Philistines are upon us and more a' coming."[29]

In desperation many Indians struck out at those at hand, their own leaders. It was impossible to get satisfaction from Washington by hiring an attorney to "*write* & *write* & *write* the Indian Bureau," but Bushyhead and Phillips might be reached and hurt. Under the newly installed electric lights at Tahlequah, the Cherokee Council debated upon the loyalty of Bushyhead and Phillips. Were they keeping up a fruitless protest in order to collect fees? Did they play both sides of the fence? Bushyhead was accused of leniency in his stand against the 1886 charter for the Kansas and Arkansas Valley railroad. He wrote to President Grover Cleveland, his enemies said, threatening tomahawks and border warfare if the railroad were allowed in, and then in Arkansas spoke in favor of the branch. S. S. Stephens reported in 1885 that the Cherokee Washington delegation was "living on diamonds" and completely ineffective: "The Dept. Interior should ask them to go home—Anyway *bosh* for such an *outfit*. Men of no capacity *scarcely*. A *Bastard & the other running over the fire of prejudice. Where is the C.N. going?*" Stephens concluded this diatribe with the comment that Robert S. Stevens and E. C. Boudinot were both major contenders for the post of commissioner of Indian affairs that year and that if Stevens should be elected, he would be in line for a political appointment. Even in their attacks on each other, the Indians were not free of the stamp of the invisible helmsman.[30]

29. Ibid., Dec. 4, 1884; April 30, May 21, 1885. Ridge Paschal to J. M. Bell, May 22, 1885, box 28, Cherokee Nation Papers, OU.

30. Citizens of Cherokee Nation to Commissioner of Indian Affairs, Oct. 31, 1885, SC 102. *Vinita Chieftain*, Dec. 31, 1885; June 3, July 22, 1886.

The rank and file in Indian Territory became increasingly upset with what they regarded as secret negotiations by the executive branch and federal agents. The Cherokee National Council passed a bill over the chief's veto refusing to accept the damage allowances set by Congress as appropriate for the K&AV railroad.[31] It also refused to pass any law authorizing the new railroad to take timber for ties, stating that to do so would be construed as an acceptance by them of the right of the United States to grant railway privileges in the territory without Indian consent.[32] Through the newspapers, the Indians complained bitterly that Bushyhead and Phillips were being so secretive in their dealings that the tribe was unable to make an effective stand.[33] Union Agent Robert Owen was charged with being financially interested in K&AV townsites.[34] Finally, the tribe sued the timber contractors at the Fort Smith District Court.[35]

The most determined effort of all, what might be called the last stand on the railroad issue, was the fight against the Southern Kansas railway system. Its projected line ran from Winfield, Kansas, to Denison, Texas. First to be affected were the Poncas, whose reserve lay along the planned route. In July 1886 the Poncas had a large meeting at which they concluded they were being "worked upon" by the Kansas corporation and at which they agreed to resist the grading crews by force, if they were not given what they considered adequate compensation for damages. In November, the tribe sent its two principal chiefs and an interpreter to Washington to confer with the

S. S. Stephens to J. M. Bell, March 13, 1885, box 28, Cherokee Nation Papers, OU.

31. *Vinita Chieftain*, June 2, 1887.

32. D. W. Bushyhead to Clayton and Brizzolara, June 4, 1887, SC 146. Railroad attorneys called defeat of tie authorization a "bold attempt of the Cherokees to practically defeat the will of Congress by an absurd and untenable construction of their own laws." Britton & Gray to J. D. C. Atkins, June 29, 1887, SC 146.

33. *Vinita Chieftain*, June 10, 1887; *Tahlequah Telephone*, Sept. 2, 1887.

34. *Indian Journal*, May 19, 1887.

35. Clayton and Brizzolara to Robert Owen, June 17, 1887, SC 146.

president and departmental officials. Their agent, writing ahead, warned that they had "lost confidence in letters & all explanations" and were expecting to meet someone face to face. The National Indian Defense Association, one of a number of reform organizations that had sprung up to promote Indian causes, entered the arena at the same time, charging that the Poncas had been unduly influenced by their agent and that the appraisers, when the tribe had refused to accept the statute damages of $50 a mile, had underevaluated their lands.[36]

The Cherokees did not appreciate the policy of the Southern Kansas line either, and like the Poncas and the Otoes and Missourias, they refused to accept the statutory damage allowance. In September 1866 a commission meeting at Topeka, Kansas, decided that the railroad owed the Cherokees $93 a mile, the Poncas $117, and the Otoes and Missourias $162. But the Cherokees were not satisfied with that settlement, and Chief Bushyhead, on behalf of the tribe, filed suit that fall on the grounds that the Congress had usurped Cherokee rights in authorizing the railroad at all, and then in presuming to make judgments upon proper damages.[37]

John C. Fay was retained by the tribe as attorney in this case, assisted by Phillips. Also helping were former Sen. Joseph McDonald of Indiana and Richard Bright. Their argument was that, while the government might have the right under the power of eminent domain to take tribal land for its own use, it did not have the right to grant land to a corporation without consent by the Indians and adequate compensation to them.[38]

The move was fraught with complications. For one thing, there was the possibility that corporations might again play both sides of the fence and that the Indian defense of sovereignty would be re-

36. E. C. Osburne to J. D. C. Atkins, July 13, 1886; Nov. 22, 1886; A. I. Willard to Commissioner of Indian Affairs, Jan. 29, 1887, SC 140.

37. John Galloway report, Sept. 25, 1886; D. W. Bushyhead to National Council, Dec. 15, 1886, Cherokee Railroad File (Tahlequah acquisition), IAD.

38. John C. Fay to D. W. Bushyhead, Jan. 26, 1887, ibid.; *Vinita Chieftain*, Jan. 27, 1887.

garded as a blind for corporate interests competing against the Southern Kansas railroad and wishing thus to destroy it. Cherokee W. P. Adair turned down $100,000 from competing railroads, which was offered on the condition that he instigate the court case. Second, there was a chance that the case would be tried in the U.S. court at Wichita, Kansas, rather than at Fort Smith. Wichita was, in 1887, in the middle of a stupendous real estate boom, and its people were paying a bonus of $6,000 a mile to attract railroads. In Kansas, compensation for damage was determined by weighing the benefits against the damage, and if the benefits were the greater the railroad owed nothing. Would these people be sympathetic to the Indians' case? In addition, the case itself could prove "the neatest kind of trap." By suing, no matter how the suit came out, the Cherokees were recognizing the right of the United States to establish civil courts with jurisdiction over their country. Some natives, therefore, thought that a simple refusal to allow the railroad to pass, backed by force if necessary, was more consistent than a court case, though equally hopeless.[39]

The case against the Southern Kansas railway was completely unsuccessful in winning for the tribes any recognition of their sovereignty with regard to corporate control. It was appealed to the Supreme Court of the United States, where it was sent back to Fort Smith, not for a change in policy, but merely for an adjustment in compensation. Like C. J. Hillyer, fifteen years earlier, no one seemed to understand why, if the tribes got enough money for giving up their rights, they should not be content. In 1891, the Cherokees accepted an out-of-court settlement from the railroad. The National Council had by that time become so discouraged that it passed an act accepting the 1884 statute allowance of $50 a mile.[40]

The decade of the eighties, then, was marked by a complete loss of tribal control over railway rights of way. The consequence of this loss was a great escalation of Indian Territory corporate activity of other kinds, particularly the cattle business and the oil business. To

39. *Vinita Chieftain*, Feb. 10, 1887.
40. P. N. Blackstone to D. W. Bushyhead, May 15, 1887, Cherokee Railroad File (Tahlequah acquisition), IAD.

serve these industries there were railroads, now freely built whenever
Congress gave the consent that its feeling of the limitless needs of
commerce guaranteed.[41]

Last of the blows to Indian sovereignty of the eighties was the
Dawes Severalty Act of 1887. This act did not apply to the Five Tribes,
the Osages and several other Indian Territory groups, partly because
of the fear of tribes there that allotment would ratify the railroad
land grants, but it did settle a philosophical question in the minds of
congressmen by establishing that the way to civilization and acculturation for the Indian was the change from tribal land title in common
to individual land title in severalty. Each head of family in tribes not
excepted in the terms of the legislation was to be granted 160 acres,
thus allowing the surplus former tribal land, after the allotments
were made, to be opened to white settlement. The Five Tribes resisted the application of this philosophy to their lands, but in 1893
the Dawes Commission was created by Congress to negotiate with
them to accomplish allotment. In 1895 a survey of the land of the
Indian Territory tribes was authorized, and in 1896 the Congress
directed the Dawes Commission to make a citizenship roll of the
various tribes. Seeing this as the creation of machinery that would
make forced allotment inevitable, the various tribes began to make
allotment agreements with the government. Those who did not were
moved to it by the Curtis Act of June 28, 1898, which made clear that
allotment was terribly central to the plans of the U.S. for the Indian
Territory. Such agreements were forthcoming in the first years of
the twentieth century and actual assignment of land allotments to
individuals began.[42] The allotment issue was especially important to

41. Transcript, Case 12992, 1888–90, *Cherokee Nation* v. *Southern
Kansas Ry. Co.*, Supreme Court appellate case files, RG 247, NA. Joel Mayes to
National Council, Dec. 2, 1891, Cherokee volume 715–K, IAD.

42. Angie Debo, *And Still the Waters Run: The Betrayal of the Five
Civilized Tribes*, pp. 22, 31–38. Other material the general reader may wish
to consult on the Dawes Act and subsequent allotment legislation includes
Wilcomb Washburn, *The Assault on Indian Tribalism: The General Allotment
Law (Dawes Act) of 1887* (New York: J. B. Lippincott Company, 1975);
Robert Mardock, *The Reformers and the American Indian* (Columbia: Uni-

corporate negotiations with Indian tribes after 1887, and the government machinery created by it, as well as the tribal disunity and confusion, provided the corporation with the kind of complications upon which it thrived.

The corporate future, thereafter, came in leaps rather than steps. Before it became the state of Oklahoma in 1907, the Indian Territory had 5,488 miles of railroad track. By the late eighties, Gould's lobbyists were "around among the boys" at Indian councils regularly, and journals in England were speculating upon the worth of Territory cattle ranches. The Indians, seeing that the farm-based Granger movement in the states was having little success in regulating corporations, could only despair when realizing that they would have "to fight the same battle with less knowledge, with weaker weapons, and with fewer men." In the moral morass the railroad and territorial battles of the seventies left in their wake the flexible corporation, which was designed for such times and quite at home. It was even more powerful when compared to a "civilized" system of Indian nationality, which, in the new dispensation, was little more relevant than the war whoop.[43]

---

versity of Missouri Press, 1971); J. P. Kinney, *A Continent Lost—A Civilization Won: Indian Land Tenure in America*; D. S. Otis, *The Dawes Act and the Allotment of Indian Lands*, ed. by Francis Prucha (Norman: University of Oklahoma Press, 1973); David Halford, "The Subversion of the Indian Land Allotment System, 1887–1934," *The Indian Historian* 8 (Spring 1975): 11–21.

43. Interstate Commerce Commission, *Twentieth Annual Report on the Statistics of Railways in the United States. . . .*, p. 27. *Vinita Chieftain*, Nov. 26, 1885; *Anglo-American Times*, April 22, 1887. *Objections of the Cherokees, Chickasaws and Creeks, Addressed to the President, Against Railroads in the Indian Territory*, May 24, 1886, Cherokee Railroad Box, OU.

CHAPTER VII

THE CATTLE SYNDICATES

In no phase of the economic exploitation of Indian Territory was the influence of corporations more pervasive, but more hidden and misunderstood, than in the cattle industry. Historians of the tribal cattle-leasing business have underestimated the influence of corporations in cattle grazing because corporations often did not negotiate the original leases directly with the tribes but had secret arrangements with individuals, who appeared at Indian councils mysteriously able to offer very large sums for grazing privileges for very large herds.[1] Further investigation usually reveals that, soon after the semipublic business of making the original arrangements was concluded, the lease, held in the name of an individual or partnership, was quietly transferred to a large eastern corporation investing surplus funds. Since Section 2115 of the Revised Statutes of the United States made Indian leases technically void, the instruments of transfer were called "agreements," and since there was an effort to eliminate corporate monopoly in the eighties, corporations often masqueraded as partnerships or "associations." Behind the mask, however, the typical pattern of diminishing Indian sovereignty may be found: a breakdown of tribal control of the cattle business, followed by infighting among Indian factions, accompanied by hesitancy of Indian and federal governments concerning jurisdiction, and climaxed by

1. The most careful recent studies of Indian Territory cattle leases are William W. Savage, Jr., *The Cherokee Strip Live Stock Association: Federal Regulation and the Cattleman's Last Frontier*; Donald J. Berthrong, "Cattlemen on the Cheyenne-Arapaho Reservation, 1883–1885"; William T. Hagen, "Kiowas, Commanches and Cattlemen, 1867–1906: A Case Study of the Failure of U.S. Reservation Policy."

the ascendancy of the corporation, an institution well designed to manage vast resources and silence quarreling shopkeepers. Corporate control of the cattle business might then take the form of outright corporate ranch organization or corporate financial backing for a ranch that, in its field organization, was not corporate. It was the latter device that allowed not only railroad corporations but some of the largest manufacturing and petroleum companies in the country to acquire as sublessees a vital economic interest in the future status of the Indian Territory and to add their lobbyists to the group giving advice about the future of tribal sovereignty.

While few expected that even the most advanced tribes would be capable of building their own railroads or mining deep mineral veins, the cattle business had been, before the Civil War, the backbone of the Five Tribes economies and provided an ideal transitional activity for nomadic tribes adjusting to an intransient life. It seemed a bastion of individual enterprise. Union Agent S. W. Marston wrote in 1878 that 55,000 Indians under his control owned livestock scattered over a 200-square-mile region and that "to state the names of all the owners of domestic animals on this reservation would be to give the names of all the men and women and children, for they all have stock." Early, the only ripple on the waters was difficulty with fort sutlers and agency traders going into the cattle export business who were using Indian grass free of charge. However, the entry of the railroads in the seventies complicated things. In 1871 the Creeks passed a grazing tax of twenty-five cents a head on noncitizens' cattle driven through or held upon their lands. The Cherokees followed suit in 1878, by which time a number of ranch operators originally from Kansas had drifted across the line and were in place with their herds in the Cherokee domain.[2]

The attempt to collect tribal taxes led to the confusion upon which the corporation thrived. Given the small bureaucracies of the native governments, it became literally impossible to collect tax

2. S. W. Marston to E. A. Hayt, April 22, 1878, LR OIA Union Agency, M 234, R 870, document #M 712. Pleasant Porter, Circular, March 20, 1871, #34791; Creek Stock & Pastures File, IAD. Savage, *Cherokee Strip*, p. 19.

from all the individual cattlemen who might, at one time or another, graze animals upon Indian lands. In addition, there was evidence that Indian progressives were using the tax laws for their own ends.

L. B. Bell was appointed Cherokee tax collector. Herders complained that only the honest paid him, and, since the Cherokees had no power to enforce the tax on all equally, it was unfair. Some doubted that the Cherokees controlled the heavily grazed Outlet (the land west of ninety-six degrees) since they had agreed, in the 1866 treaties, to sell it to the United States for use of other tribes, though no money had yet changed hands and no definite arrangement had been made. Others said that the fifty-cent tax per year was too much to pay upon cattle that sold for nine dollars a head.[3]

Bell appealed to the federal government, but as usual the Indians got no consistent response. Once in a while, the military would temporarily drive out a few nontaxpaying grazers, but mail to the Indian Office contained many complaints that there was evidence of bribery; honest taxpayers were often driven off by a military paid by the delinquent ranchers. Meanwhile, those in Congress who represented the white cattlemen put pressure on the Indian governments to scuttle their attempts at regulation. Sen. Preston Plumb of Kansas wrote Interior Secretary Schurz that the Cherokee tax was outrageously high, that the tribal governments had no right to levy a tax upon U.S. citizens, and that the method of imposing it was "liable to be arbitrary and often repeated until it becomes confiscation."[4]

In an attempt to control the situation, the Cherokee National Council sent William McCracken and E. C. Boudinot to investigate Bell's activities. Boudinot, as usual, was working several schemes

3. W. P. Adair to Commissioner of Indian Affairs, June 6, 1879, LR OIA Union Agency, M 234, R 871, document # A 1127. George Orner to Carl Schurz, June 2, 1879; document # O 210. F. A. Hunt et al. to Commissioner of Indian Affairs, June, 1879, document # 51P, LR OIA Union Agency, M 234, R 872.

4. C. Schurz to Secretary of War, June 7, 1879, LR OIA Union Agency, M 234, R 871, document # I 1349; P. B. Plumb to C. Schurz, May 18, 1879, LR OIA Union Agency, M 234, R 872, document # P 516.

simultaneously, one of which was to establish a secret Cherokee colony and cattle operation in the Outlet. He hoped that the land would be allotted and then his native syndicate could lease or sell it to white cattlemen. He therefore warned Bell against confiscating cattle for nonpayment of taxes and told him to go easy on the collections. In 1881, a Cherokee nationalist group calling itself the Committee of Safety charged Boudinot with having, in this matter, acted as an "arch Traitor" to the true interests of the tribe.[5]

Confusion deepened and injustice escalated in 1880. There were charges that Cheyenne and Arapahoe agent John Miles was in collusion with the cattlemen in allowing special grazing privileges. Stockmen at Baxter Springs, Kansas, were concerned that they were unable to get permits to run cattle into the Quapaw lands. Drovers, driving cattle from Texas, wanted regularization of the various tribal quarantine and tax laws. The Kansas railroads, especially the Santa Fe, wished that a predictable settlement could be made with the Cherokees so that there might be a lucrative cattle-shipping business from the Outlet. The military, always at odds with the Interior Department over the handling of Indian affairs, wanted an entire exclusion of cattlemen because they seemed a harbinger of illegal settlement. In April 1880 the troops were told to suspend operations for excluding cattlemen, as there were plans for the cattlemen as a group to make some arrangement for renting the land and for rationalizing their relationship with the tribes. That summer the first proposals leading to a corporate solution were drawn, and the tribes once more weighed political expense against economic benefit.[6]

5. Savage, *Cherokee Strip*, p. 20. E. C. Boudinot to J. M. Bell, March 30, 1879, box 3; Committee of Safety to J. M. Bell, Sept. 12, 1881, box 28, Cherokee Nation papers, OU.

6. Stephen Conner to Post Adjutant, Aug. 17, 1879, LR OIA Union Agency, M 234, R 873, document # W 2178. J. C. Naylor to P. B. Plumb, March 25, 1880, LR OIA Union Agency, M 234, R 875, document # P 634. B. H. Campbell to Edwin Willets, April 1, 1880, document # W 756; J. F. Goddard to John Pope, March 26, 1880, document # W 699; John Pope to Assistant Adjutant General, Dept. of Mo., July 10, 1880, document # W 1547;

The election of Dennis W. Bushyhead as Cherokee principal chief in 1879 may be partially responsible for the expedition of this agreement as early as 1880. Bushyhead was accused of being overly sympathetic to corporations, though he was granted grudging praise by all as one of the best financial minds in the Cherokee Nation. During his term of office, 1879–1887, he brought the Nation from a position of being in debt $187,000 to relative prosperity. He understood American society and American corporations, as he had attended the Park Hill school in Indian Territory, college in New Jersey, and had a different sort of learning experience when he went to the California gold fields in 1849.[7]

Bushyhead could understand the view of chiefs like B. F. Overton of the Chickasaws, who joined the full-blood factions in saying that cattlemen looking for privileges were nothing but tools "in the interest of men who are ever ready to defy the free and undisturbed right of self government among the Indians."[8] Yet, Bushyhead was a realist, forced to recognize that he could play the cards only as they lay at that time. Corporations, it was true, did not have any love for the Indian or his institutions in the abstract. Neither did any other powerful group in the United States. Yet the interest of some corporations might, through judicious leasing, be tied to that of tribal sovereignty in such a way that they would join the Gould railroads in defending Indian rights. If the Indian made no accommodation to the corporation, his governments might well be destroyed quickly by a combination of settlers, corporations, and congressmen. If, on the other hand, he simply sold out his sovereignty and became a menial profiteer, the thing Bushyhead thought Boudinot was doing, the doom of his hegemony over his lands was as sure. The one way of surviving was to use the power of the American corporation to preserve what it was now the most active agent in destroying—to make arrangements to tie corporate interests to the preservation of

Alex. Ramsey to (?), April 16, 1880, document # W 877, LR OIA Union Agency, M 234, R 887.

7. *Tahlequah Arrow*, Feb. 5, 1898, copy in Dennis Bushyhead Papers, OU.
8. B. F. Overton to C. Schurz, Nov. 23, 1880, SC 23.

the Indian way, as they had been tied to its destruction by the contingent land grants to railroads in 1866. Events showed that Bushyhead's analysis of corporate malleability was accurate. Corporations interested in tribal land leases were to be among the most influential defenders, not only of the right of the tribes as sovereign governments to grant leases but also of their right to continue to control the land upon which corporate-owned cattle grazed. That they were ultimately less strong than interests tending in another direction should not obscure the fact that Bushyhead's policy may well have lengthened the tenure of the Indian nations and that all Indian deals with corporations were not alike.

In July 1880 Patrick Henry and D. J. Miller of Waco, Texas, offered to pay $185,000 for a lease of the entire Cherokee Outlet. Initially encouraged, Bushyhead vetoed the lease bill as it was finally drawn on the grounds that Henry and Miller did not have sufficiently stable backing. The partners claimed they were not a corporation but that their "association" was worth $1 million. A few years later, they claimed to represent a "limited" joint stock company with a Texas charter, partly because there was, among the Indians, an "everlasting harping about chartered and unchartered companies, and trying to make the public believe there's all the difference of responsibility." Bushyhead's objection was not that they were too powerful but that they were not powerful enough. Had he wanted petty jobbers, he could have left things the way they were. He desired a regular, large income for the tribe and a powerful lobby acting on its behalf. Far from providing that service, during hearings Henry and Miller asked the Cherokees to guarantee the cattle company protection in the Outlet when what the Cherokees needed was a cattle company that could protect them in the Outlet.[9]

Meanwhile, feuding over grass made it necessary to come to some agreement. The Chickasaws and Creeks were unable to enforce their policies of entirely excluding cattlemen, and the Cheyennes and Arapahoes, finding their herds mixing with those in the

9. Hearings, July 14, 1880, Cherokee Strip File (Tahlequah acquisition), IAD. *Vinita Chieftain*, Aug. 30, Sept. 6, 1888.

Outlet, threatened violence. The Union agent wrote in 1881 that war was a possibility in all regions, and Sen. Sam Maxey got a letter saying that Chief Overton was raising a Chickasaw Indian force to meet the cattlemen directly and physically. The Creeks were saying that unless something were done by the tribes now, the federal government would allow cattlemen to come in indiscriminately, without compensation to Indians, just as it had allowed railroads under the 1882 policy. Had the free-enterprise model of hundreds of small operators struggling for a place continued to apply in the Indian Territory cattle business, the stereotype of violent cowboy-and-Indian battle might have been a true description of the fact.[10]

After Robert D. Hunter opened large-scale negotiations by applying, in December of 1881, to lease 1.5 million acres to the south of either the Kiowa-Commanche or Cheyenne-Arapaho reservation, offers came in regularly for large acreages, predominantly from corporations. Formal proposals for the Outlet were made by E. Lynde of Kansas City, in April 1882 and by Edgar Marston in May. Marston represented a corporation that was willing to make a ten-year lease, or, if it was illegal for the Indians to enter into a lease agreement, to sign a bond with the commissioner of Indian affairs guaranteeing tax payments.[11]

Not that corporations preferred formal agreements if they could operate informally, as had the MK&T in the absence of any Choctaw coal and timber laws. There were complaints that Cherokee citizens were fencing large tracts in the Outlet on behalf of the Pennsylvania Oil Company, which wanted to run a ranch there. This went on for

10. *Indian Journal*, Jan. 13, 1881; Richard Berryhill to Samuel Checote, Sept. 3, 1880, #34747, Creek Pastures and Stock File, IAD; C. Wheaton to Assistant Adjutant General, Dept. of Mo., Aug. 1, 1880, LR OIA Union Agency, M 234, R 877, document #W 1828; Berthrong, "Cattlemen," pp. 7–8. John Tufts to Commissioner of Indian Affairs, Jan. 24, 1881; G. B. Hester to S. B. Maxey, April 1, 1881, SC 23. I. G. McIntosh to Samuel Checote, May 9, 1882, 34772, Creek Pastures and Stock File, IAD.

11. R. D. Hunter to Secretary of Interior, Dec. 30, 1881, SC 9, tray 2. E. Lynde to D. W. Bushyhead, April 11, 1882; S. W. Marston to D. W. Bushyhead, May 17, 1882, Cherokee Strip File (Tahlequah acquisition), IAD.

more than a year before, in March 1883, the corporation openly confessed it was the backer of these activities, agreed to make cash settle-
ments with those whose small pastures the fencing project had enclosed, and admitted it would be wise to ask permission of the
Cherokee government before fencing more land. The Standard Oil
Company also enclosed large areas in the Outlet. It hoped to fence a
twenty-five-mile square and to graze twenty thousand cattle. Ob-
viously, these were not shoestring operations run by small-time
entrepreneurs drifting in from Kansas.[12]

Even without considering the effects of the giants and the important industrial and political figures (steelmaker Abram Hewitt,
Sen. Preston Plumb) who had investments in Outlet companies,
incorporation and consolidation were undoubtedly important. The
corporation, "invisible" as it often was at early stages of a new move,
was there trying to acquire a vested interest before revealing itself.
There was, for example, never a formal grazing agreement made
between an Indian Territory tribe and a petroleum corporation.
Yet two of the largest oil companies in the country were fencing in
the Outlet, and the historian finds agents of small tribes making
mention of "oil company" pastures in their domain, as though this
oddity were familiar at the time. Fencing cost $200 a mile, even using
Cherokee timber, and by the spring of 1883 there were 959 miles of
it in the Outlet.

This fencing by corporations that did not have formal leases might
have led to corporate domination without Indian control, as had
happened with the railroads, except that the federal government
intervened decisively. Secretary of the Interior Teller ordered that all

12. H. Price to Secretary of Interior, March 14, 1883, ibid. B. H. Campbell
to H. Teller, Jan. 2, 1883, SC 9, tray 2. For examples see SR 1278, 49th Cong.,
1st sess., 1886, pt. 1, vol. 2, p. 144 (Serial 2363), p. 13. Occasionally, as in the
case of the Peorias, all the elements were mixed. A cattle lease was held by an
oil company backed by a railroad. SR 1278, pt. 1, vol. 2 (Serial 2363), p. 335.
H. Price to Secretary of Interior, March 14, 1883, Cherokee Strip File (Tahlequah acquisition), IAD; SR 1278, 49th Cong., 1st sess., 1886 (Serial 2362), pt. 1,
p. 35.

the fences be removed because such improvements implied ownership by the party that installed them.[13] Teller may not have been so
concerned had the corporations merely been stealing land that belonged to the Indians, but the Outlet was promised to the United
States by the terms of the 1866 treaty and the government wanted to
be free to do with it as it wished. The cattlemen were surprised and
annoyed. B. H. Campbell of Wichita, Kansas, wrote that, while cattlemen were taking their chances with the Indians, "we never did
reckon on our own Government being against us."[14]

The antifencing decision did not damage the corporation so
much as it did the small operator, who was unable to mark his claim.
It made informal ranching more difficult and led to the establishment
of formal leases of large acreages to large companies. The cattlemen,
in joining to fight the antifencing rules, formed a corporation,
the Cherokee Strip Live Stock Association (chartered in 1883), which
soon was working on an arrangement with Bushyhead to lease the
entire 6 million acres of the Outlet and to include in the agreement
permission to fence. If the federal government were to object to
that, it would be denying Indian sovereignty, an issue that could
confuse action for a long time.

To the casual observer of the actions of 1883, there may seem
to have been a sudden coincident interest on the part of a large number of small businessmen in negotiating leases. This accident is made
less remarkable, however, by an account of the few and not un-
acquainted corporate officers into whose files most significant grazing
agreements eventually made their way. The pattern is well illustrated
by the lease of the Cheyenne and Arapaho reserve in 1883. Robert D.
Hunter, a beef contractor, met with Interior Department officers in
1879 and received informal assurances that if cattlemen negotiated
agreements with Indian councils the Interior Department, though

13. Savage, *Cherokee Strip*, p. 47. Rather than to repeat available information upon the maneuvers leading to this, the reader is directed to Savage's
book, which concentrates particularly on the roles of the federal government
and the boomer element.

14. B. H. Campbell to H. Teller, Jan. 2, 1883, SC 9, tray 2.

it could not formally recognize them, would not actively interfere. Hunter returned to Washington in February 1883 with several draft agreements with tribes, and in the company of members of Congress and potential corporate backers, like George Blanchard, vice-president of the Erie railroad, to whom he had peddled his influence with the Indians and their protectors. The arrangements that Hunter and men like him were able to make with the government gave the big money the security it needed to invest quietly, while richly rewarding individuals who had smoked the pipe at the tribal council. They were in a position to lease the lands, thanks to covert agreements to sublease them immediately to corporations, and collect a large fee in the gamble. "Are you a corporation?" a senator asked. "No sir," Hunter could calmly reply.[15]

Of seven lease agreements sent to Washington in 1883, only two of the original lessees stocked their ranges; the rest sublet to corporations, whose credentials were never examined by the Indians in council. In the spring months of 1883, a lease for 500,000 acres given to an individual was transferred to the Standard Cattle Company of Boston, a corporation; 1,064,000 acres, representing the tracts of two individual lessees, to the Cheyenne and Arapaho Cattle Company of New York, a corporation; and 336,000 acres from an individual to the Commanche Land and Cattle Company of St. Louis, a corporation. Albert Babbitt, manager of the Standard Cattle Company, had been with Hunter at meetings in Washington. George Blanchard, the Erie railroad vice-president, who was also there, became the treasurer of the cattle company. William Weld and Nathaniel Thayer, well-known sources of capital for corporate ventures, were on the board. The name of this company caused no little speculation among those who believed that the Standard Oil Company, frustrated in its fencing designs, was still interested in Indian Territory cattle. The C&A cattle company, like Standard, was associated with Hunter in that its manager, Edward Fenlon, was Hunter's old partner in the Cheyenne and Arapaho annuity beef contracting business. The C&A company was capitalized at $1 million and graced by an investment

15. SR 1278, pt. 1, p. 64; p. 163; p. 62.

of $250,000 from the estate of late industrialist Peter Cooper. Fenlon stated that it was best the land should be held by large companies, because their huge investments would cause them to be more careful of Indian rights—an opinion Bushyhead shared. The Commanche Land and Cattle Company, the third of the 1883 corporate triumvirate about which something is known, was itself a subsidiary of a larger corporation controlled by St. Louis banker H. L. Newman, who had been with Hunter at the 1879 Washington meeting and who already operated lands in Montana and Nebraska. That the historian is able to sort out anything at all about these transfers is partly the result of the complaints to Washington of B. H. Campbell, a would-be R. D. Hunter. Campbell represented a Chicago-based syndicate that wished to lease 2.4 million acres in Indian Territory and asked that the government investigate the backing of those who had defeated him.[16]

As William Savage has recently pointed out, political understandings were of the utmost importance in the Outlet negotiations, just as they were in other tribal areas. Bushyhead visited Washington with the intent of gaining some informal understanding with officials there that they would not interfere with any lease that the tribe made. He reported that the secretary of the interior and commissioner of Indian affairs not only agreed with his plans but encouraged him to put them into operation. Certainly, the Cherokee Strip Live Stock Association had good political connections. It moved early for a lease partly due to a warning "on account of my friendship" from Sen. Preston Plumb that the president was about to propose that the federal government exercise its right to buy the Outlet and move in settlers, thus ruining the area forever as a cattle range. While Plumb had to take a public stand in favor of his boomer constituents, he promised the Association he would help in "all proper ways" in Washington.[17]

16. Berthrong, "Cattlemen," p. 16. SR 1278, pt. 1, pp. 32–34, 49–55, 163–64; pp. 163–64; pp. 49–55, 60; pp. 32–34. B. H. Campbell to Hiram Price, April 27, 1883, SC 9, tray 2.

17. D. W. Bushyhead to National Council, May 2, 1883, Cherokee Strip

Even the bitterest later opponents of the CSLSA admitted that, due to difficulties in collecting tax, the chance to receive $100,000 a year from the Association, which would then itself attend to the matters of subleasing to those who would stock the range and protect the area, was very attractive. Competing offers at the time were less desirable. The Cragin Cattle Company, represented by Edgar Marston, son of the Union agent, made a bid. That corporation, however, wanted to lease by the acre, and, although its offer might have aggregated $150,000 a year, it would have necessitated surveying the land. Another offer, of up to $125,000 a year, came from W. T. Adair, who represented a company of Cherokees. That group, however, had no capital and was depending upon sublease income, which realistic members of the tribe thought it was not likely to collect as easily from white cattlemen as was the Cherokee Strip Association. Some at the time charged that the Live Stock Association won through bribery. Large amounts of cash were circulating, but this was partly due to a recent payment of $300,000 made by the government to Cherokee citizens for a part of the Outlet already settled by plains tribes. What was doubtless more important to those in attendance was that the Association, and every other bidder, recognized that the tribe had a fee-simple title to the land and was willing to tie its fortunes to that of the tribe. Late in May, the lease to the Association passed the Council. On June 1, the *New York Times*, whether from confusion or superior knowledge, reported that the 6-million acre Cherokee Outlet had been leased for five years at $100,000 a year to the Standard Oil Company.[18]

The Indian public had mixed feelings about the decision. William Savage documents that Bushyhead made some changes in the

File (Tahlequah acquisition), IAD. Preston Plumb to E. M. Hewins, Jan. 19, 1883, Cherokee Strip Live Stock Association File, Sec. X, case 2, drawer 1, IAD; for boomer complaints about Plumb's double dealings, see Carl C. Rister, *Land Hunger: David L. Payne and the Oklahoma Boomers*, p. 150.

18. SR 1278, pt. 1, p. 83, vol. 2 (Serial 2363), p. 130; pt. 1, pp. 230–37; vol. 2 (Serial 2363), pp. 128–29; *Vinita Chieftain*, Jan. 22, 1885. SR 1278, pt. 1, pp. 189–90; p. 151. *New York Times*, June 1, 1883, 4–4.

lease passed by the Council before he signed it.[19] That was bound to increase suspicions of the executive by the legislative branch, which would soon arise again in the K&AV railroad fight. Also, some enterprising natives with ranches in the Outlet were most upset with the lease and inquired how the tribe could claim to own this land when Cherokee citizens were now barred from using it.[20] Other natives tried to make the best of it, with sometimes embarrassing results. Robert Owen, a mixed-blood later to become Union Agent and U.S. senator from Oklahoma, gathered a group of citizens who, a few days after the lease was signed, got grazing licenses in the Outlet from a compliant Cherokee treasurer. Bushyhead said that the treasurer had not been authorized by him to issue any licenses, and that the whole affair was a "blackmailing scheme" by men who wished to put themselves in a position to be bought off by the new corporation. CSLSA lobbyist John Lyons was not, however, worried. In response to Owen's request for troops to put him in possession of his land, Lyons commented:

> The indications are that he will get them, if he will only wait until a commission can be arranged to enter into a contract with the King of Dahomey for the loan of his household troops. If this can be done, and the party has not sought greener pastures before the negotiations can be finally consummated, why he will then be commissioned as the Commander in Chief and he can then with drum and fife, flag flying and spearheads shining march on and take possession of his only 250,000 acres. The young man, to use a homely expression, is evidently a "little off."[21]

Whatever the state of Owen's sanity, many were upset for what they considered good reason. When Cherokee cattlemen escaping the Outlet moved onto Creek lands, the Creeks did not let a common Indian heritage interfere with the collection of a tribal tax on all

19. Savage, *Cherokee Strip*, p. 63.

20. James Critchfield to D. W. Bushyhead, June 30, 1883, Cherokee Strip File (Tahlequah acquisition), IAD.

21. John Lyons to Charles Eldred, July 21, 1883; Aug. 26, 1883, CSLSA File, Sec. X, case 2, drawer 1, IAD.

stock. Cherokee newspaperman Augustus Ivey sent documents to Washington in August 1883 indicating that the Association lease was gained by fraud. These charges were kept under wraps in Washington for a year but emerged after the 1884 election returned a Democratic administration no longer bound by informal arrangements regarding leasing. A number of members of the Cherokee Council became so dissatisfied that they introduced bills in the fall of 1883 to sell the Outlet. For stopping moves like this, CSLSA lobbyist Lyons was given a bonus and a gold watch by his employers.[22]

Nor was the CSLSA itself without difficulties in administering its new empire. Most bothersome of its subleases was one to the firm of Windsor & Roberts, so close to the Kansas border that it was nearly impossible to defend it from intruders. This firm was regarded as a front for the Standard Oil company's cattle interest. In 1884, two independent cattlemen, J. D. Love and Peter Hollenbeck, attempted to upset arrangements by obtaining grazing licenses from Cherokee Treasurer D. W. Lipe, moving on to the Windsor & Roberts range, and voicing abroad the idea that the CSLSA was a tool of Standard Oil. Meanwhile officials of the Chilocco Indian school, located on the Windsor & Roberts sublease, complained that the oil company (as Winsor & Roberts were commonly called) was fencing school lands and that its cowboys had gotten into a fight with employees of the Indian industrial school when the latter tried to remove fence posts in a night raid. The CSLSA, far from taking care of things without fuss as Bushyhead had hoped, asked the Cherokees for help. The Cherokees in turn appealed to the federal government for troops, while trying to keep the whole operation secret in order to prevent Love and Hollenbeck from withdrawing into Kansas when they learned of it. The superintendent at Chilocco was far from sure he wanted Windsor & Roberts protected. He wrote: "A very bitter feeling has grown up with the people along the line against the

22. D. W. Bushyhead to Samuel Checote, #34788, Creek Pastures and Stock File, IAD. Augustus Ivey to Secretary of Interior, Aug. 23, 1883, SC 12. J. Lyons to C. Eldred, July 11, Aug. 15, Dec. 5, 1883, CSLSA File, Sec. X, case 2, drawer 1, IAD.

Oil Company. The mention of the company has very much the same affect upon the line people as shaking a red flag before a cross bull has upon them, they get ready for battle at once."[23]

W. B. Roberts wrote a long letter to the secretary of the interior in 1885 denying that his firm was backed by Standard Oil, or that it was actually a powerful, monopolistic corporation. He and his son ran the cattle operation, he said, from headquarters at Roberts's bank at Titusville, Pennsylvania. Since they came from the oil region, they had chosen the brand O.I.L., thus leading boomers and alienated Cherokees to fabricate a rumor about Standard Oil.[24] The fact remains that during the fencing controversy Standard Oil had been running cattle in the same area covered by the Windsor & Roberts sublease, and a great number of analysts other than boomers and Cherokees were of the opinion that the corporation had not simply quietly withdrawn, although it was, to be sure, keeping quiet.

In addition to these difficulties, the Association faced insecurity in its tenure, based as it was on a series of informal compromises with the federal government on Indian sovereignty. In 1884, it was forced by federal officials to remove some fencing. There was widespread unfavorable comment when in the same year the Association leased ten thousand acres of the Quapaw reserve. At a national cattlemen's convention in St. Louis in November 1884 the view was expressed that, in the atmosphere of land reform that was growing more prevalent in the country, the very magnitude of the CSLSA interest was likely to excite alarm and lead the federal government eventually to destroy the arrangement.[25]

23. SR 1278, pt. 1, p. 466; Hollenbeck et al. petition, March 4, 1884; J. M. Haworth to H. M. Teller, June 5, 1884, SC 12. B. Miller to D. W. Bushyhead, April 14, 1884, Cherokee Strip File (Tahlequah acquisition), IAD. J. M. Haworth to H. M. Teller, June 5, 1884, SC 12.

24. W. B. Roberts to L. Q. C. Lamar, April 6, 1885, SC 111, tray 5; (?) Lee to Commissioner of Indian Affairs (telegram), n.d., SC 9, tray 2.

25. H. Price to Secretary of Interior, July 3, 1884, #L 1073; A. B. Upshaw to H. B. Crowell, Oct. 13, 1885, #L 23736; J. D. Atkins to Secretary of Interior, Sept. 18, 1885, #L 21333, LR OIA, chronological file, RG 75, NA. *Vinita Chieftain*, Nov. 6, Dec. 18, 1884.

The first move in this direction was a series of hearings upon the cattle-lease question conducted by the Senate Committee of Indian Affairs in 1885. It was occasioned both by pressure from boomers and by escalating complaints of fraud in dealing for the grass of the western Indian Territory tribes. Also, there was the matter of Ivey's charges of fraud at the 1883 Cherokee council.

At the hearings, thanks to pressure from boomers saying that monopoly was holding them back, information about the true extent of corporate subleasing in the Territory became available to the Congress at large for the first time. In the Territory, the *Cherokee Advocate* generally defended the lease, but a new newspaper, the *Vinita Chieftain*, took as its only purpose for several years the necessity for destroying "cattle kings and syndicates." The official Cherokee delegation in Washington followed the line of the *Advocate*, questioning the right of the congressional committee to investigate at all the internal affairs of the sovereign Cherokee Nation and warning that this "new phase of the Indian question must...be carefully watched, lest the tribe be the victim of it."[26]

The disagreement about leasing was represented on an individual level by the arguments, at the 1885 hearings, between Augustus Ivey and John Lyons. Lyons, despite the fact that his wife was dying, was diligent in collecting evidence in favor of the Association and in enlisting the aid of Kansas Sen. John Ingalls to make sure that the list of witnesses to appear before the committee was balanced. He blamed the trouble upon the selfishness of Ivey. Ivey, on the other hand, believed that Chief Bushyhead and the editor of the *Advocate* were in league to try to discredit antilease testimony. "Now mark it down," he said, "when you kick at me I propose to kick back, and when the people are being duped and wronged I propose to raise my voice in their defense whether it suits certain officers and big men or not." The *Chieftain* agreed: "Are we, like a little family of silly spendthrifts, going to work and dicker our land away for a few dozen jewsharps, or as many dead dog skins . . . and thus beggar ourselves

26. Ibid., April 2, 1885. Cherokee delegates to National Council, Oct., 1885, Cherokee U.S. Government Box, OU.

forever and turn our children and children's children out into the world as penniless tramps?"[27]

As the result of information on corporate leasing discovered by the committee, President Grover Cleveland began to investigate all laws on leases from Indians and to prepare to employ the military to drive out any lessee, no matter how powerful, that did not comply. It was disturbing to Cleveland to learn, for example, that member of Congress and industrialist Abram Hewitt had acted as trustee for the bondholders of the Cheyenne and Arapaho Cattle Company and had used the prestige of their names to attract investors.[28]

R. D. Hunter, the Cheyenne and Arapaho operator now a director of the CSLSA, tried to defend the status quo. He noted that the case of *Boudinot* v. *Hunter* in the U.S. District Court for the Eastern District of Missouri had declared the leases legal and that complaints against them were coming not from those interested in preserving the tribes, but from competing corporations and boomers.[29] The *Ft. Worth Stock Journal* took the broader ground by saying that the idea of the "noble savage" was a myth anyway, and Indians were as prepared to take their chances in the business world as anyone else.[30]

But the propaganda for the other side was stronger still. Politicians of note wrote to Washington that the leases were illegal and the compensation inadequate. One man wrote directly to the president, saying that the only reason the cattlemen could survive in the Indian Territory was their power in Congress. He then proceeded to list a number of members of Congress with investments in cattle

27. John Lyons to C. Eldred, Jan. 29, Feb. 14, 1884, CSLSA File, Sec. X, case 2, drawer 1, IAD. *Vinita Chieftain*, Feb. 26, 1885; May 5, 1885.

28. Ibid., July 2, 1885. Abram S. Hewitt to L. Q. C. Lamar, June 30, 1885, SC 9, tray 3.

29. R. D. Hunter, H. B. Denman et al. to Commissioner of Indian Affairs, July 7, 1885, SC 9, tray 2. The argument in *United States* v. *Hunter*, 21 Fed. Rep., 615, decided in Sept., 1884, was that the Revised Statutes declared illegal only Indian contracts conveying title or looking toward purchase, not including leases. The federal government disagreed.

30. Quoted in *Vinita Chieftain*, June 18, 1885.

corporations, suggesting that, if only the matter could be viewed by uninvolved men, the Indian question would not be difficult to resolve. In August 1885 the attorney general ruled that all Indian leases were void. President Cleveland began issuing orders to the military to remove the stockmen.[31]

The president received hundreds of letters praising the action and thanking him for standing against the "marauding bullock barons."[32] Especially the writers were glad that Cleveland had not folded to pressure from "monster corporations," which they said now would be forced to compete on an equal basis with the small ranchman and the farmer.[33] The Cherokees, besieged by offers from corporations to buy the Outlet at a much higher price than the government intended to pay, asked Cleveland to annul the CSLSA lease on the grounds that it was made by the chief without the consent of the general membership of the tribe.[34] In August 1885 the commissioner of Indian affairs received a letter from the Pennsylvania Railroad Company asking if the recent order to remove cattle from the Cheyenne-Arapaho reservation was the first step toward annulling all Indian Territory leases. If so, the company would not stock its Indian Territory range.[35]

In light of these moves, the CSLSA tried in 1886 to re-lease the Outlet upon a more secure basis. This attempt was made especially difficult, not only because, as in 1883, other corporations competed for the lease but because many were interested in buying the region outright. The government was also a competitor, with its treaty

31. Ibid., July 9, 1885. A. Churchill to Grover Cleveland, July 13, 1885; A. H. Garland to Secretary of Interior, July 21, 1885, SC 9, tray 2; *Vinita Chieftain*, Aug. 6, 1885.

32. Clipping in L. E. Forsyth to Grover Cleveland, Aug. 14, 1885, SC 9, tray 3.

33. J. B. Porterfield to G. Cleveland, Aug. 10, 1885, ibid. In this file tray are enough letters to the president on this subject to form a study in themselves.

34. *New York Times*, July 30, 1885.

35. Charles Sloan to Commissioner of Indian Affairs, Aug. 1, 1885, SC 9, tray 2.

promise to be allowed to purchase the Outlet and open it to settlement. Again, the question of sovereignty became central in the question of corporate development. Charles Cragin, representing the Cragin Cattle Company, wrote Bushyhead that if Cleveland's anti-lease policy prevailed, "your example of independent government will be lost to the word."[36] Yet one man wrote to Washington that the Cherokees had no more right to lease or sell the outlet "than to run the U.S. Post Office Department."[37] Factionalism was also important. E. C. Boudinot, hoping for a lease to a company composed of tribal citizens to which he belonged, argued that the land must be held for the U.S. government, even if the tribe were offered twenty dollars an acre for it. Others felt that even if they rejected syndicate offers such as the profitable proposals of a New York conglomerate prepared to use money from Leadville mining to pay three dollars an acre for the Outlet, these offers would place the tribe in a better bargaining position when it came time for the United States to appraise the land.[38] It would also push the price of a re-lease to the CSLSA higher. It was no exaggeration when Bushyhead said of the 1886 council: "This will be the biggest contest ever held by the Cherokees ... it will require statesmanship, patriotism, and foresight to deal with the questions so as not to endanger our country."[39]

In the fall of 1886, lobbyist Lyons engaged a "good and convenient" room at the National Hotel in Tahlequah, where he met with Bushyhead and the Cherokee delegation to plan strategy. The group

36. Charles Cragin to D. W. Bushyhead, Aug. 14, 1885, Cherokee Strip File (Tahlequah acquisition), IAD. The Cragin company, which had bid for the Outlet in 1883, was now a CSLSA sublessee but was interested in bidding for the complete franchise again.

37. A. G. Lordly to G. Cleveland, Oct. 27, 1886, SC 12, tray 2.

38. Again, the syndicate bid is a story in itself. Some sources are: F. W. Stout to Commissioner of Indian Affairs, Dec. 3, 1886, SC 12, tray 2; *Vinita Chieftain*, Oct. 28, Nov. 11, Nov. 18, Dec. 3, 1886, Jan. 6, 1887; *New York Times*, Nov. 1, Nov. 3, Nov. 4, 1886; John Bissell and J. W. Wallace to D. W. Bushyhead, Nov. 9, 1886, CSLSA File, Sec. X, case 2, drawer 1, IAD.

39. *New York Times*, Nov. 1, 1885.

was liberally supplied with whiskey, about $125 worth according to later testimony. Despite this, the council was split, asking for amendments raising the lease price to $300,000 a year. All bills failed to pass, and the question was carried over to the next year. The *Chieftain* observed that "a lugubrious crowd 'pulled their freight' from Tahlequah with redoubtable John as chief mourner."[40]

Mr. Lyons did not, however, intend to give up. By December, he reported to the CSLSA directors that he thought he had lined up the votes for passage of the lease in the next session. Leo Bennett, a candidate for chief in the coming election, was in favor of the lease, and Lyons thought he could be sure Bennett would win. Because of Lyons the syndicate, which was complicating things by trying to buy the strip, was exposed as a fraud. Over the Christmas holidays, Lyons said, the "boarding house conclave" had begun to operate again in Tahlequah, "and 214 dollars fell mortally wounded."[41]

That same December 1886 new arguments about Indian sovereignty were introduced by reformers into Congress, designed to show that the CSLSA was the best guarantee of continued respect for the tribal government. They claimed that declaring the lease invalid produced the same effect as confiscating the land, as the Indian could not use it himself and was thereby denied the chance to gather revenue from it. It would also put the Indian in an unfair position in regard to federal negotiators trying to buy the Outlet, as he would be forced, for lack of alternative uses, to sell at any price. Lyons observed, however, that the tribes were in an awkward legal position. If they claimed a fee-simple title for the purpose of demonstrating their right to lease, it might be argued that eminent domain for railroads therefore applied, as it did to other such titles. Oppo-

40. John Lyons to Charles Eldred, Oct. 20, 1885, CSLSA File, Sec. X, case 2, drawer 1, IAD; Robert Owen to J. D. C. Atkins, April 29, 1887, marked "strictly confidential," SC 12. *Vinita Chieftain*, Dec. 2, 1886.

41. John Lyons to Charles Eldred, Dec. 4, 1886, CSLSA File, Sec. X, case 2, drawer 1, IAD. *Vinita Chieftain*, Dec. 3, 1886. John Lyons to Charles Eldred, Dec. 20, 1886, CSLSA File, Sec. X, case 2, drawer 1, IAD.

sition to leasing the area, however, had to admit that in making the Outlet valuable to themselves, the Association had made it valuable to the Cherokees as well. That had been a justification for corporate intrusion since 1870.[42]

At the key Cherokee elections in 1887, things did not go perfectly for the Association. Bushyhead was replaced, not by Leo Bennett but by Joel Mayes, who, while not against leasing in principle, was neither especially bound to the CSLSA. The election was so controversial that the results almost caused a tribal civil war. There was talk of sending federal troops and ending Indian sovereignty right there.[43] To offset its political defeat, the Association hired William A. Phillips, former tribal attorney, to act for it.[44] The Union agent at this time was Robert Owen, who had tried in 1883 to bypass the Association lease for his own benefit as private Cherokee citizen.

Mayes wanted a system of competitive bidding to guarantee the highest possible price for a lease. He vetoed several bills in the early months of 1888, under which a new lease would have been granted to the CSLSA. John Wilson appeared representing the North and West Live Stock Company of Dallas, Texas, a $1 million corporation, and bid $160,000. That offer was refused when Wilson admitted that Robert Owen "might be" a stockholder in this company. Also there was Patrick Henry, who had been trying to lease on behalf of his Waco corporation since 1880. He bid $175,000. The CSLSA matched this bid.[45]

42. *Congressional Record*, 49th Cong., 2d sess., XVIII, 338. John Lyons to Charles Eldred, Dec. 20, 1886, CSLSA File, Sec. X, case 2, drawer 1, IAD.

43. *New York Times*, Dec. 10, 1887, 4–7, Dec. 12, 1887, 1–6.

44. William A. Phillips to E. M. Hewins, Nov. 29, Dec. 7, 1887, CSLSA File, Sec. X, case 2, drawer 1, IAD. Phillips noted that he could do some good working for the company "privately and confidentially."

45. *Cherokee Advocate* (Tahlequah), Feb. 1, July 11, 1888; *Vinita Chieftain*, May 17, July 12, 1888; Savage, *Cherokee Strip*, pp. 106–8. *Vinita Chieftain*, July 12, 19, Nov. 8, 1888; Hearings before the Cherokee Senate Committee on Public Domain, July 10, 1888, Cherokee Strip File (Tahlequah acquisition), IAD. Savage, *Cherokee Strip*, p. 107.

That was heady stuff, and the *Chieftain* warned that it would be better that the land be left vacant than that Cherokees be tempted to compromise their independence in exchange for money. "Such corporations, benefited by the use of national interest," the paper exclaimed, "is safe in a nation of Spartans, whose highest aim is national strength and unity." The members of the council, cigars in their mouths, exchanging bribe money, did not exactly present the image of Spartans. There "the votes of members were mere matters of traffic," and some lease bills, which the *Chieftain* thought were ruinously corrupt, failed by only the narrowest of margins. At last, the Outlet was leased, in December of 1888, to the Cherokee Strip Live Stock Association for $200,000 a year. The secretary of the interior, however, made it clear that the United States would not recognize the lease. Negotiations for United States' purchase of the Outlet were already in progress.[46]

The long contest over the lease revealed to the Cherokees characteristics of themselves they preferred not to recognize—greed and violent, often selfish, divisions within the tribe. It was said that in the council "the roar, sweat and fume were tremendous . . . the appearances were those of a raging cyclone, thunder and general destruction." The *Chieftain* stated that the legislature, placed in the limelight by corporate competition, had become "ravenous as a wild beast when he approaches water. . . . See how he plunges and snaps after the pet company; it is involuntary, unreasoning, purely physical movements, and drinks and drinks, till it is sick and distressed." Land monopoly continued, railroads were driving surveying pegs in all directions, and unprecedented pressures raised strife and confusion among the tribes. Yet they went on mechanically. One man wrote: "The music is a dead march, but step to it they must."[47]

The last chapter in the story of the cattle corporation concerns its effect upon the sale of the Outlet to the federal government. Wash-

46. *Vinita Chieftain*, Feb. 9, Feb. 23, Dec. 6, 1888; Savage, *Cherokee Strip*, pp. 108–11.
47. *Vinita Chieftain*, July 5, Sept. 20, July 19, 1888.

ington officials blamed the length of the negotiations and Cherokee intransigence about price upon the cattle interests. If the Association were not to damage the negotiations by outbidding the United States for the land, the federal government had to make more definite statements about its sovereignty, and lack of Indian sovereignty, than it ever had before. The lease to the Association was described by the *New York Herald* "as impudent a fraud as though he [Bushyhead] should undertake to lease to some body any empty house he might find on a New York street."[48]

The CSLSA said that it had not made great profits and would be happy to withdraw if given time. The corporation, officers said, had been deceived by the vascillating policy of the government, first encouraging with informal détente, then after a political election acting righteous and judgmental. It was claimed that the character of the investors in the Association prevented it from mud-slinging at its detractors, but that opposition to it was largely a cheap trick to deprive the tribe of revenue and force sale at an unfair price.[49] Recent court decisions have confirmed that the tribe was underpaid by the government for the Outlet.

When the Association was ordered to remove all its cattle by October 1, 1890, Chief Mayes defended its right to stay, and lamented that the Cherokees no longer had any warriors with which to defy the United States.[50] He changed his mind, however, when the Association, short on funds, refused to make its semiannual payment to the tribe on the ground that the lease was not binding.[51] In December 1891 the Cherokees sold the Outlet to the United States for $1.40 an acre. "It is evidently a utilitarian age," mused one Indian, "and we

48. Quoted in *Oklahoma War Chief*, April 15, 1886.

49. John McAltee et al., *A Memorial to the President of the United States from Members of the Cherokee Strip Live Stock Association* (Kansas City, 1889), copy in CSLSA File, Sec. X, case 2, drawer 1, IAD, reprinted in *Vinita Chieftain*, Jan. 23, 1890.

50. J. B. Mayes to E. M. Hewins, Feb. 11, 1890, CSLSA File, Sec. X, case 2, drawer 1, IAD.

51. E. C. Moderwell to A. Drumm, Feb. 10, 1892, ibid.; Savage, *Cherokee Strip*, pp. 117–18.

realize that . . . the acquisition of money seems to be . . . the ruling passion of the age."[52] Still, some things, like patriotism, should not be sold. "If Congress can so dispose of the Strip [Outlet]," a *Chieftain* editorial ran, "can it not so dispose of the nation proper?"[53]

Considering that the cattle-leasing question was simultaneous with the railroad right-of-way battle, not to mention the oil controversy, it was little wonder that Indian delegates to Washington in the late eighties were described as wearing a "somber, half-stern, half-sad look." The combined delegations met in their tailored clothes in a cozy hotel parlor two blocks from the Capitol, and there discussed what they had learned about the relationship between tribal sovereignty and industrial civilization. Their conclusion, looking back upon the hidden corporate influences brought to bear in the cattle situation, was that Indian policy in the eighties had resembled a "Mailed Hand," using as its legions the boomer "wrapped in his own disgust for the God who created him" and the capitalist who "has spread himself over the territory with the hope of capturing a fortune in a single day." As to the corporation, they could only say, "The white man has cut his blame dog loose and we as a nation are afraid to tangle with him." Most distressingly, some of the corporate push had come from within, for good and ill. Oil derricks were being constructed on former Chief Bushyhead's stone quarry lease, and it looked as though moderation among the progressives was at an end. "Wild Cherokees are in the saddle," the delegations concluded, "and have accomplished their scheme." Bushyhead, wrote the *Cherokee Champion* in 1895, was an intelligent man who had "posed in all attitudes and played all kinds of games" in an attempt to manipulate corporations in the interest of the tribes. But he was not, at last, equal to the situation, and finally lost most of his once-considerable nerve.[54]

52. Transcript of Cherokee Commission negotiations, Dec. 10–17, 1890, Nov. 24, 1891, ISP, file 310, shelf 6, p. 71. This transcript provides great evidence of the skill of Cherokee negotiators, hardened by years of dealing with corporations.

53. *Vinita Chieftain*, May 22, 1890.

54. *Indian Champion*, Feb. 14, 1885. *Cherokee Advocate*, May 23, 1888.

You should never name your children after the living great. Wait until your ideal has played his full hand and lays mouldering in his tomb; the game is never played out until it is played out; and the man you venerate to-day, may prove himself a poltroon and knave tomorrow.[55]

The corporate Indian Territory game was not by 1890 fully played out, but Indian sovereignty had yet to take a trick.

Vinita Chieftain, July 3, July 17, 1890. *Cherokee Telephone* (Tahlequah), March 5, 1891, clipping in Bushyhead Papers, OU.

55. *Cherokee Champion* (Vinita), June 5, 1895, clipping in Bushyhead Papers.

CHAPTER VIII

THE POLITICS OF PETROLEUM

Gerald Nash has written that the "unexplored field" of the history of petroleum in the West would provide new perspective on the "fascinating theme of the interplay of law and new economic resources."[1] Doubly so with the history of corporate oil activity in the Indian nations, where there were dual sets of laws and dual philosophies of resource exploitation. Exploitation of petroleum resources was the last major type of corporate activity with which the sovereign native governments of the Territory had to deal. The stakes here were potentially richest of all, while the structure of the intruder was the most complex yet, and the nature of its activities most thoroughly screened from the minds of the uninitiated. Development followed the familiar pattern: intertribal conflicts, avoidance of Indian law by whites, inadequate enforcement machinery, unwillingness by the federal government to take a definite stand, limited access to markets, all leading to organization, simplification, and exploitation by the corporation. When the derrick joined the steam locomotive, the slag pile, and the roll of barbed wire in the vista of the frightened full blood, it seemed to him the equipment of doom was complete.

The Indians had been aware of the existence of oil for a long time. The Choctaws were using petroleum oozing from the ground as a rheumatism remedy in 1853. However, it was not until the sixties that the commercial possibilities were appreciated. Inquiries came to the Indian Office in 1867 about leasing portions of the Quapaw reserve, south of Baxter Springs, Kansas, where there were

1. Gerald Nash, "Oil in the West: Reflections on the Historiography of an Unexplored Field," pp. 193, 198.

oil springs. In 1872, Robert Darden of Missouri organized the Chickasaw Oil Company after signing a contract with leading Choctaws and Chickasaws at the home of Winchester Colbert. Under that contract the Indians were to receive the proceeds from one half of the total production of the wells. But Darden did no drilling. The Virginia company and its failure have been discussed earlier. Likewise in 1872 Dr. I. L. Kilby drew a lease with George Colbert, a Chickasaw. Erastus Wells, one of the directors of Kilby's corporation, wrote the Office of Indian Affairs in Washington asking its opinion "in regard to the authority to occupy said land & move the produces there from and if the government will approve said leases." The Indian Office replied negatively to all these inquiries. Government officials considered inappropriate corporate development beyond the building of railroads as provided in the treaty that had just been signed, even if some Indians agreed to it.[2]

The difficulty the Choctaws had in adjusting their coal regulations to corporate mining has been discussed. The mining laws of the Cherokees and Creeks, where the first shallow oil wells were drilled, were designed to regulate individual citizens taking coal from outcrops for home use and so were not adequate to control oil activity. The 1875 Cherokee mineral law made no mention of "Rock Oil" and excluded corporations and whites from obtaining licenses to mine. Most Cherokees did not bother to apply to the treasurer for a license, and whites simply stole coal. The result was that total mineral royalty paid to the Cherokees (5 per cent of gross revenue) for the year 1883 was $14.60. There were reports of bogus royalty collectors harassing honest miners while whites from Kansas brought in machinery and paid no tax at all. Cherokee Chief Bushyhead pursued the same course here as he had with cattle. Somehow the corruption must be stopped and the tribal revenues increased. One

2. C. B. Glasscock, *Then Came Oil: The Story of the Last Frontier*, p. 113. James Sloan to Major Mitchell, n.d. [1867], box 415040, Osage Administrative File Misc., FRC (for "Abbreviations in Footnotes," see p. vii). *Cherokee Advocate*, March 2, 1872. Erastus Wells to F. A. Walker, Jan. 21, 1872, LR OIA Choctaw Agency, M 234, R 180, F 0388–89.

answer was to deal with white corporations seeking permission to drill for oil.[3]

An early mining possibility was an inquiry to Bushyhead from A. V. Weise of the Granby Mining and Smelting Company of Missouri, a profitable concern along the Frisco railway. Weise wrote in 1880 that a friend of his had "accidentally" discovered lead ore in the Cherokee Nation. Playing upon the legislative-executive split among the Cherokees, Weise offered to let Bushyhead and "such other gentlemen as you would think proper" become investors in a corporation to mine this resource. "The greater your progress is," Weise explained, "and the more means you have at command; the more successful, in the same propartion, will you be in opposing encroachments on your rights."[4] Consistent with his past behavior, the chief was amenable to the idea that corporations might be used to protect Indian sovereignty by tying it to large economic interests.

A second approach along the same lines was made by William Everett, an employee of the *Chicago Tribune*, in December 1882. Everett, in writing a series of articles on the Indian Territory, had noticed the potential for an oil industry in the region and asked that he be granted a lease. As Weise, he emphasized that some corporation was bound to enter the field and that his would be less dangerous to the Indians than others. He reported that the Standard Oil Company was trying to obtain drilling privileges in the Territory by working through the Interior Department and was bypassing the tribe completely. How much better "to operate through your people if it can be done."[5]

Bushyhead scribbled on the back of Everett's envelope a large "No." Tribal rules would not permit such enterprises as his and

3. Article XVIII, Chapter XII, *Constitution and Laws of the Cherokee Nation* (St. Louis, 1875), pp. 226–28. Revenue Report, 1883, Cherokee Officers' Reports, 1880–1885, Cherokee vol. 402, p. 78, IAD. George Walker to D. W. Lipe, April 8, 1881, F. H. Wasson to D. W. Bushyhead, Aug. 15, 1882, Cherokee Minerals (Tahlequah acquisition), IAD.

4. A. V. Weise to D. W. Bushyhead, Feb. 12, 1880, ibid.

5. William S. Everett to D. W. Bushyhead, Dec. 28, 1882, ibid.

Weise's. But the offers set all to thinking, combined as they were with the corporate organization of the cattlemen and the debates under way in Washington about the Frisco right of way that combined to make the early eighties such a crucial time. Cherokee progressives were typically active. Spencer Stephens wrote in October 1882 that he had been looking over the country for eight days with a gentleman representing a large Pennsylvania oil company—"Rich." Whether the man was interested in cattle ranching or oil wells, or both, Stephens did not say, but noted it "promises well." He closed his letter, "P.S. Somewhat ennebriated [*sic*] but I know what I'm doing."[6]

Actual changes in tribal law, however, were not enacted until 1883 and coincided with the interest of Dr. Hiram W. Faucett from New York City, who was financially backed by the Northern Pacific Railway. Faucett contacted Chief Allen Wright of the Choctaws and Bushyhead of the Cherokees in July of 1883 with the suggestion that they and other tribal progressives form petroleum companies, take out licenses under their respective tribal laws, and then sublease to Faucett's corporation, which would drill for oil. Both executives found the proposal exciting and allowed native companies to be organized by E. N. Wright and Robert Owen respectively. Changes in the rules to accommodate these men included an 1883 amendment to the Cherokee mineral code to include oil at a royalty of ten cents per forty-gallon barrel and to allow Cherokee lessees to associate with noncitizen mining interests "if necessary to raise sufficient capital to successfully work [the leases] . . . and thereby to increase the revenue of the nation." The next year, both the Choctaws and the Cherokees passed laws more favorable yet to the corporation, giving a complete monopoly on the production, transportation, and refining of oil in their respective regions to any company that would begin work within one year. Tribal leaders stated that in order to build better schools, they needed oil revenues, and in order to get oil revenues, they must "offer proper privileges to justify any one in

6. Spencer Stephens to James Bell, Oct. 16, 1882, box 28, Cherokee Nation Papers, OU.

risking the large am't of money required." Faucett's privileges while
subleasing from the native companies included a monopoly on all
Cherokee land east of the ninety-sixth meridian and on the whole
Choctaw Nation—a total of 20,000 square miles or 13 million acres.
It was the first in a line of stupendous corporate leases of Indian lands
for the purpose of exploring for oil.[7]

The native corporation organized in the Cherokee Nation was
called the Cherokee Petroleum Company. The original lease, given to
this concern in 1884, listed Bushyhead's name with those of two other
incorporators of one-sixteenth Indian blood. But just before the
law giving the company an exclusive monopoly passed, Bushyhead's
name was taken from the list of principals. The company did, however, get inside information, which Bushyhead was in a position to
give. It was aware in advance that a law was to be passed granting
a monopoly on oil and so had the first and only application. The same
day that Bushyhead signed the new law (December 13), he sent to
his friends authorization to drill, at which point they transferred the
whole thing to Faucett.[8]

Faucett's position seemed good. But there was a new administration in Washington, and President Cleveland's attitudes toward
cattle leasing were not a favorable indication of his potential position
toward any oil scheme. Dr. Faucett therefore inquired of the Interior
Department, and got equivocal answers that were no comfort to
investors. In February 1884 Bushyhead and the Cherokee delegation
wrote to the secretary of the interior asking that Faucett's lease be
recognized. In May, all the documents connected with the transaction
were sent to Washington.[9]

Indian Commissioner J. D. C. Atkins concluded in July 1885

7. Carl C. Rister, *Oil! Titan of the Southwest*, pp. 16–19. Act of Dec. 15,
1883; Act of Dec. 13, 1884, Cherokee vol. 284, Cherokee Mineral File (Tahlequah acquisition), IAD. Rister, *Oil*, p. 17.

8. Cherokee Oil Co. to Henry Chambers, Jan. 1, 1884; Cherokee Petroleum Co. to D. W. Bushyhead, Nov. 14, 1884; Attachment to act of Dec. 13,
1884, Cherokee Mineral File (Tahlequah acquisition), IAD.

9. J. D. C. Atkins to Secretary of Interior, July 2, 1885, ibid.

that the Indians had title to the land and the right to create an oil franchise, but he recommended that the federal government formally commit itself to that principle. Informal encouragement was given to Faucett, as it had been to cattlemen like R. D. Hunter before him, but any official approval, Adkins thought, would "establish a hazardous precedent, which might be productive of serious embarrassment to the Department in the future." Washington, in short, would confirm or deny nothing. It was noted that the 1866 treaties spoke of the Indian right to create "such works of internal improvement as they may deem essential to the welfare and prosperity of the community," and that oil leases might fall under that elastic clause. Also, officials said that the oil arrangement was a sublease through Indians rather than a direct agreement by the tribal government with noncitizens. Therefore, it could technically be regarded as an internal matter beyond the range of the federal government.[10] But would it be, now and in the future, or not? No one would say.

Faucett did do some drilling, as did Michael Cudahy, an Omaha packer who had gotten a lease on all the Creek lands, also in 1884. Faucett reached fourteen hundred feet at a well east of Atoka, Choctaw Nation, in 1885, and the same year assembled a rig in the Going Snake District of the Cherokee Nation. Cudahy drilled an eighteen-hundred-foot test well near Muskogee, Creek Nation. All these wells failed to produce. In 1888, Faucett contracted typhoid fever and died. The Cherokees quickly repealed the monopoly bill over the veto of Chief Mayes, leaving the first flurry of oil activity in Indian Territory a complete failure.[11]

Still, the oil was there, and still, the Indians had neither the capital nor the technology to bring it out. It was ruining their water wells. Vann Chambers wrote to his father, then Cherokee treasurer, in 1887, that a friend of his had struck oil and gas in a water well. "The man that dug it Droped [sic] a match Down in the well & it exploded & came verry [sic] near killing Him. His face & Hand

10. J. D. C. Atkins to Secretary of Interior, July 10; July 2, 1885, ibid.
11. Glasscock, *Then Came Oil*, p. 114; Rister, *Oil*, pp. 16–19. Act of Nov. 28, 1888, Cherokee Mineral File (Tahlequah acquisition), IAD.

are Peeling off yet."[12] The answer to this problem was the corporation.

The step of drilling the first well with a regular commercial production was taken by Edward Byrd, a Cherokee citizen by marriage, and Martin Hellar, a white man residing in Wichita, Kansas. They drilled a number of wells near Chelsea in the Cooweescoowee District, Cherokee Nation, and in 1889 began to pump a half barrel of oil a day from a well thirty-six feet deep.[13] The results were less than overwhelming, but when the Cherokee treasurer Robert Ross was invited to see it, he was very impressed. Hellar reported that Ross told the two that they had "done more in this short space of time on this small lease than anyone had ever done in this country before even when he had leased the whole Nation to a company to go on any land they pleased and prospect for oil."[14] It did not matter to Ross that Hellar had doubtless made the discovery and brought in Indian citizen Byrd merely to get a license.[15] For here was oil. The coal banks were already coming into the control of outside syndicates, and the better the tribe prepared for the same development in oil, the greater chance to control it. One of the coal corporations was comical in its perfect reflection of the fictional stereotype of the Gilded Age corporation. It was called Timpson, Horsefly & Co., and its president was a man named Butler Brassfield.[16]

The Byrd and Hellar discovery, as had Faucett's interest, resulted in changes in Indian mineral law. In 1890, the Cherokee code

12. Vann Chambers to "Father" [Henry Chambers], March 9, 1887, ibid.

13. *Tulsa Daily World*, Sept. 4, 1932; Rister, *Oil*, p. 20. Rister's account of the discovery is based upon Byrd's reminiscences for the Oklahoma Geological Society Bulletin. Byrd there claimed he had an oil lease as early as 1886 and brought in Hellar later. I have been unable to locate such a lease in the Cherokee archives. Hellar claimed that he discovered the well and brought in Cherokee citizen Byrd in order to get the lease, which seems more likely.

14. Martin Hellar to Secretary of Interior, May 23, 1904, box 328, ITD.

15. Martin Hellar to Theodore Roosevelt, Feb. 25, 1905, ibid. See explanation in note 12.

16. Timpson, Horsefly & Co. to R. B. Ross, March 10, 1889, Cherokee Mineral File (Tahlequah acquisition), IAD.

was revised in order to grant corporations free entry into the Nation with all the men and equipment necessary to work the oil fields. These men were to be immune from prosecution as trespassers under the Intercourse Acts. Timber could be taken from the Indian lands freely, and Cherokee citizens were given the express right to sublease their mining land to corporations composed of noncitizens. At this juncture, leases began to be granted to associations of five to twenty Cherokees, whereas before the maximum allowed to join in a lease was two or three. In this way it was possible to bypass tribal restrictions on individual holdings in order to control a field large enough to make a sublease feasible. Byrd himself organized such an "association," calling it Hugh B. Henry & Co., and took a lease to several large tracts totaling 740,000 acres, which were then subleased to the United States Oil Company, Martin Hellar, general manager. The pioneers had struck oil, and, suddenly, they were a corporation.[17]

John Adair, a Cherokee delegate in Washington, was completely taken aback by the latest developments. He had been instructed to lobby against a bill then pending in the Congress to allow Indians to sublease coal banks to corporations, on the grounds that corporate leases would compromise Indian sovereignty. He made eloquent arguments and had just reported that the bill was "a dog too dead to skin" when he got news that the Cherokee National Council itself had approved the 1890 bill providing for subleasing to oil corporations.[18] How then did Congress view his credibility? He found himself in a position similar to members of the tribe who complained about railway entry in 1866, only to find that other members of the tribe were actively promoting it. Such disunity over what actually constituted the collective will of "the Indian" continued to be an important reason for corporate success in influencing federal policy.

17. Act of Dec. 6, 1890, Cherokee vol. 295, pp. 133–37; Cherokee National Register of Mineral Licenses Issued. . . . 1884–94, Cherokee vol. 336, IAD. *Tulsa Daily World*, Sept. 4, 1932.

18. John Adair, *Protest Against Joint Resolution 114 and House Joint Resolution 193*, July 25, 1890; John Adair to "Harris," Aug. 6, 1890, Cherokee Mineral File (Tahlequah acquisition), IAD.

United States Oil Corporation was not very lucky in finding oil. It employed W. B. Linn and J. B. Phillips of Pennsylvania as drilling experts but still lost three strings of tools in dry holes in the year 1893 alone. Byrd's mineral report to the Cherokee for the last quarter of 1891 listed twelve barrels of oil pumped, and enclosed a royalty payment of $1.20, the first evidence of commercial production. The company did have high hopes. It was capitalized at $1 million and attracted as investors a number of prominent Wichitans, including Finley Ross and William C. Woodman. But failures in the field caused a reorganization in 1895. The company sold its eleven wells for twenty-five cents on the dollar to the Cherokee Oil and Gas Company, which had more wealthy backers.[19]

These initial acts to establish corporate petroleum operations within the framework of tribal sovereignty were jeopardized by efforts in the U.S. Congress to pass a bill that assigned to the federal government the right to regulate mining operations in Indian Territory. Rep. Charles Curtis of Kansas, himself part Indian, was the major sponsor of a bill known as "An Act for the Protection of the People of the Indian Territory, and for other Purposes" (commonly called the Curtis Act), which not only gave the secretary of the interior control of mineral leasing but confirmed Choctaw and Creek agreements to allot land in severalty and set policy for what, it was hoped, would be immediate allotment agreements from other tribes. The mineral clause of the bill, as it was in the final version passed in 1898, ruled that leases not approved by the secretary of the interior, regardless of approval by Indian legislatures, were void.[20]

The most eloquent Indian arguments against the Curtis bill came from D. W. C. Duncan of the Cherokee Nation, writing under the name Too-qua-stee. It was, he said, another device for disin-

19. *Tulsa Daily World*, Sept. 4, 1932. Edward Byrd to Treasurer, Jan. 9, 1892, Cherokee Mineral File (Tahlequah acquisition), IAD. *Tulsa Daily World*, Sept. 4, 1932. For more detail on this phase, see H. Craig Miner, "The Cherokee Oil and Gas Co., 1889–1902: Indian Sovereignty and Economic Change," pp. 54–55.

20. U.S., *Statutes at Large*, XXX, 495.

heriting the Indian under the guise of protecting him. What did it matter that the bill made provision for payment of Indians for land taken for mining? What did it matter how exalted was the federal officer put in the place of the tribal will? Whites seemed to labor under the delusion that official dignity could change evil into good "by a kind of moral magic . . . as if homeless starvation were a misery less to be dreaded when brought on under governmental supervision, than it would be as the result of depredations committed by a Dalton gang." It was like telling people it was fine to die because they could look forward to a nice funeral. Would the Congress authorize the tearing down of President McKinley's home so that the coal under it could be used "to set the furnaces of industry ablaze, and to send the cars of commerce abroad"? Duncan concluded, sadly, that the only reason this state of affairs ever developed was that in 1866 "the backbone of patriotism" was broken within the tribes "and speculation took the saddle." But this last indignity, at least, should not be taken smiling, should not be counted up to promotion and consent on the part of the Indians. If the Indian could no longer stand up for his rights, let him lie down beside them "and let the car wheels of ruin drive over us," keeping in the end, at a minimum, some shred of dignity. Wrote Too-qua-stee: "The fawn in the clutches of the panther will bleat for mercy; and it is useless to coax it to hold its peace by telling it that its bleating is useless, in vain. . . . When death gets hold of a man and begins to drag him down, he is pretty apt to bring a groan or two in the time of it."[21]

When the Curtis bill was debated in Congress in June 1898 its direct relationship to the question of Indian sovereignty did not go entirely unnoticed. The debaters, however, failed to meet the philosophical question directly, but talked, as practical men will, of symptoms. Tribal authority was being abused by intermarried whites and Indian speculators who, in the manner of Hugh B. Henry & Co., had fenced large tracts, thus cutting out the full blood, "the real Indian whom we undertake to protect by this legislation." "It is well known," cried one congressman during the debates, "that these tribal

21. *Vinita Chieftain*, Sept. 1, 1896; June 10, 1897; Jan. 20, 1898.

governments are corrupt; it is well known that nearly all the property of the tribes heretofore has been absorbed by a few." Duncan wrote, from his seat in the gallery, that the Indian Territory was regarded as a prize for raffle "and the number of gamesters that are competing in order to win, the subtle influences brought to bear to mislead the legislative mind . . . are not only amazing, but to one without special culture in that kind of business, quite incomprehensible." [22]

These interests determined the direction of debate. Lobbyists from a corporation wished to sell land in Mexico to the Indians in case the new bill entirely disinherited them. [23] Also, naturally, there were the men who wanted to get in on the leasing that would follow passage. Duncan commented that the surface of the country would then be dotted with leases as

> thick . . . as pocks on the wings of a guinea hen; there will be oil leases, asphalt leases, gold leases, stone leases, marble leases, granite leases, air leases, and possibly the very blessed light of the sun (should it prove capitalizable) may be captured and monopolized by some shrewd speculator under one of Charlie Curtis' wonderful lease-traps. [24]

The Cherokee delegation could obtain no access to the rooms of committees deliberating upon the bill, and two letters which they wrote were unanswered. Meanwhile, corporate representatives went in and out at will. [25]

The measure was called to a vote as members of the second session of the Fifty-Fifth Congress were packing their trunks and getting ready to go home. The galleries were almost empty that day in late June, except for a few Indian delegates who looked over the railing at the mostly empty seats below. There was no quorum; a roll call would have revealed that there were only a dozen men in the Senate. For two hours a Senator introduced amendments, which routinely

22. *Congressional Record*, 55th Cong., 2d sess., XXXI, 5552–54. *Vinita Chieftain*, March 31, 1898.

23. Ibid., March 26, 1898.

24. Ibid., Aug. 25, 1898.

25. Cherokee delegation to National Council, Aug. 1898, Cherokee-U.S. Government box, OU.

passed "with little outside of the Indian ring, besides the gloomy walls of the old chamber, to witness, or care for what was going on." The Indians sat, said Duncan, "with mingled feelings of helpless contempt upon the false assumptions of fact, the hypocrisies of argument, and the injustice of conclusions, which pushed on to consummation, this most remarkable act in the great drama of civilization."[26] The Curtis bill became law.

Nor was there rejoicing in the offices of Cherokee Oil and Gas Company. This legislation voided all tribal contracts unless approval of the Interior Department could be obtained. The company applied and got vague answers. It was caught in the middle of a sovereignty fight, with its fate in the hands of a group of overworked Interior Department clerks, themselves unsure of a proper interpretation of the Curtis Act.[27]

To complicate things further, the Cherokees decided to take this chance to stop oil development altogether. Meeting with the Dawes Commission (created in 1893 to negotiate the Five Tribes' allotment) shortly after passage of the Curtis Act, Cherokee representatives asked that all existing leases be voided and that the secretary of the interior be denied authority to grant any additional leases.[28] The Cherokee Oil and Gas Company viewed this as blatant irresponsibility, a playing of what businessmen called the "baby game."[29] The new Cherokee resolution, submitted to Congress in 1900 as an "Agreement" (treaties were not negotiated after 1871), cost CO&G the chance to sell its potentially rich wellsites to a British corporation, the Cherokee Exploration Syndicate Ltd., 4 Bishopsgate Within, London. It also made it less likely that the American company would ever be able to pump and ship the oil behind the caps of its abandoned wells.[30] But

26. *Vinita Chieftain*, June 21, 1900.
27. SMD 213, 56th Cong., 2d sess. (S 4043), p. 12.
28. Proceedings, Joint Sessions of United States and Cherokee Commissions, Dec. 28, 1898, Dawes Commission Cherokee File, IAD.
29. SMD 88, 55th Cong., 3d sess., 1899 (S 3731), p. 15.
30. SMD 213, 56th Cong., 2d sess. (S 4043), pp. 41–43.

the Cherokees had been unprepared. One of them told the Dawes Commission in the 1898–1899 negotiations:

> It is a fact that I am illiterate as compared with the representatives of the Government of the United States. . . . I cannot understand all these questions and cannot readily grasp the situation and master it. . . . I am being shoved along too fast.[31]

The Cherokee Oil & Gas Company was not the only one thus affected. The Cudahy Oil Company had been active in trying to locate a well within the town limits of Vinita, Cherokee Nation, and had drilled at Muskogee in the Creek country. By 1899, it had spent $30,000 in the Creek Nation alone, and owned an eighteen-hundred-foot well at Red Fork and a twenty-eight-hundred-foot well at Eufaula. Both of the wells were producing, but had to be abandoned at the time of the Curtis Act until the validity of the leases for the land upon which they were located could be determined. In the Choctaw Nation, all of the equipment of the Choctaw Exploration Syndicate Ltd., which had bought in at precisely the wrong time, was sold by court order in 1899. This came at a time when at last it seemed that petroleum might pay here. In 1894 total production for Indian Territory was 130 barrels, up from 10 barrels the previous year. In 1898, it was 1,020 barrels, and the pioneer companies were not pleased that other corporations should be allowed to cash in while the explorers were denied access to the fields they had opened.[32]

The major discussion in Congress regarding the new Cherokee agreement concerned the provision to eliminate federal control of leases, while at the same time voiding leases previously granted by the tribe. Was this not perhaps a clever way to salvage sovereignty? At first the Congress refused to change anything in the Curtis Act,

31. Proceedings, Joint Sessions, IAD.
32. *Vinita Chieftain*, Jan. 14, 1897, Dec. 15, 1898. J. George Wright to Secretary of Interior, April 15, 1899, box 328; Ainsworth & Burris to J. G. Wright, Jan. 22, 1900, box 324, ITD. U.S. Geological Survey, *Annual Report.* . . . (Washington, D.C., 1895), p. 380.

but the Cherokees could not be forced to ratify such an agreement. Upon resubmission there was disagreement, and the issue went to a conference committee, which in 1901 collected information on the petroleum question in Indian Territory.[33]

William Linn of the Cherokee Oil and Gas Company told the congressmen that it was unfair to shut down the wells, as he had had informal assurances from the secretary of the interior in 1896 that the tribe had authority to lease. Linn, like the cattlemen before him, was surprised to learn that the informality of these agreements could result in their being reversed. His hope now was that the secretary would ratify the company's lease. Idle land was psychologically frustrating to men like Linn, who yearned to put the Indian oil business upon a "practical and paying basis." He did not neglect to mention, either, that in supporting the Cherokee Oil and Gas Company, the Congress would be supporting a struggling independent against the rapacious Standard Oil monopoly. As in 1882, when Gould was the diversion, in 1901, with Standard Oil the ogre of the day, the temporary economic and political balance within the United States obscured far-ranging philosophical considerations of Indian rights. "These are not speculative theories or dreams," Linn emphasized, "but facts."[34]

As though following a script, the next act of a by now familiar pattern was played out here also—the split among Indians. Richard Adams, an attorney for the Delaware Indians, appeared before the committee. The Delawares, moved from Kansas in 1866, had been promised 157,000 acres of Cherokee lands, but because of bureaucratic delays their exact location had not been determined by 1901. Adams now held that the Delawares had been farming land just where the CO&G wellsites were located and that cancellation of the lease would deprive them of their right to royalty. The Cherokees responded that the Delawares had shown no interest in the land until they began to profit from the oil and that Adams himself, if he could

33. *Congressional Record*, 56th Cong., 2d sess., XXXIV, 585, 703, 707.
34. SMD 213 (S 4043), pp. 12–14.

obtain the land for the tribe, was to get most of the mineral income.[35] Adams, the Cherokees noted, was adjusted to white civilization in much the way E. C. Boudinot was. He lived in a three-story house in Washington where he gave champagne parties and peddled influence.[36] To involve him now "would only further entangle the already wonderfully complicated situation in the Cherokee Nation."[37]

The Keetoowah Society, a traditionalist Cherokee group, thought that, at the turn of the century, it was clear enough that it was not for the welfare of the Indians "that the powerful syndicates and corporations are turning heaven and earth to get control of [our] land."[38] Rather, it was because some tantalizing developments had made vague hopes into realistic expectations. The Spindletop strike near Beaumont, Texas, had produced "spouters" flowing at many times the rate than any oil well had been known to produce before. Wells were being drilled in the Osage Nation, just west of the Cherokees, and in June 1901 at Red Fork, Creek Nation, a gusher was struck that blew thirty feet over the top of the derrick. The promoters of that well instituted a nationwide campaign of publicity that made Red Fork into a boom town and brought the attention of many around the country to the difficulties of Indian Territory oilmen.[39] Muskogee was "all ablaze" with talk and new corporations. The firm of Guffey & Galey, whom some thought were the drilling team for Standard Oil, was reported in the field.[40] Edwin Ludlow, an employee of one of the

35. Ibid., p. 22; pp. 35–39; W. A. Jones to Secretary of Interior, March 28, 1899, box 372; Frank Churchill to Secretary of Interior, Nov. 4, 1899, box 327, ITD; for Adams complaints when he later failed to collect his lands, see Richard Adams to President, April 11, 1904, box 373, ITD.

36. *Kansas City Journal*, Oct. 4, 1903, clipping in box 43, II, p. 81, E. A. Hitchcock Papers, RG 316, NA.

37. SMD 333, 56th Cong., 1st sess., 1900 (S 3868), p. 6.

38. Ibid.

39. Rister, *Oil*, pp. 80–81; Fred S. Clinton, "First Oil and Gas Well in Tulsa County." Both the OU manuscript division and the Library of the Oklahoma Historical Society have manuscript collections on the Red Fork strike.

40. *Muskogee Phoenix*, June 27, July 4, 1901.

mines in the Choctaw Nation, wrote his wife that he was afraid the new oil boom in the Territory would destroy the coal business. To be secure, he was himself investing in oil stocks "as I have been getting the oil fever since I have been reading the Texas papers and want to speculate a little myself."[41]

In this confused environment the congressional conference committee tried to make its decision about who should control mineral leases in the Cherokee Nation, and, by implication, in the rest of the Indian Territory. Important as it was to have some guidelines, the committee did not provide them. The agreement stated that Section XIII of the Curtis Act, giving the secretary of the interior control over minerals on tribal lands would not apply to the Cherokees. Its statement regarding the validity of past leases granted by the Indians was a masterpiece of evasion, "That nothing in this act shall be held or construed to change, alter or modify or impair any existing coal or oil rights heretofore acquired by lease, location, development or otherwise, or to ratify, confirm, recognize, or validate any such rights." Curtis said that by this "we simply leave the parties in their present condition." That was enough for Congress, which passed the agreement as it emerged from committee. The weary tribe ratified it. In fact, the secretary of the interior would assume control of Cherokee leasing anyway, although he admitted there was no "official information" on the subject. But no one in the federal establishment was willing to explain and to justify this course formally, important as it was to the political future of the American Indian. As had been the case since 1866, circumstance was allowed to buffet policy as it would, giving power a great advantage over justice.[42]

Lobbyists converged upon the Interior Department following the passage of the agreement seeking confirmation of 94,000 acres of

41. Edwin Ludlow to wife, [Feb., 1901], Minor MSS H–48, OU.

42. *Congressional Record*, 56th Cong., 2d sess., XXXIV, 3932. Charles J. Kappler, *Indian Affairs: Laws and Treaties*, vol. 1, pp. 727, 729. A. C. Conner to Secretary of Interior, March 3, 1899, in Grant Foreman, comp., "Transcripts of Documents in the Office of the Supt. for the Five Civilized Tribes" (typescript), Cherokee vol. XIII, p. 135, IAD.

the lease of the Cherokee Oil & Gas Company. In the spring of 1901, Interior Secretary Ethan A. Hitchcock wrote that he was "inclined to deny" this. Indian analysts also felt that the petition would fail, not because Indian rights would be considered, but because the scramble for leases, would cause breeches in party organization. However, the other side had confidence also, believing that the Curtis Act was "the key that opened the Indian nation."[43]

The Indian case was managed by a number of people with different viewpoints: Cherokee attorneys, Delaware attorneys, attorneys representing individual claimants, and Cherokee leaders like Chief T. M. Buffington and Robert Owen, both of whom were charged with secretly investing in the CO&G company. The oil company, on the other hand, presented a united case, prepared by Samuel Crawford, former governor of Kansas, and John Thurston, lately chairman of the conference committee that had sidestepped the issue. The corporation also had informal contacts with Washington. In 1899, Lizzie Shaw Turnbull, wife of a stockholder, wrote to then Secretary of the Interior Webster Davis at home. She used her maiden name because "I want to get very *near to you*," and pled that hundreds of investors could be saved by "a few strokes of your magic pen."[44]

In more formal correspondence investors took the line that the Cherokees could not so easily avoid their obligations and object to the leases just when the oil runs came in. Surely the Department could not abide a wasteful situation, especially since the company had complied "in every essential particular" with Cherokee regulations. The Indians, wrote attorney Crawford, must "be made to understand that they as well as other people are answerable to the law." Linn wrote that the well sites were such a "literal wreck" that it caused him physical discomfort to talk about it. Vandals were destroying the tanks and stealing the pipe. Edward Byrd, who was yet connected

43. E. A. Hitchcock to Commissioner of Indian Affairs, July 11, 1901, Cherokee Mineral File (Tahlequah acquisition), IAD. *Vinita Chieftain*, Sept. 24, 1901. *Bartlesville Magnet*, June 22, 1901.

44. SMD 213 (S 4043), p. 45. Lizzie Turnbull to Webster Davis, Jan. 1, 1899, box 327, ITD.

with the company, wrote that he had been a loyal Republican but might change loyalties "if my own party won't stand by me . . . in time of distress on the lines of justice and equity in my declining years with an invalid wife to care for." Byrd thought it was horrible that the first man in the Indian Territory oil business should be left "poor as a Church Mouse" because of federal maneuvering.[45]

The Indians were equally clever. A delegation called upon President Theodore Roosevelt and swapped tales of the Spanish-American War, while attorneys authored briefs.[46] In 1899, when Lizzie Turnbull was making her earthy appeal, Walter Logan, for the Delawares, was making a highly abstract philosophic plea. The Cherokee Oil and Gas Company, he argued, was part of a great unseen monopoly, maybe a British syndicate "of magnificent proportions" seeking to get control of the American economy, or maybe Standard Oil. More than that, the Indian was temperamentally unsuited to industrial civilization, as he had formed his character under different conditions. "The Indian's hatred of monopolies and the industrial system . . . is a part of the nervous structure he has inherited from his ancestors. It would take generations to remove it if it ever could be removed at all."[47] William Springer, who had once represented Illinois in Congress and sponsored territorial bills, was now also eloquent for the Indians in return for a fee. Mining losses were common, he wrote, and they must be absorbed by those who speculated.[48] Richard Adams added that it was odd that the secretary should consider giving the company 94,000 acres in several separate leases when the obvious intent of the Curtis Act, which limited leases to 640 acres, was to prevent monopolization. Would the Indians be subjected to the worst of the Curtis

45. Samuel Crawford to Thos. Ryan, May 22, 1901; W. B. Linn to Samuel Crawford, May 18, 1901, box 328, ITD. E. Byrd to E. A. Hitchcock, Aug. 14, 1900, box 325, ITD.

46. William Springer to T. M. Buffington, Sept. 30, 1901, Cherokee-U.S. Government Box, OU.

47. Walter Logan, Brief on Behalf of the Delaware Indians (page proof), Dec. 9, 1899, pp. 4, 7, box 325, ITD.

48. William Springer, *Brief and Argument of Cherokees in Response to Brief and Argument of Applicant,* Oct. 5, 1901, p. 6, box 328, ibid.

Act and be denied its protections?[49] To these arguments Chief Buffington, imposing at 6′5″ and 300 lbs., added a moving public letter:

> Let us have peace. There is no longer a question of policy, for we Indians have overwhelmingly expressed ourselves as acquiescing in the policy of your government towards us. It is a matter of detail. . . . Mr. Secretary, the good Book shows you that the alloted time of man is three score years and ten. God in his wisdom has fixed it about this way; he gives man three score years to live and ten in which to die. Remember that this nation has flourished for more than seven hundred years. Ought it not be permitted to have at least one third of the time of the human, while tottering down the hill, in settling the necessary details of the distribution of its efforts among its heirs. . . . Can you [grant the lease] and satisfy conscience because we are weak.[50]

The secretary could. In October, Hitchcock granted to the Cherokee Oil and Gas Company twelve separate leases covering 11,500 acres. An Indian editor called the decision "the entering wedge for the ultimate looting of the national estate." From the Interior Department came only the "stereotyped answer" the "existing circumstances" made this course inevitable. "This answer," reported the aggressive *Chieftain*, "encompasses all the satisfaction that the Indian has awaiting him in Washington, and any petition he may have will be railroaded to the archives, marked 'disapproved.'" It is in the archives that these memorials are today to be found.[51]

The last act of the Cherokees in the struggle over oil leases was to sue Secretary Hitchcock, attempting to get an injunction from the U.S. Supreme Court to stop him from granting oil leases. The case was heard by the high court in 1902, and it decided that Indians held title to their lands in trust, contingent upon that trust being "properly executed." The Cherokee fee-simple deed was only a piece of paper,

49. R. C. Adams, *In Answer to Brief of Cherokee Oil & Gas Company* (Vinita, 1901), pp. 7–8, box 325, ibid.

50. *Chief Buffington's Protest Against Leases* (n.p., n.d.), #1738, Cherokee Minerals File (Muskogee acquisition), IAD.

51. E. A. Hitchcock to Indian Inspector, July 12, 1902, Foreman transcript, Cherokee vol. XIII, pp. 182–93, IAD.; *Vinita Chieftain*, Aug. 29; Aug. 23, 1901.

and they were allowed to play at sovereignty only so long as it suited the United States, which held ultimate title. There was no deep questioning of what constituted "proper" use of the land. To an age that spoke of the "cash value" of ideals, proper use was oil drilling. The chief of the Cherokees was befuddled by the decision. "While the white men carry things through at railway speed," he observed, "the Indians are a little slow."[52]

In 1902, the tribes had only a few years left as sovereign groups. To complete the change of tone the corporation began in 1866, even the fading Indian political system would finally be engraved with the signs and symbols of industrial civilization. Hearings on oil pipeline rights of way were reminiscent of the old railway right-of-way debates of the seventies, except that what was then a triangle of interests narrowed to arguments between corporations and government. It was the twentieth century coming on, but coming so suddenly to the Indian that its ugly side is, in looking back, especially striking. Robert Ross, former chief of the Cherokees, compared the tribes in 1899 to a family drifting on a barge without a rudder and nearing a great cataract.[53]

There was one place in the Cherokee Nation, however, where the reaction to the Cherokee Oil and Gas decision was different—Bartlesville. Located at the northwestern edge of the Cherokee Nation, Bartlesville was booming as the result of large strikes in the Osage reserve to the west. The town was full of whites and Indian progressives who were excited by the old delusion that everyone could become rich and powerful, whether traditional Indian political forms survived or not. Gnashing of teeth at the petite leasehold of Cherokee Oil and Gas failed to put affairs in the perspective of the 1.5 million-acre Osage blanket lease engineered in 1896 by Edwin Foster. Bartlesville, with its gas lights and casually stored blasting torpedoes, depended upon oil and intended to promote corporate privilege upon Indian lands despite the "rot and mendacity" of de-

52. *Cherokee Nation et al. Appts.* v. *Ethan A. Hitchcock, Secretary of the Interior,* 187 US 183 (1902). *Indian Citizen,* Nov. 23, 1893.
53. *Vinita Chieftain,* Jan. 26, 1899.

fenders of Indian rights. Wrote the editor of its newspaper, the *Magnet*: "The 'oil pirates' are only mythical anyhow, a something after the order of big snakes and winged elephants a man is . . . apt to see after drinking a bottle or two."[54] Here at the Osage border was played the most dramatic act, the one most full of contrast, in the dialogue of corporation and Indian. Before it was over, Bartlesville would see its own visions, the Osages would dream dreams.

54. *Bartlesville Magnet*, June 15, 1901, Aug. 10, 1902.

CHAPTER IX

CABLE OSAGE, NEW YORK

The Osages were an anomaly among anomalies. Payment for their Kansas lands made them, if their trust funds in Washington were considered as available income, the richest people per capita in the world, yet they retained a primitive, traditional way of life. They were pointed to by cynics as proof that even money could not change the backward habits of the Indian race. But in the 1890s, there were signs of change. White Horn expressed it in 1895 by saying that he did not want his son to grow up to be like him, isolated and alienated from the world as it had become: "Look at me; what use am I? I am a useless man. . . . I have not any ideas and am guided by others. I hardly feel able to discuss my own rights just for the want of intelligence." Confidence was slipping. Years of being on the outside of the culture of industry, and being ridiculed for it, were taking their toll. Said White Horn of his son, "My idea is to force him into a different life and to be a different man who will not only be useful to himself, but also to his peoples."[1]

In October 1895 Henry Foster, then living in the oil equipment supply center of Independence, Missouri, made a verbal application to the commissioner of Indian affairs to contract for the exclusive privilege of prospecting and boring for oil and gas on the Osage reserve over a period of ten years. Foster had talked informally about this with Washington officials as early as 1891, when the Osages passed legislation allowing mineral leases. Commissioner D. M. Browning explained the request to Osage agent Henry Freeman,

1. Talk with Osage delegation, March 8, 1895, box 415046, Osage Admin. Misc., FRC (for "Abbreviations in Footnotes," see p. vii).

warning him to look over the proposal with great care, and to re-member, in making his recommendation, that the Osages really did not need the income oil development might bring. The agent was also asked to consider what effect oil leases might have on the tribe's attitude toward allotment of their lands and sale of the sur-plus, something in which the settlers of Oklahoma Territory were much interested. What impact would the introduction of the whites who would work in the oil industry have upon the already great difficulties of managing the reservation?[2]

Freeman's reply was positive, and in it he advised that a lease should be negotiated at a royalty for the tribe of 10 per cent on oil and fifty dollars for each gas well. Browning forwarded this opinion to Foster, noting that the agent was not authorized at this point to present the matter to the Osage council or discuss it with the Indians at all. Also, the Indian commissioner had not informed the secretary of the interior about the details of the plan, especially the provision granting exclusive rights for the entire reserve to one corporation to be formed by Foster. Even so, there was the informal governmental assurance that had played so great a role in every corporate approach to the tribes theretofore. Browning wrote Foster in late January 1896 that the latter could "tacitly understand" that the Indian Office would recommend favorable consideration for any lease he might negotiate.[3]

Things moved quickly after that at Pawhuska, the Osage capital. After some discussion, a bill leasing the whole reserve to Edwin Foster (his brother Henry had died suddenly) passed the Osage business council on March 14, 1896, by a vote of 7 to 6. It granted a nearly 1.5 million-acre lease, twice the size of Foster's native state of Rhode Island, on the conditions that oil must be discovered with-in eighteen months and drilling must not thereafter be abandoned for more than six months. If the tribe became extinct during the ten-year term of the lease, the instrument was void, but if its lands

2. D. M. Browning to Henry Freeman, Dec. 15, 1895, ibid.
3. D. M. Browning to Henry Foster, Jan. 24, 1896, ibid.

were allotted, royalties would simply go to the individual owners rather than the tribe as a whole.[4]

No proceedings for that day survive among the Osage tribal records, but the interpreter attached a certificate to the lease stating that he, along with Foster and his companion, James Glenn, had fully explained the consequences of the agreement to the Indians in their own language. It passed in competition with several hastily drawn alternative proposals for blanket leases, one presented by Osage half blood Julian Trumbly. Foster and his representatives always argued that the terms were fair, considering that there was at that time not even a way to transport the oil to any market, and that, in fact, the years 1896–1905 were for their company a period of "privation, trouble, loss and bankruptcy." Still in retrospect, the names of the two Osage lease signers, Saucy Chief and James Bigheart, have allegorical significance. Before 1952, 20,805 wells were to be drilled in the Osage Nation, and the value of the production would exceed $300 million. Forty-four per cent of all tracts subleased produced oil or gas. The Osage reserve, taken from the Cherokees for the benefit of a primitive tribe driven from Kansas by town-site speculators, was practically made of petroleum.[5]

When the lease arrived in Washington for federal approval, there came with it protests from the tribe. Saucy Chief and several others stated that the Osages had not properly understood and that the close vote of the council, with one member who would have voted against it absent, did not reflect the real will of the tribe. This document of protest had 175 signers and, although the commissioner of Indian affairs doubted its authenticity, did result in instructions to agent Freeman to investigate the matter. However, no investigation

4. Copy of lease in *Argument and Petition for Renewal of Oil and Gas Leases in the Osage Nation, Oklahoma*, box 414421, ibid.; Information on vote in F. L. Campbell to Secretary of Interior, Oct. 1, 1897, box 244, SC 191.

5. F. L. Campbell to Secretary of Interior, Oct. 1, 1897, box 244, SC 191. *Argument and Petition*, p. 42, box 414421, Osage Admin. Misc., FRC. Bureau of Indian Affairs, *The Osage People and Their Trust Property*, April 30, 1953, field report at Frank Phillips Collection, OU.

was mounted before the lease was affirmed. The request for investigation was sent on April 6, and on April 8 a clerk serving as acting secretary of the interior approved the lease. This was done in the absence of Secretary Hoke Smith, but not, one would guess, without his knowledge. Freeman's report on his investigation of the protest arrived in Washington two months later.[6]

The agent's report said that the protest was not legitimate. Since the lease had already been confirmed, there must have been officials in Washington who had some knowledge of Freeman's opinion before a single inquiry was made. The origin of it, Freeman wrote, was a meeting at the town of Cleveland, Oklahoma Territory, between some Osages and J. L. Morphis and R. L. Dunlap, traders with whom Osage agents had had much trouble. Morphis was a former congressman from Mississippi, and Dunlap was an expert whiskey trader and hog stealer, according to all reports. Dunlap, at Cleveland, made a speech to about five hundred Osages, who were reportedly drunk, asking them to defeat the Foster lease so that their friends might do better for them. They were told that former Senator Blair thought the lease could be defeated for $500 and asked for money from the Osage fund for this purpose. Blair, Morphis, and Dunlap also demanded a more careful investigation, and some senators wrote the Department of the Interior that they trusted the lease would not be affirmed until an investigation was made, not knowing how far the deal had progressed. No investigation was made by the Congress until 1898. Osages were prohibited from going to Cleveland without a permit. Meanwhile, a new corporation went to work.[7]

6. Saucy Chief et al. to Hoke Smith, n.d. [c. April 3, 1896], tray 244, SC 191. D. M. Browning to H. B. Freeman (telegram), April 6, 1896; D. M. Browning to H. B. Freeman, April 11, 1896, box 415047, Osage Admin. Misc., FRC; H. B. Freeman to Commissioner of Indian Affairs, June 6, 1896, Osage LS Misc., #18, p. 10, box 414775, FRC.

7. H. B. Freeman to Commissioner of Indian Affairs, June 6, 1896, Osage LS Misc., #18, p. 10, box 414775, FRC; H. B. Freeman to Commissioner of Indian Affairs, Aug. 8, 1896; M. F. Eliott to John Reynolds, April 22, 1896, tray 244, SC 191. Henry Blair to Hoke Smith, July 14, 1896, tray 244, SC 191; P. F. Pettigrew to Secretary of Interior, Nov. 19, 1896, tray 223, SC 191.

The lease was made to Edwin Foster, an individual. He transferred it immediately to the Phoenix (or Phenix, as Foster spelled it) Oil Company, a corporation. J. A. Glenn, Foster's operating manager, began drilling test wells along the Kansas line, though agent Freeman was suspicious of the slow pace and vulnerable to inquiries he received from richer competitors, Standard Oil, for example. On October 27, 1896, Foster sent Freeman some well logs and emphasized that the newest site "smelled strongly of the crude petroleum." The corporate letterhead was at least impressive if the production was not: "The Phenix Oil Co. Main Office 54 Broad St. New York. Branch Office 494 Ellicott Square, Buffalo. Cable Address 'Osage, New York.' "[8]

Given the magnitude of the lease, the federal government reacted slowly to the questionable nature of the operations. Freeman was called to Washington early in 1897 to report on oil leases, but he saw few people and said little. Then, in December of the same year, special investigator C. F. Nesler, who was in Pawhuska to look into fraudulent farming leases, noticed the Foster oil lease in a box filled with farming leases. The lease material is to this day filed in the same way in Washington and must have been so filed then—information upon a huge oil lease indiscriminately filed among rows of boxes containing the records of routine farming operations. Nesler immediately telegraphed Washington that he thought the terms of this lease were too broad. The response was surprise. Many officials in the Indian Office seem never to have heard of the Foster oil lease.[9]

It was found, upon investigation, that Foster had submitted no report to the Osages of striking any wells, nor had he given them

8. Frank Finney, "The Indian Territory Illuminating Oil Company," pp. 152–53. H. B. Freeman to Commissioner of Indian Affairs, Aug. 8, 1896, Osage LS Misc. #18, pp. 122–26; H. B. Freeman to E. B. Foster, Oct. 15, 1896, p. 249, box 414775, FRC. J. A. Glenn to H. B. Freeman, July 16, 1896, box 415047, Osage Admin. Misc., FRC.

9. D. M. Browning to H. B. Freeman (telegram), Feb. 9, 1897, ibid. C. F. Nelser to Secretary of Interior, Dec. 20, 1897, tray 238, SC 191.

any royalty. He quickly remedied that in January 1898 by sending the tribe fifteen dollars and a letter saying that he had struck oil near Bartlesville in October, just in time to meet the lease deadline, and that it pumped twenty barrels a day until it was shut down for lack of transportation for the product. He sent to Washington affidavits from two men who worked on the well, specifying its completion date. Nevertheless, the commissioner of Indian affairs asked Foster in February to show cause why the lease should not be cancelled. A new Osage agent, William Pollack, reported that the Bartlesville well had not been completed on time. With this report in hand and no sufficient reply from Foster, the secretary of the interior cancelled the Foster lease on June 27, 1898.[10]

But, although great emphasis had been placed upon the finality of the lease confirmation by a clerk in 1896, no such aura surrounded the decision to cancel it. The documents in the case were sent to the assistant attorney general for the Interior Department, who held in July that only the Osages could cancel the lease and that in order for them to do so legally it must be demonstrated that they themselves knew the time had lapsed. Their agent, Pollack, spoke with them about this, and convinced them to write a letter saying that the royalty they had accepted in January did not imply recognition of the Phoenix company lease. A second payment was returned. On August 30, the Osage council cancelled the lease also. It appeared Foster's chances were gone. The secretary wrote him once more, got no reply, and so, on November 11, decided a second time that the lease was cancelled.[11]

10. Edwin Foster to Osage National Treasurer, Jan. 6, 1898, box 415048, Osage Admin. Misc., FRC. Affadavits of Granville Adkins and S. O. Bapst, 1897, tray 244, SC 191. W. A. Jones to H. B. Freeman, Feb. 19, 1898, box 415048, Osage Admin. Misc., FRC. William J. Pollock to Commissioner of Indian Affairs, June 18, 1898; Secretary of Interior to Commissioner of Indian Affairs, June 27, 1898, tray 244, SC 191.

11. Assistant Attorney General to Secretary of Interior, July 12, 1898, box 415048, Osage Admin. Misc. FRC. William Pollack to Commissioner of Indian Affairs, Aug. 31, 1898; Saucy Chief to Commissioner of Indian Affairs, Sept.

Foster did not give up, however. He retaliated by claiming that he had not received some of the letters directed to him, while he was too preoccupied with moving his invalid wife to Florida to make a proper response to others. He asked for a new hearing, saying he had an agent in Europe getting funds for a pipeline and that arrangements had been made for the Kansas, Oklahoma Central & Southwestern Railway Company, a Santa Fe subsidiary, to build to the wells. A Santa Fe attorney, S. M. Porter, joined Foster in lobbying for a new hearing, and, despite two decisions to cancel, the requests were granted.[12]

The hearings were conducted in January 1899 at Pollack's office in Pawhuska. Present were Edwin Foster, S. M. Porter, A. P. McBride, Black Dog, Peter Bigheart, Julian Trumbly, No-kah-wah-tun-kah, and John Leahy. McBride (the drilling contractor) advanced the thesis that, although the well had not been completed before the deadline, oil had been discovered while the well was being built and thus was in time. Foster said that economic conditions were now better, with the country recovering from a depression, than they had been, and that his $3 million Phoenix oil company would surely hereafter prosper. The important thing about the transcript of the hearings is that it contains nothing startling, nothing that the Interior Department had not known when it cancelled the lease. Yet Pollack wrote that after the testimony he was convinced that oil prospecting in the West had "passed the experimental stage," and he was therefore willing to reverse his former opinion about the lease in order that the corporation "may be ready to supply the western world with Osage oil at low rates." Although it seems to the historian a specific wording, Pollack argued that the clause in the lease "requiring paying quantities within eighteen months" was too vague

---

19, 1898, tray 244, SC 191. C. N. Bliss to Commissioner of Indian Affairs, Dec. 24, 1898, tray 244, SC 191 (this letter contains a schematic chronology of the events connected with the cancellation).

12. Edwin Foster, statement, Dec. 14, 1898; Edwin Foster to Mr. Vandeventer, Dec. 24, 1898, ibid. S. M. Porter to William Pollack, Jan. 16, 1899, box 415049, Osage Admin. Misc., FRC.

to support a cancellation. In May 1899 the Department of the Interior advised that the lease be allowed to continue in force. Shortly thereafter Pollack resigned as Osage agent, after being convicted of collusion with cattlemen to defraud the tribe. It was the best example to that time of the way in which governmental hesitations allowed the continuance of activities by corporations that were less than clear about their exact responsibility to the Indian tribes.[13]

As an operating company, Phoenix Oil was not successful. By the second quarter of 1900, 200 barrels of oil were produced on the lease, but it was not until the arrival of the railroad at Bartlesville and the striking of several large wells by the Osage Oil Company, an operating subsidiary of Phoenix, that the boom began. In May 1900 the Osage Oil Company made the first shipment of oil, 300 barrels, by rail from Bartlesville. Prospects looked so promising that Phoenix Oil took some leases in its own name. Production went to 2,732 barrels for the quarter ending in July 1900, and natural-gas production by the end of 1900 was 7 million cubic feet a day.[14]

The new business changed Bartlesville much as the railroad had changed Atoka in the seventies. Even the newspaper, the *Magnet*, enjoyed the noise and smell of the industry and made plans to use natural gas to run its presses. Bartlesville had good water and great fuel, the town boasted. The Indian Office only needed to remove obstacles in the way of white people to live and prosper upon Indian lands. The town could even accept the rowdyness connected with a situation such as theirs and laugh at it. In 1901 the newspaper wrote, the holiday season was welcomed with "an inordinate con-

13. Transcript of Hearings, Jan. 3, 1899, ibid. William Pollack to Commissioner of Indian Affairs, April 24, 1899; A. C. Tonner to Secretary of Interior, May 10, 1899, tray 44, SC 191; A. C. Tonner to William Pollack, June 7, 1899, box 415049, Osage Admin. Misc., FRC. *Bartlesville Magnet*, April 20, 1900.

14. E. B. Foster to C. A. Mitscher, Aug, 10, 1900, box 415051, Osage Admin. Misc., FRC. *Bartlesville Magnet*, March 2, May 11, April 17, Dec. 6, 1900.

sumption of squirrel whiskey, cocain cordial, fishberry bitters, hoss liniment and the devil only knows what other beverages." Blanket Osages joined the crowd of men "drunk or delierious from loco-motor ataxia" reeling about the streets. Two days later the sheep-dip supply of the town was completely gone, and the editor exclaimed there was not enough liniment (consumed as a beverage under the name Peruna) left in the city to treat a sick billy goat.[15]

The Bartlesville newspapers kept good track of more construc-tive activity, which would pay it well for tolerating growth pains. It was stated in the *Magnet* that subleasing the tracts should begin on a large scale, as Foster and his backers at the Mechanics Savings Bank in Rhode Island had, after getting the lease, become too con-servative, too content with the small income present production provided. When Edwin Foster died of Bright's disease in December 1901 there was a special wave of interest in this sort of expansion. Michael Cudahy, the other major operator in the region, offered to buy the Phoenix and Osage oil companies and promised to spend $1 million developing the field. In contrast, there were the memorials upon the death of Chief Saucy Chief, who died about the same time as Foster and was remembered as "a leader of a people emerging from barbaric darkness." As capital from the East poured into the region, Mary Corndropper, an Osage girl, was auctioned for marriage to the highest bidder, according to a tribal tradition slow to change.[16]

Rather than turn over the lease to some new set of entrepreneurs, the directors of Foster's companies used the occasion of his death to reorganize more efficiently the corporate structure that carried the Foster lease. In the same month Foster died, a new corporation, the Indian Territory Illuminating Oil Company, was organized in New Jersey to take over the Phoenix and Osage company interests. This company made an important innovation. It decided to act as a broker for the valuable lease franchise rather than operating the wells. It therefore divided the region around Bartlesville into quarter

15. Ibid., Oct. 25, 1900, Nov. 8, 1900, Jan. 10, 1901, Jan. 24, 1901; Feb. 2, 1901.

16. Ibid., Aug. 3; June 1, Nov. 30, Dec. 21; Oct. 19, 1901; Dec. 29, 1899.

section tracts and subleased to ambitious young men whose companies would leave a permanent mark on the oil industry: James Glenn, J. M. Guffey, J. H. Galey, Theodore Barnsdall, George Getty.[17]

H. V. Foster, who was Henry's son, A. P. McBride, and ITIO president F. A. Bates, visiting Bartlesville in 1902 to locate drilling leases, were able to watch the bonanza occur. In April well number ten of the Osage Oil Company was producing 100 barrels a day. In May number eleven spouted over the top of the derrick all one Wednesday, then settled down to 150 barrels of oil and ten million cubic feet of gas a day. Representatives of New York syndicates were seen about town inquiring for leases. The Almeda Oil Company and the St. Louis Asphalt Mining and Manufacturing Company took leases. The ITIO company offered free gas to all farmers on the reservation who would furnish piping to their homes. In August Osage Oil number thirteen became that company's fourth success in a row, and oil was selling for ninety cents a barrel on the loading rack. The same month Almeda number one flowed 40 barrels in nineteen minutes, the best well yet struck in the United States outside of Texas. "It won't be long," said the president of Almeda Oil, "before the Almeda company is shipping oil out of Bartlesville in solid train loads." Standard Oil believed it, and it was rumored that the company was willing to pay $3 million for the Almeda lease. The *Magnet* predicted mass immigration from California to Oklahoma Territory, a kind of dust bowl migration in reverse, to a place where, despite a faint smell of petroleum, "life is like a summer dream." The Indian must stand aside, like a dead man whose affairs are being taken care of by an administrator, "merely a voiceless, passive object oblivious to all that once concerned him."[18]

One of the unique activities connected with this boom and seen in Bartlesville by many whites, not to mention Indians, for the first time was the "shooting" of wells. This was a technique to loosen the formations and allow oil to flow more freely. Osage Oil number

17. Finney, "Illuminating Oil," p. 156.
18. *Bartlesville Magnet*, Feb. 8, April 5, May 10, Aug. 2, Aug. 23, Aug. 30, Sept. 20; July 19; May 17, 1902.

ten was shot in early April, and the affair became a social event, drawing a large crowd intent upon seeing whether nitroglycerine could
be safely handled. George Perry of Neodesha inserted a tube in the
well, poured twenty-five quarts of the "liquid death" into it, and
lowered it 1,345 feet to the bottom of the well. Then a charge was
sent down, and after several false tries there came an explosion and
a thick stream of oil which spouted over the derrick and covered
the watching ladies and gentlemen.[19] Going to a shooting, of the
new frontier type and occasionally the old, became the thing to do
at this extremity of the Indian nation.

Despite the subleasing success of ITIO (it was collecting bonuses
for rentals, no percentage of which it was required to pay the Indians), the Interior Department questioned the chain of title leading
from Edwin Foster to this corporation. The Roosevelt administration
was upset at what came to be regarded by Progressive muckrakers
as "scandalous" behavior on the part of former Interior Secretary
Smith in allowing the original lease to go into force. This new attitude was reflected in a decision not to allow a coal lease upon one
third of the reservation submitted by Charles Reeder in 1903, even
though the terms were exactly the same as the Foster oil lease. It
was, said the Department, "not practicable" to tie up so much land
in any one lease. Vested interest, however, was already in place in the
oil business, and so, following the pattern set earlier in other industries, the government not only allowed it to continue, but to bring in
subsidiary industries necessary to its prosperity. For example, Prairie
Oil and Gas Company, a subsidiary of Standard Oil, was granted
the right to handle and market Bartlesville oil. Attorneys at Washington doubted that this was proper action as policy toward the
Osages, but there was no other way to market the oil in which so
many U.S. citizens had a financial stake.[20]

19. Ibid., April 5, 1902.
20. HD, 376, 58th Cong., 2d sess., 1902 (S 4832), p. 19. Department
officials confessed that they had "very little information" about the nature of
title passed by the Phoenix Oil Company. Also see p. 23 of HD 376. A. C.

The Osages themselves complained about the oil lease in cases when it seemed that the activity ruined the value of the land surface. The arguments about this brought into view again the question of the exact nature of Indian title and Indian sovereignty. The lease prohibited drilling in enclosed pastures, and there were time-consuming hearings to determine what constituted an enclosed pasture or demonstrated Indian occupancy of a tract. Then there was the matter of taking timber for derricks and drill floors. The Osage agent said that timbers were not part of the well and that the companies would have to import them by railroad. Furthermore, he ruled that the drilling companies could not buy timber from individual Indians for this purpose unless the timber were being cleared by him for genuine agricultural purposes and not just to start a business selling rig timbers. The Department at Washington, of course, vacillated. The Office of Indian Affairs first ruled that timber cutting was permissible, thus overruling the agent. The Osages responded that this would result in denuding the land and in increasing the power of oil companies, already acting "like they owned this Osage Country, body, soul and breeches." The timber ruling was therefore changed. In 1904 the assistant attorney general for the interior department ruled that neither the ITIO company nor any sublessee had the right to cut timber for improvements other than those that would remain with the land and become the property of the tribe. By the time of this decision, however, the original lease was running out and operators were turning their attention to terms for a renewal.[21]

Tonner to O. A. Mitscher, Feb. 4, 1903; A. C. Tonner to O. A. Mitscher, Feb. 18, 1903, box 415053, Osage Admin. Misc., FRC.

21. HD 376 (S 4832), 114. The Osage Admin. Misc. document group is filled with arguments upon this issue. W. C. Tucker to E.A.H. [Hitchcock], June 25, 1904, tray 223, SC 191. A. C. Tonner to Frank Conser, July 2, 1904, box 415054, Osage Admin. Misc., FRC. O. B. Clevenger to Commissioner of Indian Affairs, Sept. 27, 1904, box 415054; A. C. Tonner to Frank Frantz, Nov. 9, 1904, box 415055, Osage Admin. Misc., FRC.

The first questions about renewal of the ten-year lease came from sublessees who were afraid to make large investments when the whole franchise might be cancelled in 1906. They therefore wanted "informal assurances" of the type upon which so many businessmen before them had depended. Most persuasive was George Getty, who had organized the Minnehoma Oil Company to operate sublease number fifty on the Osage reserve. Getty sent a barrage of letters arguing that the best petroleum operators in the country were working the Osage field and had already been "repeatedly told" by government officials that their interest would be protected through a renewal. The Indians wanted the royalties. Most important, failure to renew would mean that the field would be open to the "speculator, be he Indian or Caucasian, to attempt to reap an unjust reward at the expense of those whose investment of capital and labor has made the property valuable." The official response was that no guarantees could be given because circumstances might change with regard to government policy toward the Osages before 1906, and the government was, to be sure, much influenced by circumstances.[22]

By the beginning of 1905, the sublessees were "on nettles" about the lease renewal. Standard Oil was lowering the price it paid for crude oil, due to the oversupply from the Osage field, and perhaps, some said, to squeeze out independents in order to take over drilling operations there once the lease expired. By 1905, 361 wells had been drilled on Osage land with only ninety-seven dry holes, and an astonishing investment made—$1.5 million for drilling, a like amount for machinery, and the same for the pipeline. The production was about 115,000 barrels a month, and Osage royalties were running $20,000 a month. Kansans, themselves involved in a giant legislative battle with Standard Oil, were upset that the company could get cheap oil in Oklahoma Territory in order to starve out those pushing regulatory legislation in the north.[23]

22. HD 376 (S 4832), pp. 45–46, 59, 62–64.
23. *Bartlesville Enterprise*, Dec. 23, 1904. Papers accompanying S 6658 (58th Cong., 3d sess.), Records of the U.S. Senate, RG 46, NA. *Bartlesville*

At congressional hearings upon the question of whether the lease renewal should be attached to the 1905 Indian appropriation bill, the divisions so apparent in every tribe made their appearance. Two delegations were sent to the hearings claiming to represent the Osages. One was headed by James Bigheart and the other by Frank Frantz, then Osage agent and later governor of Oklahoma Territory. Both claimed to represent the tribe, both protested the lease, and each objected to the presence of the other. Getting a finer resolution upon the situation, however, reveals some subtle differences. It was charged later that the Frantz group, knowing that it could not, in the 1905 climate of opinion toward trusts, come out in favor of renewing the lease as it stood, opposed that alternative only in order to introduce a scheme to re-lease part of the reservation to ITIO and the rest to James Glenn and George Craig, who were closely bound to the Illuminating Oil Company, and already had proposals in hand. This would provide the appearance of reform without the reality. It was reported in a later full-scale investigation of Frantz that he had spent a great deal of time just before going to Washington with officials of ITIO, including one late-night meeting in his office where there was heavy drinking. Frantz said he merely wanted information, but Secretary of the Interior Hitchcock was suspicious. Hitchcock would not grant Frantz official authority to leave the reservation to come to Washington for the hearings, and, when the agent did so anyway, the secretary for a long time refused to pay his expenses.[24]

The supporters of the corporation were, as usual, united in facing these divisions and therefore gained an advantage. Many congress-

Enterprise, Feb. 17, March 31, 1905. See Francis Schruben, *From Wea Creek to Eldorado: Oil in Kansas, 1860–1920.*

24. Hearings on HR 17478, pp. 4, 34–38, 53, in papers accompanying S 6658 (58, 3), RG 46, NA. William Burns and James McLaughlin to Secretary of Interior, Aug. 14, 1906, box 775, SF 30 (boxes 775–76 contain extensive hearings, depositions, and letters concerning the Frantz investigation). Frank Frantz to Secretary of Interior, Aug. 6, 1906, box 776, SF 30. William Burns and James McLaughlin to Secretary of Interior, Aug. 14, 1906, box 775, SF 30.

men spoke in favor of some sort of lease renewal, even if diminished from its previous size. Edward Vreeland, representing an oil district in New York, said that cancelling the lease would result in a shameless speculation by Osage progressives. "My information is that those Indians who have perhaps a little white blood in them, can scent a dollar perhaps further than a full-blood can." Rep. Joseph Sibley of Pennsylvania chimed in, calling frontier oilmen "rough diamonds." Lewis Emery noted that the United States needed a steady supply of oil to run naval ships and keep the economy going. It was widely believed that the supposed representatives of the Indians were really speaking for Standard Oil. This last argument served the diversionary purpose in the same manner as the argument concerning Gould's railroads had in 1882, insuring that talk never came around to matters of sovereignty, rights, principles. The committees listened politely, not pressing circumstances one way or the other as they developed. Charles Curtis, a committee chairman, admitted that, although he had written the clause providing for release to the Indian Territory Illuminating Oil Company, he knew very little about the implications concerning activity of oil interests upon Indian lands. One of his colleagues replied that "the chairman of this committee is not excelled by any other member of Congress in drawing bills where he does not have knowledge of the subject." The committee room, at that, broke into good-natured laughter.[25]

Company witnesses took up this theme of governmental inability to control relations between numerous companies and numerous individual Indians as a way of justifying the arrangement between the tribe and a single company that existed at the time. In the region of the Five Tribes, as land there was allotted in severalty under several agreements dating from 1897 to 1901, the federal bureaucracy had more than it could do to try to regulate contracts between thousands of individual Indians and thousands of potential users of the land. The Illuminating Oil Company was one identifiable entity and could be held responsible. Secretary Hitchcock said that he got forty-four telegrams in one evening from all parts of the country, all ask-

25. Hearings on HR 17478; pp. 55, 71–72, 139–40; p. 61, RG 46, NA.

ing for renewal of leases and all following a form prescribed by the corporation's public relations department. Commissioner of Indian Affairs Francis Leupp testified that a "large force" of attorneys for the company filled his office "afternoon after afternoon." As a result Hitchcock agreed, in February 1905, to renew the lease for ten years on 640,000 acres. The unified front was as successful as could have been expected. As one businessman put it: "If I am successful here, be glad of it. If my neighbor is not, be sorry, and help him and stay together, and come here with clean hands and ask the government upon what terms we are going ahead to do business." The tribes might have profited from the same spirit.[26]

Neither corporation nor Indian tribe was completely satisfied with the new arrangement. The company did not like the clauses requiring regular drilling, because they limited its options to control supply, and therefore the price paid for oil, by leaving its huge field idle at times. The interests of the Indian as well as the company were best served, representatives of ITIO said, by guaranteeing the best price and therefore the best royalty for every barrel taken out, rather than forcing the rapid depletion of resources sold at a low figure. Part of the tribe was annoyed that any further lease should be made to this company, and the rest pressed for an increase in royalty to the tribe. The company paid the Osages one-tenth of the price realized from oil taken out, while it charged the sublessees one-sixth. The wording of the renewal legislation did provide that the Interior Department could set the rate of royalty, and after some negotiation, it was raised to one-eighth.[27]

In September the second phase of the 1905 leasing campaign began. The Osage Council met to consider propositions to lease the section of the reservation not covered by the revised Foster lease. The action of Frank Frantz in calling for this council without the

26. Ibid., pp. 79–83. SR 4240, 58th Cong., 3d sess., 1905 (S 4756), p. 189; p. 156; p. 11. Hearings on HR 17478, p. 127, RG 46, NA.

27. *Bartlesville Enterprise*, March 3, March 31, 1905. W. S. Leahy to Commissioner of Indian Affairs, April 5, 1905, box 415055, Osage Admin. Misc., FRC; Frank Frantz to F. Leupp, April 12, 1905, tray 238, SC 191.

authorization of the Interior Department directed new suspicions his way. Later investigation provided sworn testimony that a "corruption fund" of $47,000 was arranged by James Glenn, one of the applicants and vice-president of ITIO. This money was reportedly then divided among Frantz and three prominent mixed-blood Osages, two of whom had been members of the Frantz delegation to Washington. Government agents concluded that a similar procedure was followed in December when another large tract was leased. Frantz was, according to the investigator's report, presented with shares in the stock of new companies formed by Glenn and George L. Craig to operate the new leases, and he registered them in a relative's name to conceal his own involvement. It appeared that Frantz had been secretly working on behalf of corporations since before the lease renewal. It was testified that when he went to Washington to protest the renewal, he carried with him $5,000, which he passed out to those most likely to agree to the compromise he was really promoting. This was at a time when his personal finances were in a shambles.[28]

The specific incidents that occurred during the days the new lease instruments were considered by the Osages form a revealing study. Frantz did not submit the lease agreements to the first Osage Council that met after the renewal compromise passed, for fear that there would be competitive bidding. Even so, on September 19, the second day of debates upon the 300,000-acre Glenn lease, Herbert Auerbach, an associate of Buffalo, New York, oil operator Frank Bapst, heard from his room at the Pawhuska House Hotel the bell that announced an Osage Council meeting. He discovered it was called to approve an oil lease. Auerbach first visited his friend H. H. Brenner, president of the First National Bank at Pawhuska. Brenner had investments in ITIO and so told Auerbach that the lease had already been granted and it was too late for new bids. The lobbyist, however, persevered and went to Frantz, who told him to come back later. Auerbach then wired Bapst, threatened publicity, and was al-

28. William Burns and James McLaughlin to Secretary of Interior, Aug. 14, 1906, box 775, SF 30.

lowed to speak to the council, which voted 5 to 3 for a week's delay to allow Bapst to prepare a bid.[29]

The small size of the Osage Council, a body never designed for dealing with corporate pressures, and the established connections among the members of the Illuminating Oil Company insured that this outside threat would fail. A committee of Bacon Rind and other Osages were taken on a tour of the oil fields by Glenn and other ITIO officers. All the advantages of Glenn's new proposal, including a provision for constructing telephone service on the reservation, were explained. Just to insure that the arguments got through, however, some money changed hands. Investigators found that the chief received $500 cash and the promise of $1,000 more. Just before the council reconvened, Bapst's attorney saw the president of the Illuminating Oil Company in earnest conversation with council member Charles Me-she-tse-he, whom, upon inquiry, he found could control the vote. Agent Frantz arranged to be away at a Masonic convention when the council reconvened. Bapst offered a better royalty, but Glenn got the lease.[30] In fairness, it should be said that whatever the power of corruption money there were some legitimate objections to the Bapst proposal recorded in the council proceedings. It asked for a chance to renew at the end of ten years and provided that materials used should revert to Bapst.[31] It was not a matter of practical moment at any rate. In May 1906, when the Office of Indian Affairs got wind of the Glenn and later Craig leases, Interior Secretary Hitchcock refused to approve them.[32]

A number of the friends of Frank Frantz argued at the time of

29. Ibid. Bapst was president of the Barney Oil Company, the German Rock Asphalt Paving Co., and the Buffalo Expanded Metal Company, according to an October 1906 interview with him, Exhibit B in the Frantz investigation.

30. Ibid. Burns's and McLaughlin's fifty-five-page letter of conclusions is an excellent guide to the testimony. One may go, however, to the testimony in the same file for more detail on this.

31. Proceedings of Osage Council, Oct. 1905, tray 246, SC 191.

32. E. A. Hitchcock to Commissioner of Indian Affairs, May 26, 1906, ibid.

the investigation of him that this description of his role was unfair and that the investigation and its conclusions had a political motivation designed to damage Frantz, who was by 1906 the governor of Oklahoma Territory. Their arguments, however, were based upon the fact that Frantz had a lovely wife, three bright children, and an affectionate mother, and therefore could not be "innately bad."[33] There was no positive evidence introduced in response to specific charges. His most powerful defender was President Theodore Roosevelt, interested in protecting the good name of Republican governors and particularly of Frantz, who was a former Rough Rider. He claimed that William T. Burns and James McLaughlin, who conducted the investigation of Frantz in the summer of 1906, were eager to gain power and publicity and so "repeated vicious gossip, and then patched the gossip up by wild guesses of their own."[34] The transcript of the testimony taken by the two, however, remains in the National Archives and speaks for itself. It would be straining to come to any other conclusion than the one reached by Burns and McLaughlin. Certainly, the Osages failed to comprehend the full significance of the series of moves made by Frantz and corporate strategists in 1905. Tradition had little to offer in the face of efficiency. "It is like this," said Bacon Rind in the council, "we are up here to make inquiry into this matter—the people is getting so that they know a little more than they have been—heretofore they never made any inquiry into anything... but right now at the present time they want to look into everything before they make any kind of trade." Frank Bapst turned to the interpreter, "Tell him we know that."[35]

Although the next and last debate about the extension of the

---

33. J. W. Buford to Theodore Roosevelt, June 30, 1906, box 776, SF 30.

34. Theodore Roosevelt to F. E. Leupp, Sept. 18, 1906, Oct. 2, 1906, in Elting E. Morison, ed., *The Letters of Theodore Roosevelt*, vol. 5, pp. 438, 471.

35. Interview transcript, Sept. 28, 1905, tray 246, SC 191. Bapst went on to say, perfectly seriously, that he represented only himself, and no corporation. Bacon Rind knew better, and said, "Of course there is a good many companies and you belong to a good many companies."

Foster lease took place after statehood, it focused again upon the events of the early years in an attempt to destroy at last the scandal of 1896. By 1913, when these discussions began, Osage oil had become a kind of romance of fabulous fortunes and exotic tribal traditions, which was making the Osage Nation a mecca for used car dealers and vendors of expensive gimcracks. "Here are the original natives of the Territory," mused one man, "They are probably as typical a race of Indians as exist in American today." This appealed to the imagination and caused "the gold to flow from the pockets of the unsuspecting, who are always wanting to get into big things." Opponents of any continuance of the Foster lease pointed out that the Wilson administration was pledged to the New Freedom based upon healthy competition, a goal inconsistent with the existence of such a monopoly.[36]

The most colorful attack upon the image of ITIO came from the Oklahoma Independent Producers Association. They argued that, far from being a problem, the Osages would benefit from "the opening of this magnificent domain to the great democracy of wit, energy, and independence of the oil producing public, on equal footing." The defense offered by the Illuminating Oil Company, with its appeals for the welfare of Foster's widow and heirs, was not, said the Association, at all "illuminating." The company merely sought "to foist for a longer period this hoary and sucking barnacle that for nearly twenty years has clutched itself upon the very vitals of this fabulous wealth of the Osage Indians." Attorneys for the association did not find it unusual that in the course of such a time "the grim reaper . . . clipped one or two of the sagacious promoters, who obtained in the first instance, and have kept for so long, the softest, brightest and most priceless article of velvet ever woven in the loom of promotion from the rich fibers of others." T. N. Barnsdall, who held the most ITIO stock, had been loaned $7 million by Standard

36. John Brennon et al. before Secretary Franklin Lane, March 8, 1915, "In the Matter of the so-called Foster lease on Oil Property Owned by the Osage Indians of Oklahoma" (3 vols.; typescript), II, 136, III, 334, 448, box 414421, Osage Mineral Branch, FRC.

Oil, a favor it would not likely have done for an enemy. Even if
ITIO and Standard were enemies, it did not imply that the former
was virtuous because of the latter's excesses. That the Foster lease had
not yet paid its promoters for their efforts was considered by the Association the most ridiculous argument of all. The great sums the company had spent were, to one who knew the capital requirements of the
oil business, "childish pipings and vain vaporings." The Illuminating
Oil Company was actually a holding company, nothing but "a cog
in the immense wheel constructed by these 'promoters.'" Might
someone forbid that they "conceal themselves within its fairy framework," and play out a continued story "in the likeness of Tennyson's
brook to 'go on forever?'"[37]

The company published a series of pamphlets in response to this,
the most extensive of which was called "Myths Dispelled by the Illuminating Oil Company." There it was said that the higher royalty
set in 1905 was arbitrarily arrived at by the President without hearing
and that it reduced the profit margin of the corporation to a narrow
limit. That little was deserved by the heirs of "the pioneer advance
guard of daring speculators and oil men that presumed to advance
across the Kansas line, before the advent of railroads and . . . test an
unknown and untried country for oil." Relations with the government were good, and business had gone more smoothly and honestly
than any other operations conducted on behalf of the Indians. The
company employed 1,000 men and had a $75,000 monthly payroll.
Its early activity, resulting in the booming of Bartlesville and Tulsa,
had increased the value of Indian lands. For this, the company merited
a continued chance to benefit from the lease.[38]

All attempts to defend the position were futile. In 1916, the
Foster lease ended, royalty to the Osages for oil was raised to one-
sixth, and the leaseholds taken by various producers were limited to

37. *Reply to Argument and Petition of Indian Territory Illuminating
Oil Company for Second Renewal of Foster Lease*, May 29, 1913, box 414421,
Osage Minerals Branch, FRC.

38. *Argument and Petition for Renewal of Oil and Gas Leases in the
Osage Nation, Oklahoma*, ibid. The interior title was "Myths Dispelled. . . ."

4,800 acres apiece.[39] It is worth noting that it was in this period, immediately after the cancellation of the lease, that the financial benefits to the Osages from oil royalties reached their spectacular height, becoming almost legendary by the early twenties.

The Indians, in speaking about the possibilities in their council predicted this, and concluded that it would be due to the diminished power of large corporations in the oil fields. Osage Charles Revard thought tribal members should form their own oil companies and eliminate the white middleman completely:

> They have done things their own way for many years. What have the Osage people got? If they had losed [sic] millions of dollars, would they be after this property so bitterly; so strong? We have gotten the crumbs and we are not going to take that any more. It is not the millionaires that altogether can be depended upon. It is the people. . . . Not those great corporations, because if we do we will be placed upon the ground under their feet and tramped.[40]

In doing this, the tribe would put its faith in government, to eliminate unscrupulous operators from A-she-gah-hre saw were "taking advantage of my people every day; every day that comes." The secretary of the interior promised the full bloods that he would help them better regulate their oil and gas affairs and "treat them like men." The Osages were in about the same position twenty years earlier when White Horn had told a government officer, "We think of you as tall trees." What intervened was a strange institution, the corporation, described even by matter-of-fact businessmen as "an intermediary, a kind of web a ghost." But the tribe had not been prepared by gradual change to deal with it. "It is a hard situation, if you will think about it," said A-she-gah-hre in 1916, "and it is getting worse every day; as time passes, it is getting worse."[41]

39. Council Proceedings, March 17, 1916, pp. 20–22, ibid.
40. Ibid., March 20, 1916, pp. 32–34.
41. Ibid., March 16, 1916, pp. 15–16; *Reply*, p. 16, ibid.

CHAPTER X

"A CORPS OF CLERKS"

The prediction made by the Illuminating Oil Company that the government, in trying to control business in Indian country, would soon find itself snared in a web of its own creation was accurate prophecy. The Union Agency at Muskogee received twelve letters a day in 1880, one thousand a day in 1900. So powerful did the hierarchical, rule-oriented federal bureaucracy become that both Indians and businessmen complained that they were being treated as wards—the former as incompetents and defectives, and the latter as robbers and scoundrels. The government, said one oil operator, had gone into the business of trying "to legislate forethought," in order to protect the Indian, and, in so doing, was attempting to "reverse the laws of nature." One Indian Territory observer compared the rule of the secretary of the interior after the Curtis Act was passed with the control by the Russian csar and complained that "the administration by a corps of clerks ... at Washington, D.C. ... of the private business of 85,000 peoples [is] unAmerican and absolutely senseless." It is well, therefore, in viewing the corporate aspects of the final destruction of tribal sovereignty in the early twentieth century to place alongside the figures of the corporate officer and the nonfeathered reservation Indian that of another central, but neglected figure—the department clerk. He was at the center of things, filling out oil leases, slashing at his enemies with a sharpened pencil, or charging with fixed spectacles into a range of filing boxes—a hero when heroes were gone.[1]

1. *St. Louis Republic*, May 13, 1906, in box 43, III, p. 92, E. A. Hitchcock Papers, RG 316, NA (for "Abbreviations in Footnotes," see p. vii). SR 5013, 59th Cong., 2d sess., pt. 1, 1907 (S 5062), pp. 600, 688. U.S., Congress, House,

Involvement of the clerks with corporations escalated with the railroad right-of-way decisions of the 1880s, which had represented a decision by the federal establishment to take a much more active role in corporate-Indian relations than it had since 1866. The decisions on cattle operations and the moving of corporations out of the Cherokee Outlet contributed to the centralizing tendency. But it was in facing the difficulties created by the powerful railroad-coal cartels and petroleum corporations of the two decades preceding Oklahoma statehood that the governmental bureaucracy grew most. By then, corporate vested interest in the Indian Territory was established, Indian institutions were daily becoming less capable of coping with more modern systems, and the tribal landholding system was being revolutionized by various allotment agreements.

The government had been trying to convince the Five Tribes to allot their lands since the Dawes Severalty Act, providing a general philosophy of individual rather than tribal land ownership, but excepting a large number of tribes from its practice, had passed in 1887. Between 1897 and 1902, allotment agreements were made with the last of the tribes, including the stubborn Cherokees, but they created new corporate problems of their own. Mineral and timber reserves, for example, were often withdrawn from allotment, so the corporation still had to deal with the sovereign tribe. At the same time the government's responsibilities to individual Indian landholders under the new system were not precisely defined. It was faced with the red tape of allotment and subject to pressure from corporations wishing to acquire land piecemeal from individuals that they had been unable to obtain in toto by dealing with tribal legislatures. Most of the twentieth-century frauds involving corporations and clerks, therefore, were the direct result of the immense complications introduced by the incongruous allotment process.

The Indian Office was challenged in 1889 by the activities of the Choctaw Coal and Railway Company. This corporation was par-

---

Statehood for Oklahoma: Hearings Before the Committee on the Territories of the House of Representatives, Jan. 20, 1904, p. 276.

ticipating, it seemed, in every sort of violation of the department's Indian Territory regulations. It sold potatoes from its cars in violation of the Intercourse Acts, it illegally developed townsites, it fenced much more acreage than its right of way allowed it, and it negotiated coal leases with Indian minors, including an eighteen-month-old Creek girl, who received one dollar for her "consent," such as it was. This company sent representatives to Congress in 1890 asking that its mineral claims be affirmed and that subleasing to it by Indian individuals be authorized after the fact. Cherokee lobbyist John Adair noted that "it is certainly questionable, if nothing more serious, that Congress, in any sense of accommodation or alleged necessity, can assume the right . . . to separate the natural products of a country from its lands." Agent Leo Bennett was more direct, "If the Indian Office is powerless to protect the Indians . . . it seems to me that justice demands that the fact be made known so that the wards of the Government may appeal to a higher power if one can be found."[2]

Bennett, however, was unable to "ventilate the swindle" operated by company lobbyists. The corporation threatened, and Bennett believed, that it had enough influence in Washington to have him removed from his job if he caused trouble. It used all the old tricks. Creek and Choctaw citizens were hired to send memorials to the Indian Office saying that Bennett was only the cat's paw of a competing corporation and that the objections were coming from self-constituted tribal leaders, who objected to the Choctaw Coal and Railway Company because it dealt directly with the Indian people rather than enriching the clique. The company had broken the coal monopoly of the MK&T railroad and was depended upon by Texas for cheap coal.[3]

2. Files full of charges against the company include box 338, ITD; papers accompanying S 2580, RG 46, NA; and the extensive 1893 hearings into the activities of the railroad in ISP, file 310, shelf 7, #414, 33–93. John Adair, protest, July 25, 1890, H.R. 52A–F19.5, RG 235, NA. Leo Bennett to Commissioner of Indian Affairs, July 21, 1890, SC 156.

3. Leo Bennett to Commissioner of Indian Affairs, Jan. 14, 1892, LR OIA Choctaw Agency, # 2086–92–L, RG 75, NA. John Lowrey and Johnson Hijo

The officials of the government were, however, reluctant to support a corporation so unpopular with many Indians and to give it what amounted to a "gigantic monopoly" of the Choctaw coal fields. This would, said an officer in the Interior Department, "put the Choctaw government at the mercy of this private enterprise," and create "a grating between it and the National Government." Secretary John Noble noticed that this lease was to be for ninety-nine years, thus bypassing, by special congressional legislation, the ordinary rule limiting leases to ten years. It would prevent the Indian tribes from developing their own industry and being self-supporting for several generations. Despite this, the commissioner of Indian affairs supported the lease bill, and reformer Henry Dawes worked in the Congress for a compromise that would not deny the road altogether. The Senate and the House passed joint resolutions affirming a number of the company's leases, and, after it responded by sinking into receivership, extended several times the deadline allowed in its charter for completion of the railway line.[4]

It took the company six years to build 100 miles of railroad, while it was mining coal. "When it comes to asking priveleges [*sic*]," said Creek Chief L. C. Perryman, "this seems to be a great corporation, but its performance is about the poorest I have ever known in this country." Francis I. Gowen, a Pennsylvanian who had investments in the road, blamed bank failures in England and the general depression of the economy for missed deadlines, but emphasized that the company was as good at mining as it was poor at railroad building. Also used was the standard argument that large corporate leases would simplify regulation of tribal lands exploitation and prevent an undemo-

---

to T. J. Morgan, Aug. 10, 1890, SC 156. E. D. Chadick to H. L. Dawes, Aug. 28, 1890, S 2580, RG 64, NA.

4. George Chandler to Secretary of Interior, n.d.; John Noble to Chairman House Commission on Indian Affairs, Aug. 20, 1890; T. J. Morgan to Secretary of Interior, Aug. 14, 1890, H.R. 52A–519.5; H. L. Dawes to Secretary of Interior, Sept. 30, 1890, SC 156. Leo Bennett to Commissioner of Indian Affairs, Aug. 2, 1890, SC 156; Francis Gowen to James Jones, Sept. 21, 1893, H.R. 53A–F18.1, RG 235, NA.

cratic bureaucracy building in Washington. These considerations outweighed charges of "scandalous" mismanagement of the Choctaw company. It was given its privileges, even granted a new federal charter in 1894 and renamed the Choctaw, Oklahoma and Gulf.[5]

While this way of dealing with a particular company might relieve the federal government of some administrative trouble, the general situation regarding corporations, coal, and allotments assured that the size of Washington staffs dealing with Indian Territory grew apace. For example, great effort was required to deal with exceptions to the general allotment policy for the benefit of corporations, in much the same way as exceptions to the general homestead policy upon the public domain were handled, as is well documented by historians of land law.[6] The Choctaw coal regions were surveyed and 440,000 acres of these "segregated coal lands" withdrawn from allotment entry. This left a large area in the Nation, which contained most of its mineral resources, unavailable to the individual Indian title that was so touted by reformers as a way of making a civilized businessman out of the western aborigine. There were constant complaints that the operators upon these lands were all tied to a few railroad companies and that these companies were manipulating the coal supply to create winter shortages and consequent high prices in the Southwest.[7] These factors made the coal issue as delicate in 1906 as it had been in 1871, but the greater number of investors, clerks, and complications made the sorting out of justice more difficult than it might once have been.

Estimates of the total wealth represented by underground coal alone in the Indian Territory ran as high as $4 billion, making it little

5. L. C. Perryman to James Jones, Oct. 4, 1893; Francis Gowen to James Jones, Sept. 21, 1893, H.R. 53A–F18.1. C. A. Maxwell to James Pugh, July 28, 1894, SC 156.

6. See, for example, the classic account Paul Gates, "The Homestead Law in an Incongruous Land System." Much government intervention resulted also from coal strikes in Indian Territory in 1898–1899. See Aldrich, "A History of the Coal Industry in Oklahoma to 1907."

7. U.S., Congress, House of Representatives, Statehood for Oklahoma . . . , pp. 91ff.

wonder that, as D. W. C. Duncan put it, the real concern of the federal allotment commissions was to see that the special interests were taken care of, "town-lotters, mineral leasers, churches and missionary societies, railroad corporations and monopolists." By 1906, there were almost 200,000 people living upon the segregated lands, and whole towns had grown up containing immigrant miners that were outside the control of the tribes. Congress was favorably disposed to selling the surface of these lands to settlers, at the same time allowing mining corporations to continue working the veins while paying royalty to a skeleton tribal committee created to collect the last dues of the five Indian Nations, which would be terminated by federal fiat in their long sovereign and landholding existence. Most businessmen and Indians had given up trying to understand what was now best left to the clerks. "We have all fretted and worried over it," said one resident of the segregated lands, "until we don't know any more where we are at, and if something ain't done with it there will soon be more call for a lunatic asylum down here than anything else."[8]

While others were willing to let a 1906 bill for terminating the Five Tribes take its accidental and complicated course, complete with whatever advantages for corporations it might contain, Robert LaFollette of Wisconsin was one Progressive who believed that complications might very well hide unconscious or purposeful fraud. LaFollette, though considered by some a "crank" for doing so, spent a long time sorting through dull statistics and the rulings of dozens of agencies affecting Indian coal rights. He found that under the proposed thirty-year lease arrangement railroad corporations would monopolize the new state and defraud the Indians. So well publicized were his charges that plans for selling to coal lands were scrapped, although LaFollette did not succeed in getting into law his plan for the federal government to operate the Indian Territory coal lands as a means of price control on energy. The lands remained with-

8. SR 5013, 59th Cong., 2d sess., pt. 1, 1907 (S 5062), p. 752; *Vinita Chieftain*, Jan. 28, 1897. SR 5013, 59th Cong., 2d sess., pt. 1, 1907 (S 6062), pp. 801ff; 886; 838. This document is filled with accounts of life on the segregated lands, called by one man "a kingdom in itself."

drawn from allotment entry at the time Oklahoma became a state in 1907. "If we paid what Senator LaFollette says they [the lands] are worth," said one man, "we will be accused of robbing the Government, and if we paid what the Indians will take we will be said to be robbing the Indians." It was one of those dilemmas in which it was decided to let circumstance take its course until some policy might force itself upon the principals in the future.[9]

The corporation and the government clerk were related on other allotment matters in a way more direct and obvious than the coal imbroglio. S. M. Brosius, special agent for the Indian Rights Association of Philadelphia, reported to his superiors in 1903 that members of the Commission to the Five Civilized Tribes (Dawes Commission), which was responsible for alloting land in Indian Territory, were enriching themselves by forming trust companies to lease allotted lands in ways that amounted to a promise to sell, often to an oil corporation. The commissioners were in the wrong not only in the investment in the trust companies, which represented a conflict of interest, but also because the companies were themselves acting in violation of laws that prevented the restricted Indian ward from alienating his allotment. No agency escaped compromising connections. Pliny L. Soper, the U.S. District Attorney for the northern district of Indian Territory, who was to represent Indians in disputes with corporations, was a stockholder in the Indian Territory Development Company (a trust company) as well as chief attorney for both the Cherokee Oil and Gas Company and the Frisco railroad company, corporations that were daily in court with Indians. Guy Cobb, Creek revenue inspector, was the major stockholder in the Tribal Development Company; P. S. Mosley, the Chickasaw tribal governor, was an officer of the same concern; Tams Bixby, chairman of the Dawes Commission, was vice-president of Muskogee Title and Trust; and J. George Wright, Indian inspector for the Territory, was an offi-

9. Clipping, scrapbook B–260, LaFollette Family Papers, Library of Congress; Belle and Fola LaFollette, *Robert M. LaFollette, June 14, 1855–June 18, 1925* (N.Y., 1953), p. 209. SR 5013, 59th Cong., 2d sess., pt. 1, 1907 (S 5062), p. 902.

cer in the same company, to mention only a few of the prominent. Brosius blamed the House Committee on Indian Affairs, and particularly its chairman, Charles Curtis, for giving friends "the places where corruption has grown." In a broader sense, however, the situation in 1903 must be attributed to the whole history of the involvement of progressive tribesmen and government officials in the tempting business of corporate development of Indian lands since the Civil War. So intertwined had these various types become in the great dance of greed that the question of honor had disappeared and even separating interests was problematical.[10]

The Interior Department was unnerved by Brosius's revelations. There had been charges within the bureaucracy about fraud in the allotment of lands, but this had been attributed to corrupt agents or minor officials. There were even complaints about the trust companies in 1902, but the Department had simply turned them over to the Justice Department as a matter of routine, and there they had stayed for two years with no further investigation. The Dawes Commission had made a point that all leases, particularly in areas around Bartlesville with its excitement about drilling for oil, should come through it so that they could be checked against the allotment, land classification, and tribal membership rolls in its possession. No one imagined that the Commission itself might be using its inside information for fraudulent purposes. Clarence Douglas, head of the Creek land division operated by the Dawes Commission, was removed from office for allotment fraud in July 1903, while Brosius was in the Territory, but the commissioners doubted that their involvement would be suspected. Commissioner T. B. Needles wrote vacationing Tams Bixby less than a month before the Brosius report: "Douglas is stirring up quite a tempest in a tea-pot because of his removal. . . . we will hold the fort until you find it convenient to return so don't hurry."[11]

10. S. M. Brosius to Phillip Garrett, Aug. 12, 1903, box 437, ITD. Clipping from *Leavenworth Times*, Aug. 18, 1903, box 43, I, E. A. Hitchcock Papers, RG 316, NA.

11. E. A. Hitchcock to P. Porter, Sept. 6, 1902, Dawes Commission Creek

The Interior Department took the public stand that the whole matter was a creation of yellow journalists and that Brosius was a troublemaker whose report was based upon "insinuation and innuendo." Officials said that the Department had known of these sorts of charges for a long time and had been following every lead to make sure things were honest. Privately, all took the turn of events more seriously. A great number of clerks were assigned to an investigation of all the past activities and investigations of S. M. Brosius, beginning with his 1899 exposure of teacher-student immorality at the Puyallup Indian school. It was hoped that some evidence damaging to Brosius's reputation could be unearthed or that it could at least be shown that he depended upon "malcontents and busy bodies to tell him their tales of woe." In the Indian Territory Division of the Interior Department in a new file was started, simply marked "Frauds."[12]

The Dawes Commission quickly made a defense. Bixby said that the charges upset "a work unparalleled in the history of civilization," and asked for an investigation to clear the air.[13] Some of his friends said that they had been elected to the trust-company directorships without their knowledge.[14] Commissioner C. R. Breckenridge wrote that Brosius was honest, but made "the usual errors of impressionable persons, not acting under official responsibility, and relying upon rumors and the statements of interested and baffled persons for their data instead of going directly to the record." The trouble, of course, was that the records were in the possession of the body under investigation. True, Breckenridge said, mistakes had been made, but

---

File, IAD. Tams Bixby to Secretary of Interior, Dec. 24, 1902, box 359, ITD. Clipping from *Muskogee Phoenix*, July 5, 1903, in box 43, I, E. A. Hitchcock Papers, RG 316, NA. T. B. Needles to Tams Bixby, July 24, 1903, Dawes Commission Choctaw File, IAD.

12. *New York Times*, Aug. 18, 1903, 6–6; A. B. Pugh to Secretary of Interior, Aug. 25, 1903, box 437, ITD. Clarence Allen, Memorandum of Charges Made by S. M. Brosius, box 438, ITD.

13. Tams Bixby and T. B. Needles to Secretary of Interior (telegram), Aug. 26, 1903, box 437, ITD.

14. For example J. G. Wright to E. A. Hitchcock, Aug. 21, 1903, box 438, ITD.

they were no purposeful fraud. The commissioners did have stock in the trust companies, but these were corporations legally chartered and represented only a "normal business interest" on the part of the investing government officers—"The law never authorizes anyone to violate the law."[15]

The press had other information. The *Chicago Record-Herald* printed a damaging story in August. The Canadian Valley Trust Company (Tams Bixby was its president) had its offices in the building where the Dawes Commission was headquartered. According to the account, one night the commission and the trust-company offices, which were located on different floors of the same building, traded places. The Indians arriving the next day, and seeing the same men in the same room as always, signed up with what they thought was the Dawes Commission for what they thought were allotments, while they were in fact signing leases with the trust company. The accuracy of this story may have been questionable, but the humor of it made a laughing stock of the Commission. A cartoon showed "pilot" Bixby floating around on the "political sea" in the Dawes Commission ship surrounded by leaping "sharks" and "grafters" and setting sail for "success" with canvas patched by the "Brosius report." In the prow was a blanketed Indian saying, "He suits me." The *New York Evening Post* wrote that when Bixby said that his trust company investment was, after all, small, it was like saying it was fine for the U.S. marshall to be involved in a moonshine still if it were a little one. "It is deplorable enough to find a commission in a position of particular trust as regards the wards of the nation deeply involved in equivocal transactions; even more alarming is the brazen display of intolerably low standards of official honor." The *Kansas City Star* was encouraged only in the fact that the Indians were responding to this fraud with fraud of their own; one tribesman had leased his allotment twenty-five times, each time to a different trust company. The *Watchman* at St. Louis, in Secretary Hitchcock's own district, called him an "ignorant, narrow-minded bigot" and estimated that "these

15. C. R. Breckenridge to Secretary of Interior, Aug. 29, 1903, box 437, ITD.

government land sharks could carry away the whole territory from the face of the earth, and he would not know that any injury had been done save to the map makers and school book publishers." The *Herald* of Gloversville, New York, used the same devastating humor in noting that investigations of the trust company had given new meaning to Grover Cleveland's phrase "a public office is a public trust." The country was laughing, and it was the laughter that the pretensions of the federal officers could least afford. Even its own investigation into these affairs was widely regarded as a mere cover-up. The head of the Indian Rights Association wrote in response to Hitchcock's criticism of independent snooping, "Too often these officials appear to be under the influences from members of Congress interested in them, and I am bound to say that Inspectors too often seem to whitewash men utterly unfit for their position."[16]

Despite this suspicion, the dispatching of a departmental investigating team headed by Charles Bonaparte and the slow realization that so many people were involved that it would be impossible to prosecute them all cooled the ardor of the indignant and allowed the practical types once more to hold the day. The Bonaparte report was a sort of whitewash in that, although it offered proof that officers had participated in questionable activities, it questioned whether they realized they were acting illegally and whether anything could really be done about it. The *Okemah Journal* granted, "There is no statute against playing politics, and it is no crime for a man who is drawing a good salary to feather his nest." The *Topeka Herald* agreed that it was perhaps best to let the business of doing away with the tribes proceed without becoming too annoyed at the motives of officers dealing with a complex situation. It wrote, "To believe that half the population lies awake nights planning schemes for beating the Indians

16. Clipping, *Chicago Record Herald*, Aug. 27, 1903, box 43, I; cartoon from *Muskogee Phoenix*, March 16, 1905, box 43, II; clipping from *New York Evening Post*, Aug. 27, 1903, box 43, I; clipping, *Kansas City Star*, Aug. 31, 1903, box 43, I; clipping, *Watchman*, Sept. 3, 1903, box 43, I; clipping, *Herald*, Sept. 16, 1903, box 43, I, E. A. Hitchcock Papers, RG 316, NA. *New York Times*, Sept. 7, 1903, 1–7; 2–1.

is as absurd as to believe that half your neighbors are lying awake planning how to get into your chicken coop and not get caught." Complaints against Bixby were still coming in when he resigned from the Commission in 1906 to devote full time to business. There were still advertisements then for the International Bank and Trust Company of Vinita, which once claimed as a vice-president Thomas Needles, member of the Dawes Commission, and had the slogan, "Every courtesy extended consistent with sound business principles."[17]

The trust company scandals did have their effect, however, upon other corporations operating in the Territory in that President Roosevelt and Secretary Hitchcock seemed to think that their own guilt might be assuaged by a loud persecution of "grafting" corporations. Wrote the *Oil City Derrick*: "Any absurd story from an Indian will be considered by the Department, but oilmen are on the blacklist. . . . They are simply wards . . . just like the Indians."[18]

In April 1906 Hitchcock ordered James M. Guffey of the firm of Guffey and Galey to answer charges that he was a secret agent for the Standard Oil Company in leasing in the Cherokee and Osage Nations. Guffey and Galey had transferred some leases to Theodore Barnsdall, although Barnsdall already held more than the leasing limit of 4,800 acres and was believed by many to be in the pay of Standard Oil.[19] The transaction was hidden from the government. Hitchcock found that Barnsdall controlled 55,660 acres in the Osage lands by sublease from ITIO, 1,650 by assignment (such as that from Guffey and Galey), and 12,000 by drilling contract.[20] The last technique was to take 80–90 per cent of the production of an oil well to pay for drilling it while assigning the lease itself to a dummy cor-

17. The Bonaparte hearings are in file 4412–1904, ITD. Both newspapers quoted in HD 528, 58th Cong., 2d sess., 1904–95 (S 4675), p. 14. Anonymous to E. A. Hitchcock, Nov. 21, 1906, box 436, ITD. Unmarked clipping in box 43, II, E. A. Hitchcock Papers, RG 316, NA.

18. Clipping, April 2, 1906, in box 43, III, ibid.

19. Clipping, *Baltimore Evening Herald*, April 28, 1906, ibid.

20. Statement of chief of Indian Division, May 24, 1906, box 26, case B, ibid.

poration, thus slipping around departmental rules limiting the number of acres of formal leases held by a single company. Hitchcock got nowhere in talking to Guffey. He and Barnsdall regarded the baroque set of rules spewed from Washington as an unjustified curb upon legitimate enterprise, and they believed they could not afford to interrupt their dream of providing inexpensive gas to St. Louis and Wichita by pipeline in order to read all the fine print in government regulations.[21]

In May, Hitchcock tried again, this time calling all the oilmen in Indian Territory to Washington for informal hearings designed to encourage independent operators to put more pressure on Barnsdall and to build an independent pipeline to compete with the marketing monopoly of Prairie Oil & Gas (Standard Oil). The independents, however, were uninterested in taking on Standard Oil unless the government gave them special privileges, such as the lifting of the 4,800-acre leasing restriction to allow them to fight abuse with abuse. Although Hitchcock could not oblige, he called the information coming to him about Standard Oil "simply monstrous" and promised to do all he could that was fair to all in backing the independents. The oilmen saw this as an empty pledge. "We are not in a position to compete," said one, "unless we can prepare to-day before we show our hands." Hitchcock dismissed them.[22]

Next came Barnsdall himself. Hitchcock was most curt with him, not allowing him to explain his motivations but simply demanding that he "undo what you have done." It was not the government's problem if Guffey and Galey would not pay the full price for the return of the lease in question. "Nobody can defy this Department, or the Administration, in such a matter." Barnsdall tried to explain that he had never looked at the leases, and that, although he knew there

21. Memo, April 28, 1906, ibid. Guffey & Galey were operating as a corporation, The Arkansas Valley Oil Company, and continually tried to separate themselves personally from the corporate shield.

22. *Hearings Before the Secretary of the Interior on the Leasing of Oil Lands and Natural Gas Wells in Indian Territory and Territory of Oklahoma* (Washington, D.C., 1906), pp. 22–63, in box 53, ibid.

was something in them requiring Interior Department permission, he had assumed that Guffey would "fix" that. As to the drilling-contract device, Barnsdall could say only, "I took the best advice I could on that." Hitchcock snapped back:

I don't care what advice you took; such advice is not worth a cent. The only advice you ought to have had was right at the top of that lease. Now, I don't want to say anything harsh or discourteous or that will hurt your feelings, but that drilling contract was simply a device to get around our restrictions and limitations as to acreage.

"I took the chances," replied the man in the hot seat. "We do not allow such chances here," came the answer. When Barnsdall expressed a desire to make a "gentlemen's agreement" to smooth the matter with Hitchcock, the Secretary exploded: "We will talk frankly. You say you have not done anything dishonestly. You tried to whip the devil around the stump. We can not treat you differently from what we treat anybody else." The interview ended with a curt "Goodbye" and an invitation to test the administration's resolve in the courts if the oilmen dared. Excerpts from the interview were placed in a number of newspapers, and the whole published as a pamphlet. One angry comment in a newspaper in the oil region concluded, "Secretary Hitchcock . . . would do well in Russia right now." Hitchcock clipped that piece and pasted it in his private scrapbook, no doubt getting hotter under the collar in the process.[23]

Unsuccessful at argument, Barnsdall tried political influence. Former Sen. James K. Jones, now representing Barnsdall, appeared in August 1906 at the home of Theodore Roosevelt at Oyster Bay. The newspapers, consistent in their opinion that Barnsdall *was* Standard Oil, had a lively time with this, as Jones had been chairman of the Democratic National Committee in the campaigns of William J. Bryan, one of the prime smiters of the Standard monopoly.[24] These

23. Ibid., pp. 62–66. (?) to E. A. Hitchcock, n.d. [May, 1906], box 43, III, E. A. Hitchcock Papers, RG 316, NA.

24. Clipping, *New York Herald*, Aug. 10, 1906, ibid. Clippings of the next day for the *New York Sun* and the *Press* of Portland, Maine, ibid., take up the chorus.

events, combined with the publication of the hearings, returned to
Hitchcock much of the public reputation he had lost in the 1903
trust company scandals. It could be that the special harshness was designed exactly to do this. The editor of the *Bartlesville Enterprise*
congratulated the secretary on his "splendid attitude," and said that,
while the paper had been critical of department rules in the past, the
hearings were a real "eye-opener."[25]

Jones tried to convince Roosevelt that while Barnsdall had
made a mistake he should not suffer undue financial loss from it.
He claimed the oilman had done people a favor by taking drilling
contracts and would never have taken them had he known the government objected. But now he was owed money and could not stop.
As a result, Roosevelt asked Hitchcock to inform him more completely
on the matter and suggested it be taken up in a cabinet meeting. He
reminded his interior secretary that the purpose of the administration
was not to prevent combination but to regulate it on behalf of the
public "and of course doubly in the interest of the Indians." Roosevelt
wrote that he was "by no means sure" that the drilling contracts were
simply a device to avoid rules and was influenced by Jones's argument that it allowed men of small capital, whom the administration
wished to encourage, to enter the field. The president was upset also
that Hitchcock, in the hearings, had published a letter showing that
Republican Gov. Frank Higgins of New York was acting as a lobbyist for Barnsdall with the White House. Had there not been enough
political turmoil connected with the Frantz revelations of three years
earlier? While justice must be done at whatever political cost, Roosevelt advised his hot-headed secretary, "We do not wish either wantonly
or foolishly to invite such disaster."[26]

Thanks, however, to the arguments of Hitchcock and of E. B.
Butler, representing independent oilmen in Washington, the president

25. Thomas Latta to E. A. Hitchcock, Aug. 16, 1906, box 26, ibid.
26. James Jones to T. Roosevelt, Aug. 15, 1906; Theodore Roosevelt to
E. A. Hitchcock, Aug. 18, 1906, ibid. Theodore Roosevelt to E. A. Hitchcock,
Aug. 27, 1906, in Elting E. Morison, *The Letters of Theodore Roosevelt*, vol. 5,
pp. 386–88.

was convinced that Barnsdall was in the wrong.[27] By September, he wrote that the affair was "clear as a bell" to him, and that he was hesitant only because the administration "should not only be right but should be clearly shown to be right, and that our enemies shall not be able to say in this movement we merely represent 'the usual heedless antagonism' (as they style it) of the administration toward corporations."[28] Later information made all glad for that decision. One of the leases transferred to Barnsdall was from Delaware attorney Richard Adams. Jones himself held illegal leases. The government here took a firm stand and prevailed. Barnsdall wrote in October that he was now willing to act under departmental rules. Hitchcock replied that trouble would have been saved had he said that long ago.[29]

The issue in the Barnsdall case was monopoly. A similar confrontation between Roosevelt's New Nationalism and Indian Territory corporations took place over another prime area of Progressive concern—conservation. In 1905 the Interior Department was contacted by Jack Gordon of Texas who wished to buy 100,000 acres of Choctaw pine lands to establish a game preserve and hunting and fishing club in the wild Kiamichi mountains. Gordon was recommended by his friend, Frank Frantz, Osage agent. He outlined a plan for a hunting corporation that would enclose the whole area with a fence and practice strict rules of game management. Almost immediately, seeing the news in the papers, another Texan, John Bailey, proposed that the area should instead be made a national park or forest preserve. It had been appraised at only twenty-five cents an acre by the Dawes Commission, was too poor for farming, and would provide a recreation area for thousands rather than the hundreds who

27. For example, Butler's long attack on Barnsdall in A. B. Butler to Theodore Roosevelt, Aug. 24, 1906, box 26, E. A. Hitchcock Papers, RG 316, NA. Butler's most important point was that the government could not be neutral. If it allowed a monopoly to form, it was responsible for it.

28. T. Roosevelt to E. A. Hitchcock, Sept. 5, 1906, E. A. Hitchcock Papers, RG 316, NA.

29. E. A. Hitchcock to T. Roosevelt, Sept. 26, Oct. 29, 1906, ibid.

might belong to a private club. Timber corporations offered a third alternative—to cut off the timber, or at least continue to cull it, in order to meet the country's need for lumber.[30]

There was already debate raging within the government on the proper attitude to be taken toward timber lands, and the Gordon and Bailey letters sparked an investigation of this area. Chief McCurtain of the Choctaws had no objection to a forest preserve as long as Indians living in the region were paid for their improvements, and the Secretary of Agriculture, after consulting with his forestry staff, agreed that this arrangement would be ideal.[31]

Jack Gordon did not, of course, wish his plan to be ignored in the rush for a national forest. He went to Washington in the fall of 1905 and gave honorary memberships in his club to Hitchcock and Roosevelt. He had a way of getting around the Curtis Act restriction limiting the leases of individuals to 640 acres, a way he may have learned from Cherokee Oil and Gas. Each of the three hundred members of his hunting corporation would apply for one section each and deed the block of land to the club. This would give it 200,000 acres (his appetite had grown by this time) subject to taxation and protected from the sawmill. The Gordon corporation had a capitalization of $150,000 and was chartered to build a clubhouse, keepers' houses, and boat houses, and to stock the land with fish and birds. The Gordon Choctaw Game Preserve, as it was called, would not allow anyone to hold more than one share of stock, would allow no gambling with cards or dice, no liquor or beer, no hunting on Sunday, and no sale of timber. It was full of attractions and romance to the middle-class reformer of the day.[32]

As a first step Hitchcock withdrew the area from allotment in

30. C. F. Larrabee to Secretary of Interior, Feb. 20, 1905; Frank Frantz to T. Roosevelt, Oct. 29, 1906; John Bailey to E. A. Hitchcock, March 27, 1905, box 445, ITD.

31. Green McCurtain to J. G. Wright, April 11, 1905; Secretary of Agriculture to Secretary of Interior, Jan. 13, 1906, ibid.

32. Jack Gordon to Theodore Roosevelt, Nov. 30, 1905, Oct. 22, 1906; Bylaws, Choctaw Game Preserve, n.d., ibid.

December 1906, noting that the region was being considered as a national forest or private game preserve. The timber interests were enraged and the departments received letters of protest from congressmen in Missouri, where most of the timber corporations operating in the Choctaw country were located.[33] Forest inspector William Cox was quick to point out, however, that in keeping with the ordinary policy of the Roosevelt administration designation as a national forest would not prevent controlled cutting of timber but would only stop the present tendency toward consolidation of leases in the hands of a few large corporations, like the Chicago Lumber and Coal Company and the Southern Trust Company. This statement effectively combined conservation with antitrust and gave the measure double political credentials. Last, the withdrawal of the area eliminated Indian interest in it and the "unsatisfactory and annoying relations between the Indians and the government over land." Cox was much against the Gordon plan of wilderness preservation "especially when there is a merchantable stand of hardwood over nearly all of it and great quantities of pine." He recommended the patenting of home lots within any forest reserve created, so "people from the thickly settled States round about may actually own homes here in the hills where they can breathe in air that is pure and enjoy mountain scenery which compares favorably with the best of the Appalachians."[34] It was a solution that satisfied political interest on several sides, but it was a far site from what Gordon had had in mind when he talked of creating an area where "the almighty dollar will be as far from the scene of the transaction as a snow flake in July."[35] But such changes often took place when ideas were taken up by the corps of clerks.

33. J. H. Hamilton to Charles Curtis, Dec. 16, 1906; W. W. Hastings to E. A. Hitchcock, Dec. 20, 1906, ibid.

34. William Cox report in James Wilson to Secretary of Interior, Dec. 14, 1906, ibid. For a good account of the general methods of the Roosevelt administration in balancing demands of corporations and conservationists, see Samuel P. Hays, *Conservation and the Gospel of Efficiency: The Progressive Conservation Movement, 1890–1920.*

35. Jack Gordon to E. A. Hitchcock, Jan. 10, 1907, box 445, ITD.

All things Indian had in fact become complicated matters of the weighing of large interests by a broker government. There was always a certain abstract argument between the West's cynical evaluation of the native and the East's Fenimore Cooper images, but more central was the interest of lobbyists who thought little about the Indian at all. One observer of the passage of the 1906 bill to close the affairs of the Five Tribes said that the legislation was "like a rudderless ship without a captain," subject to so many amendments to please lobbyists that "even its author would not have known it had he met it stranded on the beach or a floating derilict." The Senate investigating committee sent to gather information in 1906 was said to be in the control of corporations, while all hearings were characterized by the presence of "the railroad attorney trying to continue the 'protection' of his company, the attorney for this or that other corporation making the effort of his life for his oil or gas leases and land, and the townsite delegate wanting to smash everything in sight that did not put his town in the exact geographical center of the future country."[36]

On the whole, it may be concluded that the departmental corps of clerks did a better job of protecting Indian rights than did the Congress, which was responsible for the major diminutions of Indian sovereignty, from the 1866 land grants to the Curtis Act. Yet the "web" of red tape in which the departmental bureaucracy was entwined hid courage in complexity, blunted resolve in compromise, and embarrassed virtue through opportunism to such an extent that it commanded little respect among either Indians or corporations. The regulatee became involved with the regulator, and pulling the mask off once too often revealed the face of the other. The very complexity of the relationship between corporations and clerks suggested to Indians, accustomed to vividly clear oral images, an intent to deceive. The "file of clerks" seemed to operate within a closed system, according to logic no ordinary man could fathom. To be "tied up

36. William Finn to E. A. Hitchcock, Jan. 31, 1907, box 26, ibid.; *Muskogee Phoenix*, April 19, 1906.

in swaddling clothes" by such as these was not really a respectable form of transition for the Indian from tribal independence to U.S. citizenship. Secretary Hitchcock was criticized as harshly by Indian newspapers as by white. He was called Mr. "It's Cocked" and derided for the oversimplification of trying "to wrap all who have Indian blood in their veins in a blanket and adorn them with paint." Could the Indian trust a man who rode over their territory in a private railroad car provided by Adolphus Busch, the St. Louis brewer, while purportedly seeking out illegal trade in alcohol and mischievous corporate dealings?[37]

The bureaucratic tangle that was associated with the experiment of assimilating the land and people in Indian Territory into the contemporary United States was a model for structures and attitudes that would become national. Its patterns in dealing with the corporation have been repeated in assimilation experiments since—of the poor, of ethnic minorities, of political dissenters. The "New Indian" faced very modern problems when dealing with those who on the one hand taunted him with letting the government treat him like a child, and on the other bypassed institutions representative of his sovereign will in order to acquire his property. It has become a standard approach to history to disbelieve that the U.S. government ever practiced a "laissez-faire" philosophy, but the clerks in the Indian Territory, representing both government and corporations, did amount to "a new wrinkle in modern government." Both the corporate and the governmental bureaucracies had an inaccessible institutional physiognomy—"no body to kick or soul to damn." Responsibility could be hidden in hierarchy, suggestions of change smothered in complexity, and the "native hue of resolution" go begging in the "pale cast" of rules legalistically interpreted. The tribes in the Indian Territory, as they left the world of their own past and turned

37. Clipping, *Oklahoman*, June 10, 1905, box 43, III; clipping, *Okemah Journal*, July 9, 1903, box 43, I; clipping, *Muskogee Evening Times*, May 7, 1903, box 42, E. A. Hitchcock Papers, RG 316, NA; SR 5013, 59th Cong., 2d sess., 1907, pt. 2 (S 5063), p. 1323.

to find themselves set upon by the most baffling set of powers ever created, were the first to know the twentieth-century world as everyone since has known it—the abstract world in which sensation must be sought in artificial situations, and where success and failure are matters of conjecture—the world of fewer "edges and corners and things."[38]

38. "The New Indian," *Nation* (July 21, 1904), p. 47; clipping, *Oil City Derrick*, April 2, 1906, box 43, III, E. A. Hitchcock Papers, RG 316, NA.

CHAPTER XI

THE SYNDICATED INDIAN

To design a single "thesis" or "model" about the way in which corporations and Indians interacted—to designate group heroes and villains—would be to repeat the shallow thinking of past propagandists, to which historical research should be an antidote. Therefore, while we may speak of patterns of action and causes of specific results, to speak of *the* corporate impact upon Indian sovereignty, *the* Indian response, *the* nature of western economic development, and *the* American experience, separate from the documentation of precise historical situations in their complexity, is compelling only to those more interested in intellectual security than truth. No one knows better than the author of a historical work how much he has simplified actuality (already condensed by being limited to its written remains) when he reduces it to a few shoeboxes full of note cards and weaves those fragments into a comprehensible text. Arthur Schlesinger once wrote that, after serving in the Kennedy administration and seeing the actuality of governmental process first hand, he was amazed at how neatly he had categorized motives and causes in his classic *Age of Jackson*, and how unsatisfactory that study was.[1]

Among modern American historians, the Consensus School would like to homogenize the past to demonstrate a base unity, the New Left looks for conspiratorial exploitation of one group by another, while the Myth-Symbolist school finds men behaving erratically and inconsistently with a world situation of which they perceive only parts. The last approach best fits this work.[2] The cor-

---

1. Arthur Schlesinger, Jr., "The Historian and History," in Thomas Guinsburg, ed., *The Dimensions of History*, pp. 65–71.

2. It will be noticed, however, that the title of this book "*The* Corporation

poration was both the chief despoiler of Indian sovereignty and its most powerful supporter. The Indian was both a promoter and an opponent of corporate privilege—even a single Indian might be each at different times, in different situations, or at different levels of perception. The government was often simultaneously friend and foe of a development and worked at cross purposes within itself. In fact, the full realization that Indians, and all other parties facing corporate issues in Indian Territory, had to deal with a complex and paradoxical reality using an extremely limited store of knowledge and perception, does more to "explain" the process than any neat model that suggests that reform of this or that could have prevented it or will prevent it in the future.

History is still being written, this one is largely written, as though the universe of human behavior paralleled the mechanistic physical universe of Isaac Newton. What is needed is a theory of historical relativity and ways of describing man in the flux of time such as Einstein formulated in mathematical symbols for describing space and objects. At this point in the evolution of a conservative discipline, however, all one can say is that the events described in chapters 1–4 of this book and again in 6–8 were happening simultaneously, that participants could not and did not isolate the corporate issue, as this book does, from myriad other events in their lives, and that the way the text is presented, and even more the way the following conclusions are presented, is a pedagogical device designed to point at a reality they certainly do not contain. The medium is *not* the message. The most important thing about any historical work is the previously unknown and documented facts it contains.

In sorting the facts of corporate involvement with Indians in Indian Territory presented in this book at this maximum responsible level of generalization, one may point out six major fact constructs as important in analyzing how corporate intrusion and the decline in Indian sovereignty were connected:

---

and *the* Indian" is a concession to the consensus thinking that so pervades the field that one is hard pressed to invent another sort of title that would sound right to potential readers.

1) Tribal citizenship, not degree of blood or cultural integrity was the operative determinant of "Indianness" when it came to corporate dealings.

2) No tribal group in Indian Territory expressed, through its constituted government or otherwise, consistent, unified opposition to development of its lands by white corporations.

3) The federal government, in dealing with this problem, allowed circumstance rather than principle to dictate its course.

4) Tribal sovereignty came to be widely regarded in the United States as contingent upon American industrial needs. Ethnocentric observers regarded Indian nationalism merely as the interest of one set of corporations opposing another.

5) Informal détentes with government allowed corporations to gain vested interest in Indian lands before formal policy decisions were made and thus to use economic power to influence the circumstances under which those decisions were made.

6) Indians were not given enough time to understand the complexity of corporate impact upon their way of life before being asked to make irreversible decisions regarding it.

These may serve as a guide to thinking about events described in the text. While all of them may be documented with evidence of numerous events, the first and last points are perhaps most surprising and need additional comment here.

If one were to study Indian reaction to corporations by looking only at the full bloods, there would emerge a pattern much more in tune with the expectations of readers of popular histories about the greed of the white man and the exploitation of the innocent Indian. With the full bloods, there was a consistent misunderstanding of what was described as "industrial civilization" and a clinging, maybe only from fear and ignorance, but noble nevertheless, to the sovereign tribal structures in the face of everything. Rather than compromising in the hope that the newcomers would be appeased or taking on protective coloration in hopes that they might pass by, the full bloods refused to go along. Had this attitude been more widespread, it would have been a powerful weapon against the corporation. Osway Porter, a full-blood Chickasaw, said in 1906 that he had taken the words of the U.S. government at face value, had not tried to speculate upon their possibilities, and therefore, unlike many of his brothers, could speak of broken promises for what they really were. The "Great Father" had said years ago, "If you never loose your hand from my hand I will never loose my hand from your hand."[3] The full blood, ignoring chances for financial gain, simply grasped the hand and treated the world thereby to the moving spectacle of a child led over a cliff by his guardian.

This was destruction, to be sure, but a death which would have returned to haunt the killer, a fate with a psychological barb. Had this simple attitude been universal among the Indians, they would have been innocent of the damaging charge that they had consented to and even promoted the corporate activities which finally damaged their sovereignty. The stance of the full blood confounded the corporate officers and government clerks who could find no foothold for their created needs against the common sense of a genuinely different culture. Washington Gladden wrote in 1885 that unless missionaries could create economic needs in the native and convince him that the things the white man craved were also necessities to him, the white man's economic system, corporations included, could never gain ground there, nor could his religion or his social and political concepts.[4] A 1902 newspaper article, despite its racist humor, described the passing in the night well when describing a full-blood reaction to new telephone lines in the Osage Nation:

James G. Blaine, an Osage warrior, endeavored to call up several full-blood Osages over the phone Sunday last. The first one he called was stretched out in the shade dead to the world, the second was sick and unable to get to the phone, the third had taken an overdose of some weak mixture and was running in a circle, the fourth had overloaded himself with roast beef and was suffering with the jerks, the fifth and last was administering to a sick brother who had drunk some unknown

3. SR 5013, 59th Cong., 2d sess., pt. 1 (S 5062), p. 105.
4. Washington Gladden, "Christianity and Wealth," passim.

lotion and dared not leave. After encountering the above difficulties James declared: "Fone no d——— good. Osages can't talk when have it, maybe so take it out."[5]

It is not popular now to advance racial interpretations of historical events, and I am personally reluctant to do so. The evidence in this study, however, suggests that the degree of corporate intrusion upon a tribe's lands was inversely related to the percentage of Indian blood that flowed in the veins of its citizens. That Indian Territory was an area of special intensity in corporate activity was of course due to many factors (the existence of oil and grass for example), but one of them may have been that tribes there were more completely "bleached out" than elsewhere. This led to the mixed-blood or even white tribal citizen through whom the corporation gained leverage. The custom of allowing intermarriage with whites and of granting full tribal rights to white husbands of Indian women assured that the corporation never faced a united front. The Osages were 92 per cent full blood in 1871. By 1906 the percentage was 38, and by 1952,9.[6] To suggest that this had less than a major impact upon patterns of dealing with them and upon the nature of their intratribal institutions would be a monumental strain. It was revolutionary.

In the course of research for this book, I discovered only one full blood, Shawnee Mathias Splitlog, who promoted a railroad.[7] Mixed bloods did, but not all of them took the line of E. C. Boudinot or Robert L. Ream, and they should not be lumped together. For example Cherokees D. W. Bushyhead and E. C. Boudinot were both mixed bloods who accepted some kind of corporate development. But they hated each other. Boudinot thought that Bushyhead was a fool and Bushyhead thought Boudinot was a traitor. Some mixed bloods were simply taking the "practical" view that accommodation would save the tribes and intransigence surely destroy them.

5. *Bartlesville Magnet*, July 19, 1902.
6. Bureau of Indian Affairs, *The Osage People*, pp. xii–xiv, Frank Phillips Collection, OU.
7. Indian Pioneer Collection, vol. 105, pp. 286–92, IAD.

D. W. C. Duncan (Too-qua-stee) was a Phi Beta Kappa at Dartmouth College but always said what he learned from the Indians was more important.[8] Mixed bloods dominated the boards of the native railroad companies of the seventies, that were organized to industrialize Indian Territory without the intervention of outsiders or damage to tribal rights. But while these mixed-blood moderates might have found the saving middle ground, the tendency of the public to characterize all mixed bloods as "tanned Yankees" speculating for their own gain upon promises made to now out-bred Indian tribes made them unable to establish their credentials as Indians. The final solution to the Indian problem, it seemed, was his racial disappearance. In 1904, mixed-blood Cherokee Robert Owen told a congressional committee that, even without inbreeding, the racial characteristics of full bloods could be changed by education and the civilization economic development could bring. He showed them a picture of the graduating class of an Indian Territory school, noting that the three full-blood girls in the picture could hardly be identified: "There is nothing in the form of the face to indicate the degree of blood; indeed, one of the full-blood girls is the prettiest of the party. It shows what education will do with the human face."[9] Noted the *Vinita Chieftain* in 1885, "Zinc Indians in front of cigar stores are superceding those made of wood."[10]

As important as race was time. The Gilded Age atmosphere of rapid and radical change put a premium on efficiency of action rather than quality of evaluation, and therefore tended, in both white and Indian culture, to place power in the hands of irresponsible individuals or small groups, not representative of the best, but only the fastest or the loudest of their type. The *Cherokee Advocate* in 1903 yearned for the "romantic and poetic" past before the white man came with his "push and dash born of conditions existing beyond the . . . sea." He created the "madly rushing, strenuous present" when "the demon locomotive with puffs and ear-splitting screams,

8. SR 5013, 59th Cong., 2d sess., pt. 1, 1907 (S 5062), pp. 182–83.
9. *Statehood for Oklahoma*, p. 5.
10. *Vinita Chieftain*, Feb. 12, 1885.

rushes madly from city to city." The promoters were men unintelligent enough to be positive and, as many studies of reform have shown, could not be effectively resisted by hesitant intellectuals. Exceptions, like Robert LaFollette, were too rare to have much impact. From the beginning it was, as one Cherokee put it, "a case of 'if-you-don't-do-as-we-want-it-will-be-the-worst-for-you,' " and in the end it was, "We are aware that you have constructed your governments, maintained courts of law, educated lawyers and judges, built towns, formed business corporations, erected schools and colleges, but we are dissatisfied, and you must give it all up."[11]

But cultures do not change at "railroad speed." Cherokee chief Charles Thompson took in 1878 a Burkean view that great changes were possible, and that his people ought to change, but that these changes could take place only "in accordance with our capabilities of appreciating them,—and by such healthy graduations as will not disrupt our social and political organization." Corporate profits, however, are always figured in the relatively short run, and this view dominated. It prevented leisurely thought and experiment about how Indian culture and white culture might accommodate to each other without fatal damage to either. Commented the *New York Tribune* late in the nineteenth century: "The attempt to veneer [industrial civilization] upon a race just emerging from barbarism must in the long run prove a failure. Some individuals may make the tremendous mental leap from the rude simplicity of their fathers to the highly complex thinking of the modern world. But a race cannot do that." Despite a hopeful 1904 artical in the *Chicago Record Herald* entitled "Syndicating the Indian," the transformation of a race and culture was not a job amenable to the techniques developed by confident men to create a capital pool, however strongly they may have believed it was. What corporate theorists and mixed-blood tribesmen may have imagined would be the emergence of a God-intended butterfly from the stiff enclosure of tradition, was ultimately a tale of force, fraud, and confusion, governed by no discernible natural

11. *Cherokee Advocate*, April 25, 1903. *Denial of Indians to Charges of Dawes Commission* (Washington, D.C., 1894), p. 15.

law save that of greed. The "Invisible Hand" did undeniably have a great grip, and those things which corporate ideas of modernity confined to the past would never return again. Creek chief Pleasant Porter encapsulated it in 1903:[12]

> The Indians seem out of place where they were supposed to be in place . . . and they haven't had time to grow up to that individuality which is necessary to merge them with the American citizen. . . . There is that sense of right and wrong which will bind men together and preserve the peace and maintain virtue and provide for offence without. That is the institution out of which a nation grows. Each of these groups [the tribes] must have had that; but you rub that out, you transplant them into what they have no knowledge of. . . . Evolving a thing out of itself is natural, transplanting it is a matter of dissolution, not growth. There may be a few that will grow; in all nature that is true; but the growth will not be natural. . . . If we had our own way we would be living with lands in common, and we would have these prairies all open, and our little bunches of cattle, and would have bands of deer that would jump from the head of every hollow, and flocks of turkeys running up every hillside, and every stream would be full of sun perch. That is what we would have. . . . But we came up against it; this civilization came up against us and we had no place to go.[13]

The history of the Indian Territory from the Civil War to statehood, then, was dominated by the rise of the corporation and the decline of the sovereignty of the tribes, the federal government standing by to watch the direction of the breeze of circumstance. It was a psychologically and culturally disorienting and intellectually twisting experience for Indians, most of whom were unsure where, in the complex detail of boomers vs. corporation, lease vs. sale, tribal vs. federal courts, individual vs. tribal ownership, their future happiness lay. By the twentieth century intelligent tribal citizens were more

12. Charles Thompson to R. B. Hayes, March 12, 1878, LR OIA Union Agency, M 234, R 870, document P354. Clipping, *New York Tribune*, Dec. 6, 1899, box 41; Clipping, *Chicago Record Herald*, March 10, 1904, box 45, 2, E. A. Hitchcock Papers, RG 316, NA.

13. Statement of Porter, Dec. 15, 1903, file 4412–04, ITD.

and more turning to those inevitable human responses in the face of the unfathomable: exaggeration, simplification, and laughter. The Indian had been promised, went the late accounts:

> Thou shalt in nowise be taken from the land of thy fathers into the evil city of Ft. Smith . . . to be bound in chains because thou wouldst not give into the hands of the white man thy fatted calves and fruitful lands in exchange for seven bottles of Jamaica giner; and the palefaced bunco steerer shall not come into thy land with revolvers of a very large bore and chase thy children into the sage brush and perforate their perleraniums because they do not favor allotments, but thine enemies shall fall by wayside, even as the price of summer underwear falleth in the month of December.

But it was not to be so, for in Washington was a corps of determined men and some in Tahlequah, Muskogee, Atoka, and Bartlesville joined their chorus.[14]

Even when it was all done, many Indians were not sure what the corporation had brought them or would bring them and which of the things were gifts and which curses. It was fundamentally paradoxical, expressed most closely in myths, like the old Cherokee legend about the Indian economy. The story had it that the tribe had once lived in a land of floods and was forced to build a storehouse to reach heaven. Each time it almost got there, great powers destroyed it and confused the language of the tribes. Then whites came. The Indians knew the whites were deceptive and wanted to resist them, but the storehouse temple had been neglected and the natives could not light its shrines with their own fire. So the Indians paid a large tribute in gold and land to keep alive their great deceiver, and to support the destroyer who would build the storehouse to heaven. All that he asked was given him.[15]

14. *Cherokee Advocate*, Aug. 1, 1894.
15. *Vinita Chieftain*, Jan, 2, 1896.

BIBLIOGRAPHY

ARCHIVAL SOURCES

NATIONAL ARCHIVES

Record Group 46, Records of the U.S. Senate
  51st Cong., 1st sess. file S 2580; 55th Cong., 1st sess. file H.R. 8581;
  55th Cong., 3d sess. file H.R. 11868; 47th Cong., 1st sess. file S 60;
  58th Cong., 2d sess. file S 2302; 58th Cong., 3d sess. file S 6658.
Record Group 48, Records of the Department of the Interior
  Microcopy 606, Letters Sent by the Indian Division, 1849–1903, reel 28.
  Special Files of the Indian Division: #30.
  Special Files of the Indian Territory Division: #4412–04, 10852–1907.
  Indian Territory Division Letters Received: boxes 328–3393–358–63,
    372–73, 410, 445, 447, 436, 440.
  Land and Railroad Division: railroad packages 126–142 (MK&T);
    142a–145 (MRFtS&G); 3–7 (AT&SF), 110–11 (LL&G).
Record Group 75, Records of the Office of Indian Affairs
  Special Cases #9, 12, 23, 51, 84, 93, 102, 119, 123, 136, 141, 146, 142,
  154, 156, 161, 166, 178, 182, 191. (These are files relating to specific
  topics mostly after 1880. They vary in size from a few inches of manuscript to #191: Osage leases which is 30 boxes of material.) Irregularly
  Shaped Papers: entry 310, shelf 6; entry 310, shelf 4, 41433–93, Microcopy 234, Letters Received by the Office of Indian Affairs, 1824–1880:
  reels 836–39 Southern Superintendency, 1865–71; 113–116.
  Cherokee Emigration 1828–54; 100–112 Cherokee Agency 1864–80;
  142 Chickasaw Agency 1867–70; 176–183 Choctaw Agency 1860–76;
  231–235 Creek Agency 1864–76; 634–41 Osage Agency 1875–80; 865–
  877 Union Agency, 1875–80.
  Microcopy 574, Special Files of the Office of Indian Affairs, 1807–
  1904: reel 24, Treaty Negotiations with the Cherokees, 1861–66.
Record Group 235, Records of the U.S. House of Representatives (used
  by permission only).

H.R. 53A–F18.1; H.R. 58A–F35.4; H.R. 52A–F19.5; H.R. 51A–F39.5; H.R. 43A–F44.4.

Record Group 247, Records of the U.S. Supreme Court
   Transcript Case 12992, 1880–90, *Cherokee Nation* v. *Southern Kansas Railway Company.*

Record Group 267, Records of the U.S. Supreme Court
   Appellate Case Files #7198, 12992, 18549

Record Group 316, Private Papers
   Ethan Allen Hitchcock Papers.

OKLAHOMA HISTORICAL SOCIETY, OKLAHOMA CITY
(Records of the Five Civilized Tribes and others, Indian Archives Division)

Cherokee Volumes 715–D, 402.

Manuscript Records of the Cherokee Nation, 1850–1907: The voluminous files of the tribe are divided by subject. The most important for this study were Railroads, Minerals, Townsites, Traders, Livestock, Cherokee Strip. The Cherokee Records are divided into two sections, one called the "Tahlequah acquisition."

Manuscript Records of the Creek Nation, 1850–1907: The same technique was used. Especially important here were files on Newspapers, Pastures and Stock and Tax Collectors.

Manuscript Records of the Choctaw Nation, 1850–1907: Especially important were Railroads, Federal Relations, Intruders, Tax Collectors, Timber, Traders and Townsites.

Miscellaneous Tribal Records: The volume of the Chickasaw and Seminole collections is relatively small, as is that of the Quapaws, though here the railroad file was of some use. The Kiowa files are largely duplicated in Microcopy 234 of the National Archives, but here conveniently broken down by subject. The "Transportation and Freighting" file was consulted.

Records of the Dawes Commission: Letters Sent, vol. 40; Letters of the U. S. Indian Inspector, vols. 105–10; Dawes Commission Letters Received, 1895–1903. (These records were deposited in Oklahoma before the formation of the National Archives, and are an important

and very little known source for late 19th and early 20th century Indian history.)
Cherokee Strip Live Stock Association Papers: Sec. X, Case 2, Drawer 1.
Creek Newspaper Special File: Sec. X. (The importance of the largely
unexploited 2 million pieces of Indian records at the Society to this
study cannot be overemphasized.)
Library, Oklahoma Historical Society.
Clippings File on Railroads.
L. C. Heydrick, comp. Collection on Red Fork Oil District, Creek
Nation.
2 vols. typescript.
Collection of Printed Laws for the Five Nations.

FEDERAL RECORDS CENTER, FORT WORTH, TEXAS

Osage Nation Field Records, Administrative Branch Misc. Correspondence: boxes 415–040–415, 064 (1860–1907)
Osage Nation Field Records, Minerals Branch: box 414, 421 (Foster Lease)

KANSAS STATE HISTORICAL SOCIETY, TOPEKA

Chester I. Long Papers, 1890–1928
Indian Pamphlets Collection

UNIVERSITY OF OKLAHOMA LIBRARY, NORMAN

J. J. McAlester Papers, 1870–1908
Edwin Ludlow Papers, 1894–1902
Cherokee Nation Papers
Printed Pamphlet file in Frank Phillips Collection
Dennis Bushyhead Papers

GILCREASE INSTITUTE, TULSA, OKLAHOMA

D. S. Stanley Journal, 1853
Grant Foreman Papers
Hargrett Indian Pamphlet Collection
(The three collections of printed pamphlets, at Topeka, Norman, and

Tulsa were of special value. They represent the finest arguments of the tribes and their attorneys on various issues and are in a more quotable style generally than that of the routine correspondence. The Gilcrease's Hargrett collection is the most useful and extensive, and the catalog for it has been recently published by the University of Oklahoma Press.)

LIBRARY OF CONGRESS

LaFollette Family Papers

GOVERNMENT DOCUMENTS

Annual Reports of Commissioner of Indian Affairs (N.C.R. Microfiche edition), 1860–1907.

Congressional Globe and Record, 1850–1907.

Federal Reporter, XXI.

House Documents: #528, 58th Cong., 2d sess. (Serial 4675); #376, 58th Cong., 3d sess. (Serial 4832).

House Misc. Documents: #88, 43d Cong., 1st sess. (Serial 1618); #13, 46th Cong., 1st sess. (Serial 1876).

House Reports: #61, 42d Cong., 2d sess. (Serial 1528); #98, 42d Cong., 3d sess. (Serial 1578); #151, 43d Cong., 2d sess. (Serial 1659), #211, 48th Cong., 1st sess. (Serial 2253); #1356, 49th Cong., 1st sess. (Serial 2439).

Interstate Commerce Commission, *Twentieth Annual Report on the Statistics of Railways in the United States....* Washington, D.C.: A.P.O., 1901. *Statutes at Large*, XXX.

Senate Misc. Documents: #90, 41st Cong., 2d sess. (Serial 1408); #66, 43d Cong., 2d sess. (Serial 1630); #72, 43d Cong., 2d sess. (Serial 1630); #79, 44th Cong., 1st sess. (Serial 1665); #41, 46th Cong., 2d sess. (Serial 1890); #88, 55th Cong., 3d sess. (Serial 3731); #296, 56th Cong., 1st sess. (Serial 3868); #427, 56th Cong., 1st sess. (Serial 3878); #423, 56th Cong., 1st sess. (Serial 3877); #325, 56th Cong., 1st sess. (Serial 3868); #333, 56th Cong., 1st sess. (Serial 3868); #213, 56th Cong., 2d sess. (Serial 4043).

Senate Reports: #156, 39th Cong., 2d sess. (Serial 1279); #744, 45, 3d sess. (Serial 1839); #1278, 49th Cong., 1st sess. (Serial 2362–63); #4240, 58th Cong., 3d sess. (Serial 4756); #5013, pts. 1 & 2, 59th Cong., 2d sess. (Serial 5062, 5063).

U.S., Congress, House, *Statehood for Oklahoma: Hearings Before the Committee on the Territories of the House of Representatives. January 20, 1904*. Washington, D.C.: Government Printing Office, 1904.

U.S., Geological Survey, *Annual Report* . . . . Washington, D.C.: Government Printing Office, 1895.

THESES AND DISSERTATIONS

Aldrich, Gene. "A History of the Coal Industry in Oklahoma to 1907." Ph.D. dissertation, University of Oklahoma, 1952.

Bailey, Minnie E., "Reconstruction in Indian Territory, 1865–1877." Ed.D. dissertation, Oklahoma State University, 1967.

Cormier, Stephen T. "Land, Currency, Cherokees and William Addison Phillips: A Study in Contradiction." M.A. thesis, Wichita State University, 1973.

Miner, H. Craig. "The Border Tier Line: A History of the Missouri River, Ft. Scott and Gulf Railroad, 1865–1870." M.A. thesis, Wichita State University, 1966.

NEWSPAPERS

Anglo-American Times (London), 1887
Arkansas Sentinel (Fayetteville)
Atoka Independent
Atoka Indian Chieftain, 1885
Bartlesville Enterprise, 1904–1907
Bartlesville Magnet, 1895–1902
Cherokee Advocate (Tahlequah, I.T.), 1860–1901
Choctaw Vindicator (New Boggy and Atoka, I.T.), 1872–1878
Emporia News (Emporia, Kansas), 1865–1875
Indian Champion (Atoka, I.T.), 1884–1885
Indian Citizen (Atoka and S. McAlester, I.T.), 1890–1900

Indian Journal (Muskogee, I.T.), 1876

Kansas Tribune (Lawrence, Kansas), 1865

Leavenworth Times (Leavenworth, Kansas), 1866

Missouri Democrat (St. Louis), 1870–1873

Missouri Patriot (Springfield), 1872

National Intelligencer (Washington, D.C.), 1850–1860

New York Times, 1854–1907

Oklahoma War Chief (Caldwell, Kansas), 1886

San Francisco Chronicle, 1882–1883

Sedalia Democrat (Sedalia, Missouri), 1869–1874

Tahlequah Telephone (Tahlequah, I.T.), 1887

Tulsa Daily World, 1932

Vinita Chieftain (Vinita, I.T.), 1884–1907

Western Journal of Commerce, (Kansas City, Missouri), 1864–1865

Wichita Eagle (Wichita, Kansas), 1880–1890

Wyandotte Gazette (Wyandotte, Kansas), 1870

BOOKS, PAMPHLETS, ARTICLES

Adams, R. C. *In Answer to Brief of Cherokee Oil & Gas Company*. Vinita Chieftain Print, 1901.

Applen, Allen G. "An Attempted Indian State Government: The Okmulgee Constitution in Indian Territory, 1870–1876," *Kansas Quarterly* 3 (Fall 1971): 89–99.

Bailey, M. Thomas. *Reconstruction in Indian Territory*. Fort Washington: Kennikat Press Corp., 1972.

Baird, W. David. *Peter Pitchlynn Chief of the Choctaws*. Norman: University of Oklahoma Press, 1972.

Beadle, J. H. *The Undeveloped West; or Five Years in the Territories*. Philadelphia: National Publishing Co., 1873.

———. *Western Wilds and the Men Who Redeem Them*. Cincinnati: Jones Bros. & Co., 1878.

Berthrong, Donald J. "Cattlemen on the Cheyenne-Arapaho Reservation, 1883–1885," *Arizona and the West* 13 (Spring 1971): 5–32.

Bureau of Indian Affairs. *The Osage People and Their Trust Property*. Anadarko, Okla.: Bureau of Indian Affairs, 1953.

Carriker, Robert C. *Fort Supply, Indian Territory.* Norman: University of Oklahoma Press, 1970.

Clinton, Fred S. "First Oil and Gas Well in Tulsa County," *Chronicles of Oklahoma* 30 (Autumn 1952):312–32.

Dawes, Anna Laurens. "An Unknown Nation," *Harpers New Monthly Magazine* 76 (March 1888):598–605.

Debo, Angie. *And Still the Waters Run: The Betrayal of the Five Civilized Tribes.* Princeton: Princeton University Press, 1940.

————. *The Rise and Fall of the Choctaw Nation.* Norman: University of Oklahoma Press, 1961.

Denial of Indians to Charges of Dawes Commission. Washington, D.C.: Gibson Bros., 1894.

DeRosier, Arthur. *The Removal of the Choctaw Indians.* Knoxville: University of Tennessee Press, 1970.

Finney, Frank. "The Indian Territory Illuminating Oil Company," *Chronicles of Oklahoma* 37 (Summer 1959):149–61.

Fritz, Henry E. *The Movement for Indian Assimilation, 1860–1890.* Philadelphia: University of Pennsylvania Press, 1963.

Gates, Paul. "The Homestead Law in an Incongruous Land System," *American Historical Review* 41 (July 1936):652–81.

————. *Fifty Million Acres: Conflicts over Kansas Land Policy, 1854–1890.* New York: Atheneum, 1966.

Gibson, A. M. *The Chickasaws.* Norman: University of Oklahoma Press, 1971.

Gladden, Washington. "Christianity and Wealth," *Century* 28 (October 1884): 903–11.

Glasscock, C. B. *Then Came Oil: The Story of the Last Frontier.* Indianapolis: The Bobbs-Merrill Company, 1938.

"The Great South: The New Route to the Gulf," *Scribners Monthly* 6 (July 1873):257–88.

Hagen, William T. "Kiowas, Commanches and Cattlemen, 1867–1906: A Case Study of the Failure of U.S. Reservation Policy," *Pacific Historical Review* 40 (August 1971):333–56.

Hays, Samuel P. *Conservation and the Gospel of Efficiency: The Progressive Conservation Movement, 1890–1920.* Cambridge: Harvard University Press, 1969.

Harsha, William J. "Law for the Indians," *North American Review* 124 (February 1882):272–92.

Hillyer, C. J. *Atlantic and Pacific Railroad and the Indian Territory.* Washington, D.C.: McGill & Witherow, 1871.

Hinton, Richard. "The Indian Territory—Its Status, Development and Future," *Review of Reviews* 23 (April 1901):451–58.

Hurst, James W. *Law and the Conditions of Freedom in the 19th Century.* Madison: University of Wisconsin Press, 1956.

Kappler, Charles J. *Indian Affairs: Laws and Treaties.* 2 vols. Washington, D.C.: Government Printing Office, 1904.

Kinney, J. P. *A Continent Lost—A Civilization Won: Indian Land Tenure in America.* Baltimore: The Johns Hopkins Press, 1937.

LaFollette, Bell, and Fola LaFollette. *Robert M. LaFollette June 14, 1855– June 18, 1925.* 2 vols. New York: The Macmillan Company, 1953.

Masterson, V. V. *The Katy Railroad and the Last Frontier.* Norman: University of Oklahoma Press, 1952.

Miles, Nelson A. "The Indian Problem," *North American Review* 128: 238:304–15.

Miner, H. Craig. "Border Frontier: The Missouri River, Ft. Scott and Gulf Railroad in the Cherokee Neutral Lands, 1868–1870," *Kansas Historical Quarterly* 35 (Spring 1969):105–29.

————. "The Cherokee Oil and Gas Co., 1889–1902: Indian Sovereignty and Economic Change," *Business History Review* 46 (Spring 1972): 45–66.

————. "The Colonization of the St. Louis and San Francisco Railway Company, 1880–82: A Study of Corporate Diplomacy," *Missouri Historical Review* 63 (April 1969):345–62.

————. *The St. Louis-San Francisco Transcontinental Railroad: The Thirty-Fifth Parallel Project, 1853–1890.* Lawrence: University Press of Kansas, 1972.

————. "The Struggle for an East-West Railway into the Indian Territory, 1870–1882," *Chronicles of Oklahoma* 47 (Spring 1969):560–81.

Moore, J. H. *The Political Condition of the Indians and the Resources of the Indian Territory.* St. Louis: The Southwestern Book and Publishing Company, 1874.

Morison, Elting E. *The Letters of Theodore Roosevelt.* 8 vols. Cambridge: Harvard University Press, 1952.

Morrison, James D. "The Union Pacific, Southern Branch," *Chronicles of Oklahoma* 14 (June 1936):173–86.

Nash, Gerald D. "Oil in the West: Reflections on the Historiography of an Unexplored Field," *Pacific Historical Review* 39 (May 1970):193–204.

"The New Indian," *Nation* 79 (July 21, 1904):47.

"Our Indian Policy," *Nation* 2 (February 16, 1866), 134–35.

Priest, Loring B. *Uncle Sam's Stepchildren: The Reformation of United States Indian Policy, 1865–1887*. New Brunswick: Rutgers University Press, 1942.

Rister, Carl C. *Land Hunger: David L. Payne and the Oklahoma Boomers*. Norman: University of Oklahoma Press, 1942.

————. *Oil! Titan of the Southwest*. Norman: University of Oklahoma Press, 1949.

Savage, William W., Jr. *The Cherokee Strip Live Stock Association: Federal Regulation and the Cattlemen's Last Frontier*. Columbia: University of Missouri Press, 1973.

Schlesinger, Arthur, Jr. "The Historian and History," in Thomas Guinsburg, ed., *The Dimensions of History*. Chicago: Rand McNally & Co., 1971.

Schruben, Francis. *From Wea Creek to El Dorado: Oil in Kansas, 1860–1920*. Columbia: University of Missouri Press, 1972.

Shurz, Carl. "Present Aspects of the Indian Problem," *North American Review* 133 (July 1881):1–24.

Stewart, Dora. *Government and Development of Oklahoma Territory*. Oklahoma City: Harlow Publishing Co., 1933.

Walker, F. A. "The Indian Question," *North American Review* 116 (April 1873):329–88.

Wardell, Morris. *A Political History of the Cherokee Nation, 1838–1907*. Norman: University of Oklahoma Press, 1938.

Washburn, Wilcomb, "The Writing of American Indian History: A Status Report," *Pacific Historical Review* 40 (August 1971):261–82.

Young, Mary. *Redskins, Ruffleshirts and Rednecks: Indian Allotments in Alabama and Mississippi, 1830–1869*. Norman: University of Oklahoma Press, 1961.

INDEX

A

Adair, John, 46, 150, 188

Adair, William, 34, 93, 95, 115, 129

Adams, Richard, 156–57, 160, 201

Age of Jackson, 207

Allotment: legislative history, 7, 48, 93, 109, 116–17, 151–54, 178, 187; tribes and, 23, 35, 48, 165; and industry, 67, 75, 82, 190, 192–97, 201–3

Almeda Oil Co., 173

Amsterdam, 91

Andrain, James, 47

Arapaho Indians. *See* Cheyenne and Arapaho Indians

Arkansas Sentinel, 108–9

Armstrong, Silas, 8

Army. *See* U.S. military

A-she-gah-hre, 185

Astor House, 88

Atchison, Topeka and Santa Fe railroad, 110–11, 114, 121, 170

Atkins, J. D. C., 147–48

Atlantic and Pacific railroad: chartered, 14–15; survey, 23, 42–43, 48, 54; right of way, 44, 47, 50, 55; at Vinita, 44–45; land grant, 78–81, 90–92, 99–100. *See also* St. Louis and San Francisco railroad

Atlantic and Pacific Railroad and the Indian Territory, 78–81

Atoka, I.T., 54–55, 148

Atoka Coal and Mining Co., 62

Auerbach, Herbert, 180–81

B

Babbitt, Albert, 127

Bacon Rind, 181–82

Bailey, John, 201

Baker, James, 93, 97

Baltimore and Ohio railroad, 72

Bapst, Frank, 18–82

Barnes, D. H., 25

Barnsdall, Theodore, 173, 183–84, 197–201

Bartlesville, I.T., 162–63, 169, 171–73, 184, 193

Bartlesville Enterprise, 200

Bartlesville Magnet, 163, 171–73

Bates, F. A., 173

Baxter, Uri, 104–5

Baxter Springs, Kans., 29–30, 121, 143-44

Beaumont, Tex., 157

Bell, L. B., 111, 120–21

Bennett, Leo, 137, 188

Bigheart, James, 166, 177

Bigheart, Peter, 170

Bixby, Tams, 192–97

Black Dog, 170

Black Hills, 170

Blaine, James G. (Osage), 210–11

Blair, Sen., 167

Blanchard, George, 127

Blunt, James, 16

Board of Indian Commissioners, 18, 50–51, 90, 98

Boggy Depot, I.T., 54–55, 84

Bonaparte, Charles, 196

Boston, Mass., 47

Boudinot, Elias C., 6, 30, 44–46, 49, 81–83, 89, 91, 95, 98, 111, 120–21, 136

Boudinot vs. Hunter, 134

Boudinot, William, 49

Brassfield, Butler, 149

Breckenridge, C. R., 194

Brenner, H. H., 180

Bright, Richard, 114

Britton and Gray, 73

Brosius, S. M., 192–94

Brown, James, 92

Browning, D. M., 164–65

Bryan, J. M., 45

Bryan, William J., 199

Buffalo, N.Y., 180

Buffington, T. M., 159, 161

Bull Eagle, 84

Bureaucracy, 186–206

Burns, William T., 182

Busch, Adolphus, 205

Bushyhead, Dennis W.: and railroad, 102, 112; and cattle, 122–23, 130, 133, 136, 140–42; and oil, 145–47; mentioned, 109, 111, 114, 211

Butler, E. B., 200

Byrd, Edward, 149–50, 160

C

Caddo Resolutions, 91

Campbell, B. H., 126, 128

Canadian Valley Trust Co., 195

Carpenter, C. C., 97–98

Cattle, 4–5, 100, 118–42

Chambers, Vann, 148

Chelsea, I.T., 149

Cherokee Advocate, 49, 83, 87, 99, 133, 212

Cherokee Champion, 141

Cherokee Exploration Syndicate, Ltd., 154

Cherokee Indians: railroads, 3, 7, 13, 16–17, 21–27, 29–32, 34, 38–41, 44–45, 52, 102, 108–9, 112–15; intratribal affairs, 4–5, 19, 40, 53, 98, 112, 193, 215; land title, 9–10, 13–14, 16, 40, 77–78, 81, 92, 98, 111–12; treaties, 12–14, 16, 169–72; timber, 35, 38, 41–42, 65, 74, 113; coal, 22, 59, 144; cattle, 119–26, 128–42, 144–63, 197

Cherokee National railroad, 109

Cherokee Oil and Gas Co., 151, 154–62, 192, 202

Cherokee Outlet. See Cherokee Indians, cattle

Cherokee Petroleum Co., 147

Cherokee Strip Live Stock Association, 126, 128–40

Chesapeake and Ohio Canal Co., 10

Cheyenne and Arapaho Cattle Co., 127, 134

Cheyenne and Arapaho Indians, 47–54, 8, 108, 121, 123–24, 126–28, 134–35

Chicago Lumber and Coal Co., 203

Chicago Record-Herald, 195, 213

Chicago, Texas and Mexican Central railroad, 102–4

Chicago Tribune, 145

Chickasaw Indians: railroads, 3, 11–12, 24–25, 28, 33, 52, 106; funds, 10; oil, 55, 59, 144; timber, 65–66; cattle, 122–24

Chickasaw Oil Co., 59, 144

Chilocco Indian School, 131–32

Choctaw and Chickasaw Central railroad, 24

Choctaw and Chickasaw Thirty-Fifth Parallel railroad, 24–25

Choctaw Coal and Railway Co., 187–90

Choctaw Exploration Syndicate Ltd., 155

Choctaw Indians: railroads, 3, 7, 11–12, 24–25, 28, 33, 35–36, 52–55; treaties, 7,

11–13; coal, 59–65; tie issue, 65–76; Frisco right-of-way debate, 101–10; oil, 143–44, 146–47, 151; forese preserve, 107, 201–3; Choctaw Coal and Railway Co., 187–90

Choctaw, Oklahoma and Gulf railroad, 190

Choctaw Vindicator, 37, 49, 64, 84

Chouteau, I.T., 45

Civilization. *See* Industrial Civilization

Civil War, 4–5, 85–86

Clarke, Sidney, 2, 5–6, 78

Cleveland, Grover, 112, 134–36, 147, 196

Cleveland, O. T., 167

Coal, 22, 58–65, 150, 174, 187–92. *See also* individual tribes

Coates, Kersey, 16

Cobb, Guy, 192

Colbert, George, 144

Colbert, Winchester, 144

Cole, Coleman, 36, 64

Commanche Indians. *See* Kiowa-Commanche Indians

Commanche Land and Cattle Co., 127–28

Commission to Five Civilized Tribes. *See* Dawes Commission

Commissioner of Indian Affairs. *See* U.S. Office of Indian Affairs

Condict, J. Elliot, 94

Conner, John, 88

Consensus School (of historians), 207

Conservation, 201–3

Cooley, Denton, 6–8, 16

Cooper, Douglas, 11, 55

Cooper, Peter, 128

Corndropper, Mary, 172

Corporation, xi–xii, 10–11, 22, 71, 77, 97–98, 100, 118–19, 122–23, 127, 141, 185, 207–9. *See also* Industrial Civilization and individual companies

Cox, J. D., 26, 32–34

Cox, William, 203

Cragin, Aaron, 16

Cragin Cattle Co., 129, 136

Cragin, Charles, 136

Craig, George, 177, 180

Craig, John, 35, 38, 40–41

Crawford, Samuel, 159

Creek Indians: railroads, 3, 23, 27, 28, 43; funds, 10; timber, 65; newspaper, 91; cattle, 119, 123–24, 130; minerals, 144, 148, 151, 155, 157, 188; mentioned, 192–93

Cudahy, Michael, 148, 172

Cudahy Oil Co., 155

Curtis, Charles, 151, 153, 178, 192

Curtis Act, 116, 151–55, 158–61, 186, 202

D

Darden, Robert, 144

Davis, Webster, 159

Dawes, Henry, 189

Dawes Act, 116, 187

Dawes Commission, 116, 154–55, 192–97, 201

Delaware Indians, 156–57, 160

Department of Interior. *See* U.S. Department of Interior

Douglas, Clarence, 193

Downing, Lewis, 19, 23, 34, 41, 81

Downingville, I.T., 44

Duncan, D. W. C. *See* Too-qua-stee

Dunlap, R. L., 167

E

Emery, Lewis, 178

Eminent Domain, 75, 105, 107, 114, 137

Emporia News, 31

Erie railroad, 127

Eufaula, I.T., 155
Everett, William, 145
Ewing, Thomas, 13

F

Faucett, Hiram W., 146–49
Fay, John C., 114
Fencing, 125–26
Fenlon, Edward, 127–28
Finn, Daniel, 85–86
Fitch, Thomas, 88
Fletcher, Thomas, 43
Folsom, Sampson, 12
Forest. *See* Timber
Fort Gibson, I.T., 23, 53
Fort Sill, I.T., 54
Fort Smith, Ark., 6–8, 102–3, 115
Fort Worth Stock Journal, 134
Foster, B. C., 70
Foster, Edwin, 162, 165–66, 168–70, 172, 174
Foster, Henry, 164–65, 173
Foster, H. V., 173
Frantz, Frank, 177, 179–82, 201
Freeman, Henry, 164–68
Frisco railroad. *See* St. Louis and San Francisco railroad

G

Galey, J. H., 173
Garland, Augustus, 107
Garner, A. B., 60
Gas, 173
George, Henry, 51
Getty, George, 176
Gladden, Washington, 210
Glenn, James A., 166, 168, 177, 180–81

Going Snake Affray, 53
Gordon, Jack, 201–3
Gordon Choctaw Game Preserve, 202
Gould, Jay, 46, 70, 100–101, 104, 106, 110, 117
Gowen, Francis I., 189
Grafton, B. F., 70–73, 93, 95
Granby Mining and Smelting Co., 145
Granger Movement, 117
Grant, Ulysses S., 30, 34, 84, 92, 102
Griffith, Theophilus, 53, 65–66
Guffey and Galey, 157, 197–98
Gulf, Colorado and Santa Fe railroad, 110

H

Hailey, D. M., 53, 62–64
Harkins, D. F., 68–69
Harlan, James, 51
Harris, Cyrus, 52
Harris, E. Poe, 91
Hawley, Joseph, 107–8
Heddon, S. P., 22
Hellar, Martin, 149–50
Henderson, John, 17
Hendricks, Thomas, 16
Henry, Patrick, 123, 138
Herald (Gloversville, N.Y.), 196
Hewitt, Abram, 125, 134
Higgins, Frank, 200
Hillyer, C. J., 78–81, 83, 99, 106, 115
Hinton, Richard, 20
Historical writing, ix, 207–8
Hitchcock, E. A., 159, 161, 177–79, 181, 196–201
Hoag, Enoch, 34
Hodges, F. S., 42–43
Hollenbeck, Peter, 131
Hubbard, Gardiner, 91, 94

Hugh B. Henry & Co., 150, 152
Hunter, Robert D., 124, 126–28, 134, 145
Hunting, 202–3
Hyatt, Thaddeus, 20

I

Independence, Mo., 164
Indian: definition, xii–xiii; distribution, x, 1, 9; Civil War, 4–5; treaties, 3, 5–8, 11–19, 79, 86, 148; factions, 6–7, 11, 18–19, 27, 34–37, 64, 86, 211–12; railroads, 15, 110–11; Indian-run railroads, 24–29; issue of territory, 85, 90; legal issues, 103; cattle, 4, 19; delegations, 141; attitudes, 160; citizenship, 209. *See also* Tribal sovereignty, individual tribes
Indian Citizen, 49
Indian Journal, 71
Indian Progress, 49, 91
Indian Rights Association, 192, 196
Indian Territory Development Co., 192
Indian Territory Illuminating Oil Co., 172–86, 197
Industrial Civilization: defined, xiv; public statements on, 2, 31, 39, 48–49, 56, 71, 74–75, 78–81, 84, 87–88, 160, 209–15; native coal companies and, 65
Ingalls, John, 107–8, 133
International Bank and Trust Co., 197
"Invisible Hand," 5, 19, 214
Ivey, Augustus, 131, 133

J

J. W. Seligman & Co., 104
Jones, James K., 199–201
Jones, John, 48
Jones, Dudley, 25
Joy, James F., 29–30, 33

K

Kansas, 31, 46, 51, 99, 115, 176
Kansas and Arkansas Valley railroad, 112–13, 130
Kansas and Neosho Valley railroad, 14–16, 29
Kansas City, 99
Kansas City Star, 195
Kansas City Times, 97
Kansas-Nebraska Act, 2
Kansas, Oklahoma Central and Southwestern railroad, 172
Katy railroad. *See* Missouri, Kansas and Texas railroad
Keetoowah Society, 157
Kilby, I. L., 144
Kiamichi Mountains, 201
Kiowa-Commanche Indians, 42–43, 124

L

Land grants, 14–16. *See also* individual railroad companies
Land, Labor and Law, 51
Latrobe, John H. B., 11
Laughlin, W. R., 86
Law. *See* individual tribes, U.S. Congress, U.S. Supreme Court
Leahy, John, 170
Leases. *See* Allotment; Cattle; Coal; Oil; and individual tribes
Leavenworth, Lawrence and Galveston railroad, 14–15, 97, 110
Leupp, Francis, 179
Lindsay, J. G., 69
Linn, W. B., 151, 156, 159
Lipe, D. W., 131
Liquor, 38, 48, 50, 85, 172
Little Rock, Ark., 25

Little Rock and Ft. Smith railroad, 33, 49, 101–2
Logan, Walter, 160
Lone Wolf, 42–43
Love, J. D., 131
Ludlow, Edwin, 157–58
Lynde, E., 124
Lyons, John, 130–31, 133, 136–37

M

McAlester, I.T., 58, 64
McAlester, J. J., 61
McBride, A. P., 170, 173
McCracken, William, 120
McCurtain, Green, 62, 202
McCurtain, J. F., 103–4, 106
McDonald, Joseph, 114
McKee, George, 89, 95–96
McLaughlin, James, 182
Manning, Van H., 64
Manypenny George W., 3
Marston, Edgar, 124, 129
Marston, S. W., 70, 95, 119
Maxey, Sam, 105, 124
Mayes, Joel, 138, 140, 148
Mechanics Savings Bank, 172
Medicine. *See* Smallpox
Me-she-tse-he, Charles, 181
Miles, John, 121
Miller, D. J., 123
Minnehoma Oil Co., 176
Missouri, 203
Missouria Indians. *See* Otoe and Missouria Indians
Missouri Democrat, 43, 84–85
Missouri, Kansas and Texas railroad: right of way, 15–16, 29–34, 36–43, 101–102; name, 29; equipment, 34; rates, 52–53; views on Indians, 56–57; and coal issue, 58–61, 188; and timber issue, 66–76; advertising, 92; lobbying, 87, 91, 94–95, 99, 104; and settlers, 97–98. *See also* Union Pacific, railroad, Southern Branch
Missouri River, Ft. Scott and Gulf railroad, 29–30, 32–33, 110
Mitchell, Maggie, 53
Mormons, 13, 95
Morphis, J. L., 167
Morrill, Lot, 20–21
Mosley, P. S., 192
Murdock, Marshall, 99
Muskogee, I.T., 53, 91, 148, 155, 157, 186
Muskogee Title and Trust Co., 192
Myth-Symbolist School (of historians), 207–8

N

Nash, Gerald, 143
Nashville and Chattanooga railroad, 10
National Agent (Choctaw), 59, 66, 68
National Cattlemen's Convention, 132
National Hotel (Tahlequah), 136
Needles, T. B., 193
Neodesha, Kans., 174
Nesler, C. F., 168
"New Freedom," 183
New York Evening Post, 195
New York Herald, 84–85
New York Times, 129
New York Tribune, 93–94, 98, 105, 213
Newman, H. L., 128
Newspaper, 48–50, 78
Noble, John, 189
No-kah-wah-tun-kah, 170
North and West Live Stock Co., 138
Northern Pacific railroad, 146
Nuttall, Thomas, 58

O

Office of Indian Affairs. *See* U.S. Office of Indian Affairs
Oil, 59, 125, 144–63, 168–85, 197–201
Oil City Derrick, 197
Oklahoma, 117
Oklahoma Independent Producers Association, 183–84
Oklahoma Journal, 212
Oklahoma Mining Co., 59
Oklahoma Territory, 88, 165, 173, 182
Okmulgee government, 24, 78
Osage Coal and Mining Co., 58–61, 69
Osage Indians, 10, 89–90, 116, 162–85, 211, 213–24
Osage Oil Co., 171–74
Otoe and Missouria Indians, 114
Overland Transit Co., 52
Overton, B. F., 108, 122, 124
Owen, Robert, 113, 130, 138, 146, 159, 212

P

Pacific and Great Eastern railroad, 111
Paiute Indians, 7
Paris, France, 91
Parker, Ely S., 26–27, 32
Parker, I. C., 103
Parker, I. N., 27
Park Hill School, 122
Parsons, Albert, 54–55, 61, 66–69, 89
Parsons, Kans., 64
Parsons, Levi, 30, 38, 40–42, 78
Patterson, John, 73
Patterson Committee, 73, 92–95, 102
Pawhuska, O.T., 165, 180
Payne, David, 97–100
"Peace Policy," 34, 84

Pearce, Roy H., iv
Pennsylvania Oil Co., 124
Pennsylvania railroad, 135
Perry, George, 174
Perryman, L. C., 189
Pettit, John, 2
Phillips, J. B., 151
Phillips, William A., 13, 28–30, 50–51, 109, 111–13, 138
Phoenix (Phenix) Oil Co., 168–69, 171–72
Pitchlynn, Peter P., 7, 28, 34, 39, 95
Plumb, Preston, 120, 125, 128
Pollack, William, 169–71
Ponca Indians, 113–14
Porter, Osway, 210
Porter, Pleasant, 214
Porter, Silas M., 170
Prairie Oil and Gas Co., 174, 198
Pusley, Joshua, 58

Q

Quapaw Indians, 29–30, 32–33, 121, 132, 143

R

Race, 18–19, 43, 89, 209–12
Railroads, 9–10, 23, 25–27, 50–51, 53, 56, 83–86, 97–98. *See also* individual companies and tribes
Ream, Robert L., 61–65, 211
Ream, Vinnie, 44
Red Fork, I.T., 155, 157
Reeder, Charles, 174
Revard, Charles, 185
Reynolds, George, 61, 69
Rhode Island, 165

Roberts, W. B., 132

Rogers, Charles, 47

Roosevelt, Theodore, 160, 174, 182, 197, 199–201

Ross, Daniel, 108–9

Ross, Finley, 108–9

Ross, John, 3–4, 87

Ross, Robert, 149, 162

Ross, William, 22–23, 30, 53, 75–76, 86–87, 95

S

St. Louis, Mo., 43, 84, 88, 99, 128, 132, 195, 198

St. Louis and San Francisco railroad, 92–93, 100–111, 192. *See also* Atlantic and Pacific railroad

St. Louis Asphalt Mining and Manufacturing Co., 173

Salina, Kans., 51

Satan, 90

Saucy Chief, 166, 172

Savage, William, 128–29

Sawmills. *See* Timber

Schlesinger, Arthur, Jr.

Scribners, 57

Sears, T. C., 70, 72, 94, 98

Seminole Indians, 12, 61

Seneca, Mo., 43

Seneca Indians, 26, 30

Settlers, 20, 31, 57, 78, 86, 97–98, 128, 133, 141, 165

Shanahan, Patrick, 47

Shanks, John P. C., 65, 83–84

Shawnee Indians, 43, 211

"Shooting" (oil well), 173–74

Sibley, Joseph, 178

Sioux Indians, 84, 97

Smallpox, 54

Smith, Hoke, 167, 174

Soper, Pliny L., 192

Southern Kansas railroad, 110, 113–15

Southern Trust Co., 203

Sovereignty. *See* Tribal sovereignty

Spindletop strike, 157

Splitlog, Mathias, 211

Spotted Tail, 84

Springer, William, 160

Standard Cattle Co., 127

Standard Oil Co.: and cattle, 125, 127, 129, 131–32; and oil, 145, 173–74, 176, 178, 183–84, 198–99; mentioned, 156–57, 160

Stephens, Spencer S., 98, 109, 146

Stevens, Robert S., 20, 43, 60, 66–70, 99, 112

Stone, 73–74

Stone Calf, 47

T

Tahlequah, I.T., 21, 94, 109, 136–37

Tahlequah Telephone, 46

Taxation, 10, 52–53, 119–21

Teller, Henry, 62–63, 125–26

Territorial government, 6–8, 48–49, 77–96

Territorial Ring, 77–78, 81, 85–86, 95

Texas Central railroad, 63

Thayer, Nathaniel, 127

Thirty-Fifth Parallel Expedition, 20, 58

Thompson, Charles, 213

Thurston, John, 159

Ties. *See* Timber

Timber: Delaware, 9; Cherokee, 31–32, 35, 41–42, 65; Choctaw hearings, 65–76, 107; and K.&A.V., 113; and fencing, 125–26; and oil leases, 150, 175; forest lands, 201–3

Timpson, Horsefly & Co., 149

Titusville, Pa., 132

Too-qua-stee (D. W. C. Duncan), 151–54, 191, 212
Topeka, Kans., 114
Topeka Herald, 196
Townsites, 40, 44–45, 48, 53–55, 113, 188
Treaties. *See* Indians and individual tribes
Tribal Development Co., 192
Tribal sovereignty: defined, xiii–xv; analyses of, 2–3, 18–19, 23, 35, 39, 50–51, 86, 88–89, 93, 95–96, 137–38, 161, 204; and tax, 52–53; and coal, 61–64; and timber, 67–68, 74–76; and bureaucracy, 84, 90, 205–6; and progressives, 91; and corporation, 100; and cattle, 118–19, 122–23; and Curtis Act, 151–54; and oil, 162; conclusions on, 209–15
Trumbly, Julian, 166, 170
Trumbull, Lyman, 16
Trust companies, 192–97
Trust funds, 9–11
Tufts, John, 62–63
Tulsa, I.T., 42, 111, 184
Turnbull, Lizzie Shaw, 159–60

U

U.S. Congress: and Kansas-Nebraska bill, 2–3; and railroad bills, 15–16, 55–56, 85–87, 101–2, 105–11; comments from, 20–21, 51; on territorial issue, 77–81, 84–95; powers of, 28–29, 84, 114; timber hearings, 66–67; cattle issue, 120, 127, 133–34, 137; and Curtis Act, 151–54; and 1900 Cherokee Agreement, 155–58; and Foster lease for oil, 177–79; and coal lands, 188–92; and termination, 204
U.S. vs. *Cook*, 72
U.S. General Land Office, 92
U.S. Department of Agriculture, 202

U.S. Department of Interior: and railroads, 13–14, 25, 32, 104–5; and minerals, 60–64, 143, 145, 147–48, 151, 154, 158–62, 167, 169–71, 174–75, 177, 179–81, 188–90; and cattle, 120, 125–28, 139–41; and trust co. scandals, 186, 193–97; and forest issue, 200–3, 205. *See also* U.S. Office of Indian Affairs
U.S. Department of Treasury, 10
U.S. Mail, 52
U.S. military, 38, 120–21, 138
U.S. Office of Indian Affairs: treaties, 5–6, 16–17; on white expansion, 7–9, 56; on funds, 9–11; and railroads, 3, 26, 32, 101; and coal, 59–65, 188; and timber, 41, 73; and oil, 144, 164–69, 175; and grazing leases, 120, 128; mentioned, 2, 43. *See also* U.S. Department of Interior
U.S. Supreme Court, 72, 115, 161–62
U.S. Territory. *See* Territorial government
United States Oil Co., 150–51
Union Pacific railroad, 7
Union Pacific railroad, Eastern Division, 9, 13
Union Pacific railroad, Southern Branch, 9–10, 15, 21–23, 29
University of Oklahoma, 46

V

Vest, George, 97–98, 107–8
Vinita, I.T., 44–45, 52, 98, 155
Vinita Chieftain, 49, 111–12, 133–34, 137, 139, 141, 161, 212
Vorhees, Daniel, 13
Vreeland, Edward, 178

W

Waco, Tex., 123
Walker, Francis A., 96

Walker, G. M., 22
Walker, Robert, 3
Weise, A. V., 145
Weld, William, 127
Wells, Erastus, 144
Western Refrigerator Car Co., 43
Whirlwind, 103
White Horn, 164, 185
Wichita, Kans., 115, 126, 149, 198
Wichita Eagle, 99–102
Wichita Indians, 54

Williamson, James, 92, 99–100
Williford, G. S., 63
Wilson, John, 138
Wilson, Woodrow, 183
Windsor & Roberts, 131–32
Woodman, William C., 151
Woodson, Gov. (Mo.), 88
Wright, Allen, 53, 82, 146
Wright, E. N., 146
Wright, J. George, 192
Wyandotte Indians, 8, 43